T0136907

Armchair Traveller
at the bookHaus

Besides the Italy that everyone visits, there is, if one goes deeper into the South, a genuinely unknown Italy, no less interesting than the other and in no way inferior in the beauty of its landscapes or the grandeur of its historical monuments.

François Lenormant, *"À travers l'Apulie et la Lucanie"*

For Andrew Ciechanowiecki

An Armchair Traveller's History of Apulia

Desmond Seward and
Susan Mountgarret

Armchair Traveller
at the bookHaus

First published in Great Britain in 2009 by Haus Publishing Ltd

This new, revised and extended edition published in 2012 by
The Armchair Traveller at the bookHaus
70 Cadogan Place, London SW1X 9AH
www.thearmchairtraveller.com

Cover image courtesy gettyimages

Maps copyright © Martin Lubikowski

print ISBN 978-1-907973-75-8
ebook ISBN 978-1-907973-76-5

A CIP catalogue record for this book is available from the British Library

Typeset in Garamond by MacGuru Ltd
Printed and bound in China by 1010 Printing International Ltd.

Contents

Author Biographies

DESMOND SEWARD, born in Paris, was educated at Ampleforth and Cambridge. He is the author of many books, including *The Monks of War: The Military Religious Orders* and *The Wars of the Roses*. His latest, *Wings over the Desert: in Action with an RFC Pilot in Palestine 1916–18,* is based on his father's experiences.

SUSAN MOUNTGARRET, educated at the London Academy of Music and Dramatic Art, is co-author (with Desmond Seward) of *Byzantium: A Journey and Guide.* Among the reasons that drew her to Apulia was a wish to study the Byzantine frescoes in its cave churches.

Foreword: Old Apulia

It is clear that the God of the Jews did not know Puglia, or He would
not have given His people Palestine as the Promised Land.

The Emperor Frederick II

APULIA (OR PUGLIA) is the heel of Italy, stretching down from
the spur of the Italian boot. Its landscape is often very beautiful
and it has wonderful old cities with Romanesque cathedrals, Gothic
castles and a great wealth of Baroque architecture, together with
'rupestrian' churches that contain Byzantine frescoes. But, although
far from inaccessible, until quite recently it was seldom visited by
English-speaking tourists. Today, however, Apulia is becoming
fashionable, "an alternative to Tuscany". It is featured on radio and
television; travel supplements describe its beaches and its cooking,
supermarkets stock Apulian wine, oil, bread and pasta. Yet almost
nothing about the region has been published in English since the
days of Norman Douglas and the Sitwells. And there is no popular
introduction to Apulian history, not even in Italian. Our book has
been written to fill this gap.

Both of us believe that to understand the present you must know
the past, and this is a portrait of the old Apulia, concentrating on its
people, its heroes and its shrines. Whenever possible, we have made
a point of using accounts by early travellers, since the landscape has
changed surprisingly little. You can still see it with eighteenth or
nineteenth century eyes.

Geographically, in northern Apulia the mountainous Gargano

contrasts starkly with the flat Tavoliere, while going south and west the stony plateau of the Alta Murgia, Apulia Petrosa, has little in common with either. On the western border great wheat-fields sweep up to the hills of Basilicata. Much of the ground is limestone karst, the Apulian Platform, through which rain-water seeps down so quickly that there are virtually no streams or lakes. The rest, which a million years ago was under the sea, is mainly soft tufa filled with fossilised shells, and gashed by long ravines *(gravine)* riddled with caves; many of the ravines are choked by prickly pear, especially in coastal areas. Everywhere the fields are divided by dry-stone walls. There are innumerable orchards; in spring you can drive through mile upon mile of blossom – almond, peach or cherry – while the ground is covered by an almost vulgar profusion of wild flowers. But the most characteristic and most prized tree in Apulia is the olive, that lives for five hundred years (some say for two thousand) and whose silver-green groves cover vast tracts of dark-red Apulian soil.

The landscape is not only unlike Northern Italy, it is unlike the rest of the *Mezzogiorno*. There is no resemblance to mountainous Calabria or harsh Basilicata. Much of the soil is extremely fertile, so that there has always been great wealth for those who own the land, while the seaports are ideally placed for trade with the Levant. The people, too, are subtly different from other Southerners, although they are no less secretive and have the same beautiful manners.

Apulia's history is one of repeated invasion and conquest. The first known settlers were the Messapians from the Balkans, followed by the Greeks in about 800 BC, both absorbed and Latinised by the Romans. Goths arrived in the fifth century AD, soon evicted by a Byzantine reconquest, but followed by a further wave of Germans, the Lombards. After this, Saracens laid the region to waste, enslaving its inhabitants and establishing short-lived emirates at Bari and Tàranto. Then came a Byzantine revival, accompanied by Greek re-colonisation.

The Norman conquest of the eleventh century established a kingdom that endured for seven hundred years. The *Regno* was medieval Italy's most feudal state and Apulia possessed its most lordly fiefdoms, with vast estates whose lords dominated the cities. The kingdom was inherited in 1194 by the Hohenstaufen, brutally displaced seventy years later by the Angevins, who reigned until 1442. Then followed the Aragonese kings, dethroned in 1501, after which Southern Italy was governed by Spanish viceroys until 1713, briefly succeeded by Austrians. From 1734 to 1860 the *Regno* was ruled by a branch of the Bourbons. The Borboni's reign was interrupted in 1799 by the Neapolitan Republic, and again from 1806–15 by a French occupation under Joseph Bonaparte and Marshal Murat.

The *Risorgimento* of 1860 was far from being a "liberation". During the late nineteenth century new speculator landlords reduced Apulian labourers to near slavery, one in ten emigrating during the decade before 1915 and many others leaving after the Second World War. During modern times, however, life here has been transformed by "the coming of the water". Formerly in desperately short supply, it came first from the Abruzzi through the Great Aqueduct completed in 1939 and then from wells sunk deep into the tufa after 1945.

The Apulians have always possessed a genius for survival. They escaped from the Goths and later the Saracens by living in cave-cities, hewing grotto churches out of the rock. In spite of their Norman conquerors' harsh rule, they amassed so much wealth from exporting oil, wine, almonds and wool to the Levant that they were able to build gleaming white towns above ground, while during the seventeenth century, despite plague and Spanish taxation they created the lovely Baroque city of Lecce. They warded off brigands or corsairs with *masserie*, fortified farms where entire communities and their flocks could take refuge.

They have learned, too, how to make an invader's culture their own, especially the Byzantine and the Norman. In many churches Mass was said in the Greek rite until the seventeenth century and, even if the Greek language is now almost extinct in Apulia, other Italians still regard certain Apulian qualities as Byzantine, whilst Norman cathedrals continue to be the most treasured feature of the Apulian landscape.

Suffering and privation, from the fire and sword of barbarian invasions to the *Risorgimento*, have also played a large part in shaping the Apulian character, instilling the endurance and adaptability that has made the economic achievement of the last half century possible.

In our book we link Apulia's history to its topography. We know the terrain well and we write from personal experience – besides living in a small Apulian town for several months we have made many visits over the years, systematically tracing the footsteps of early travellers. We would like to share not only our fascination with this beautiful land and its history, but also our admiration for its people.

Introduction

The Early Travellers

In the past, Apulia was largely avoided by sight-seeing travellers. In 1883 Augustus Hare wrote that "the bareness and filth of the inns, the roughness of the natives, the torment of *zinzare* (mosquitoes), the terror of earthquakes, the insecurity of the roads from brigands, and the far more serious risk of malarial or typhoid fever from bad water, are natural causes which have hitherto frightened strangers away from the south." None the less, a few came, and some of these recorded their impressions.

The **Abate Giovanni Battista Pacichelli** (1641–95), born in Rome though by origin from Pistoia, was an indefatigable traveller who went as far as Ireland. During the 1680s he visited every town in Apulia, however small, describing each with gusto in "Il Regno di Napoli in Prospettiva", which was not published until 1703. Antiquary, jurist, theologian, hagiographer, letter writer and a member of the Royal Society at London, Pacichelli seems to have been the only priest for whom Norman Douglas ever felt any sympathy. "I like this amiable and loquacious creature, restlessly gadding about Europe, gloriously complacent, hopelessly absorbed in trivialities, and credulous beyond belief," he wrote. No doubt, the Abate's obvious love of wine was one of the reasons that endeared him.

For over a century the literary visitors who followed Pacichelli came in search of Roman remains, presumably inspired by Livy's account of the battle of Cannae or by Horace's journey to Brìndisi. The first was an Anglo-Irishman, **Bishop George Berkeley** (1683–1753), then Dean of Derry, later famous for his 'immaterialist' philosophy – that matter exists only in so far as it is perceived – which

Dr Johnson ridiculed by kicking a stone. He came here in the course of an extended Grand Tour in 1734, when he was companion to the Bishop of Clogher's son, writing down his impressions of Apulia in terse notes, very different from his usual stately prose. He also sent letters to his friend Sir John Percival, enthusing over Lecce, which he considered the most beautiful city in Italy, amazed to come across such impressive architecture in so remote an area. He says that he has seen in a single day five fine cities built in marble "whereof the names are not known to Englishmen."

The next visitor to put pen to paper was an Englishman, **Henry Swinburne** (1743–1803), the son of Sir John Swinburne of Capheaton in Northumberland. "A little genteel young man", was how he struck the philanthropist Hannah More: "He is modest and agreeable; not wise and heavy like his books." This is unfair – even if his "Travels in the Two Sicilies" is strong on facts, it is written with a caustic wit and a keen sense of the ridiculous.

No other British travellers of this sort visited Apulia during the eighteenth century. The Swiss **Baron von Riedesel**, who came in 1767, looking for classical remains, was sometimes unintentionally comical – as when he thought *trulli* were Roman tombs or mistook quarries for ancient baths. Another Swiss, **Count Charles Ulysses de Salis Marschalins**, who toured the region in 1789 was a friend of Giuseppe Capecelatro, the free-thinking Archbishop of Tàranto. Capecelatro organised de Salis's tour, providing him with a guide and accompanying him from Naples to Tàranto. The resulting book gives a vivid picture of Pugliese rural life.

Jean-Claude Richard, Abbé de Saint-Non, who visited Apulia during the 1770s, had not much to say but commissioned a number of famous artists to illustrate his sumptuous "Voyages pittoresques ou descriptions du Royaume de Naples et de Sicile", published in 1781–86. The beautiful plates show how comparatively little Apulia has changed. Another Frenchman, the mysterious **Paul-Louis Courier**, who was afterwards murdered by his gamekeeper, was garrisoned at Foggia and Lecce as a gunner officer from 1805–7. Although brief, his letters convey the bloodthirsty mood of the period.

In the winter of 1816–17 a young Scot rode alone through Apulia, which he later revisited with his friend the Prince of Ischitella, who had estates in the Gargano. **Charles Macfarlane** is described by the "Dictionary of National Biography" as "a miscellaneous writer"; in 1856 he lamented that "literature no longer affords me the ample income I derived from it during more than quarter of a century" and he died as a Poor Brother of the Charterhouse. If clumsily written, Macfarlane's accounts of shepherds and brigands in "The Lives and Exploits of Banditti and Robbers" (1833) are of considerable interest.

As a young man, the **Hon Richard Keppel Craven** settled in Naples, where he was famous for coloured waistcoats and his hospitality at the Palazzo Craven. "A Tour through the Southern Provinces of Italy" recounts his adventures in Apulia in 1818 with ponderous humour. Ten years later the extraordinary **Crauford Tait Ramage**, tutor to the sons of the British Consul at Naples, walked or rode a mule through the region, travelling along the coast by felucca; he wore a white frock-coat and shoes, and carried an umbrella for protection from the sun and rain. His "Nooks and Byways of Italy" (subtitled "Wanderings in Search of its Ancient Remains and Modern Superstitions") was not published until 1868, a classic of travel admired by Norman Douglas and Harold Acton. **Edward Lear** confined himself to the western border during his painting tour of 1848 but his description of Venosa, in "Journals of a Landscape Painter in Southern Calabria and the Kingdom of Naples" is well worth reading. He also composed a limerick:

There was an Old Man of Apulia,
Whose conduct was very peculiar;
He fed twenty sons
Upon nothing but buns,
That whimsical Man of Apulia.

This appears to be the only English verse inspired by the region.

"A Handbook for Travellers in Southern Italy being a guide to the continental portion of the Two Sicilies" appeared in 1853. Not very much is known about the author, **Octavian Blewitt**, save that for many years he was Secretary to the Royal Literary Fund (the charity for indigent writers) and catalogued its archives. He spent the 1830s wandering through Greece, the Levant, and Italy, often returning to the *Mezzogiorno*, and certainly knew his history besides having a good eye for topography. Published by John Murray, his pioneering study went into many editions, being heavily plagiarised by Augustus Hare.

That odd figure **Charles Yriarte** went to the Capitanata with the Piedmontese army in 1861, going on to Lecce and Òtranto fifteen years later. A journalist and painter, he was inspector of France's lunatic asylums and then of the Paris Opera while contributing articles to the Press under such pseudonyms as "Marquis de Villemer", illustrating the *Monde Illustrée*, and writing a life of Cesare Borgia. From "Les Bords de I'Adriatique et de Montenegro" (1878) he obviously liked the Pugliesi.

Mme Louis Figuier, born Juliette Bouscarren at Montpellier, was the first woman to record her impressions. She also wrote novels and plays, with titles such as "La dame aux lilas blancs", which enjoyed modest success. Escorted by her husband, a distinguished scientist, she paid a brief visit to Apulia during the winter of 1864–65, at the end of the Brigands' War, seeing only Foggia and Trani. Throughout, the couple appear to have been terrified. In "L'Italie d' après nature" she gives a gruesome account of the sheer horror of Apulian inns, which goes a long way towards explaining why the region had so few visitors.

The magisterial author of lengthy studies of the Emperor Hadrian, Pope Urban VIII and Lucrezia Borgia, **Ferdinand Gregorovius** - a Prussian with a square head, shovel beard and pince-nez - rode over all Apulia during 1874–75, on a series of expeditions which he describes with Teutonic thoroughness in "Wanderjahre in Italien".

Augustus Hare travelled by rail at the end of the 1870s when researching here for his "Cities of Southern Italy and Sicily". Acid about Apulia's beggars and discomfort, the fussy old bachelor was warmly enthusiastic about its "wonderful old cities" and even pitied the labour gangs slaving in the fields. He complained bitterly about his accommodation, however: at Manfredonia, "Inn, *Locanda di Donna Pepina*, very miserable"; at Bari, "*Hotel del Risorgimento*, clean and tolerable but very dear"; and at Tàranto, "*Albergo di Roma*, poor and dirty, but endurable."

A blue-stocking virago rumoured to have the names of her lovers tattooed on her thighs, **Janet Ross** explored Apulia in 1888, collecting material for her book "The Land of Manfred", which to some extent plagiarised de Salis-Marschlins. Her reminiscences, "The Fourth Generation" (1912) are better value. "Our Tuscan friends were much excited and rather alarmed at our daring to go to such an unknown region", she recalls when describing how she first decided to visit Apulia. "I was advised by several people to leave my earrings and gold watch at home – 'those *Meridionali* are all thieves and robbers, you may very likely be captured by brigands and murdered.

It is a dangerous expedition on which you are bound.' Few of them knew where Apulia was ... The Northern Italians hardly regard them as fellow-countrymen." She got to know the Apulians well and was impressed by their honesty and gaiety.

François Lenormant, who saw Apulia shortly before Janet Ross, lectured on archaeology at the Bibliothèque Nationale in Paris. His "À travers l'Apulie et la Lucanie" (1883) and "La Grande Grèce" (1881–84) not only emphasise the region's Hellenistic links but are fiercely indignant at the plight of the miserable labourers on the *masserie*. The two books persuaded **Charles Diehl** to visit the Apulian grottoes in search of Byzantine frescoes, and then publish a pioneering study, "L'Art Byzantin dans I'Italie Méridionale" (1894). They aroused so much enthusiasm in that forgotten "psychological novelist" **Paul Bourget** that in 1890 he spent his honeymoon here, describing what he saw in "Sensations d'Italie". A would-be disciple of Henry James, a fat, red-faced little man too fond of his food and wine, he fell genuinely in love with the Apulian landscape, urging that Lenormant's books should be made compulsory reading in French schools.

Another novelist, **George Gissing**, stayed at Tàranto in 1897, but his "By the Ionian Sea" is disappointing. The eccentric, red-bearded Sir George Sitwell came down from his Tuscan castle to explore in the early 1900s, perhaps inspired by Mrs Ross's "Land of Manfred" – there was a copy in his library at Montegufoni. He may have been the first to tell his sons Osbert and Sacheverell about Apulia, although they seem to have derived their passion for Lecce from **Martin Shaw Briggs**, a Leeds architect, who in 1910 published a glowing description of the city, "In the Heel of Italy", which extolled its Baroque architecture. The brothers would often visit Lecce during the 1920s, **Sir Osbert Sitwell** praising it almost too extravagantly in "Discursions on Travel, Art and Life".

Edward Hutton was a minor Edwardian 'man of letters' (his preferred description of himself), and once well known for his Italian travel books. A young friend of Janet Ross, he came here just before the Great War. He did not particularly enjoy the experience, described in his pedestrian if still useful "Naples and Southern Italy" (1915). However, **Norman Douglas's** "Old Calabria", published the same year, contains some magnificent chapters on Apulia. The author was a deplorable figure, a sponger and a paedophile, but he was undeniably amusing and learned, his beautifully written books ranging from "South Wind" – surely the funniest novel about Capri – to a monograph on the lizards of Paestum.

Brought up to read the Greek and Latin historians, all our travellers took for granted a familiarity with Apulia in classical times (especially of the battle of Cannae, of Taras and Brundisium), which today's visitors rarely possess. On the other hand, they had certain handicaps. They were unable to appreciate Byzantine art, considered barbarous before the twentieth century, and, apart from Diehl and Lenormant, did not bother to visit the grotto churches, if they were even aware of their existence. Only the very early and the very late comers among them admired Apulian architecture, Romanesque or Baroque. They also lacked the insights that have been provided by modern archaeology. All save a handful ignored the wretched life led by the poor, such horrors as the labour gangs in the fields and why there were so many beggars. Where possible, we have tried to illuminate any blind spots of this sort.

Part I

The Gargano

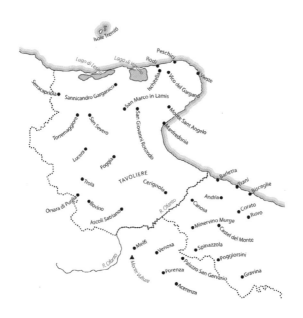

2

The Gargano

A strong people with simple customs live in these mountains...
Gregorovius, "Apulische Landschaften"

THE THREE PROVINCES of Apulia are the Capitanata, the Terra di Bari and the Terra d'Òtranto, also known as the Salento – north, centre and south. In classical times the inhabitants were all known as Iapygians but were divided into three tribes – Daunians, Peucetians and Messapians. Although they were almost certainly Illyrians from the Balkans across the Adriatic, legend claims that they came from Greece in groups led by three fugitive sons of Lycaon, King of Arcadia: Daunus, Peucetius and Iapyx. Lycaon, together with fifty of his sons, had sacrificed a child (or a plate of human flesh) to Zeus, for which they had been changed into wolves. Only these three brothers escaped. Until recently, lycanthropy – belief in werewolves, men who change into wolves at night – was prevalent throughout the wilder regions here. None could be wilder than the inner Gargano.

In the extreme north of the Capitanata, the Gargano is the 'spur" of the Italian boot, but totally different from the rest of Apulia. Since ancient times it has had a sinister name, Horace writing of fearsome north winds that strip the trees of leaves and drown men off its coast. They still blow, so curiously that winter seems to linger long after it is over. "Spring hesitates to smile upon these chill uplands" was Norman Douglas's impression. Its woods and caves have attracted pagan deities, witches and saints, and even today the Gargano remains among the mysterious places of Italy, despite the holiday makers on its enchanting shores.

One of the Tremiti Islands long ago, it is now joined to the mainland, a great mountainous promontory about thirty-five miles by twenty-five, 3,400 feet above sea-level at its highest, that juts out into the Adriatic, with the same geological structure and configuration as those of the Dalmatian mountains. There are dense forests, mainly of chestnut, and wild, steep-sided glens, deep gullies, bleached cliffs and sandy beaches, many of which are only accessible from the sea. The western half consists of stony fields and limestone pavements, with pockets of good grazing in little valleys, where the grey cattle's bells sound mournfully through the mist.

In spring, the Gargano's limestone pavements are full of blue, white and yellow dwarf-irises, while orchids grow everywhere, cross-pollinating to an alarming degree. The sheer number of rare plants creates a botanist's paradise in the area, where 2,000 species have been recorded. Four of these, including the charming *campanula garganica*, are found nowhere else in the world.

Much of the woodland described by ancient writers has disappeared, cleared for agriculture or felled for export to shipbuilders on the far side of the Adriatic. Even so, the Foresta Umbra, now managed by the state, covers 24,000 hectares; most of the trees here are beech or oak instead of chesnut, many as tall as 130 feet, so that the forest lives up to its name of "shady". Until the 1950s it was inhabited by wild boar and wolf, but only a few wild boar remain while the wolves seem to have vanished. During the Middle Ages large areas of Apulia were covered by woodland of this sort, very unlike today's treeless landscape.

"Whoever looks at a map of the Gargano promontory will see that it is besprinkled with Greek names of persons and places – Matthew, Mark, Nikander, Onofrius, Pirgiano (Pyrgos) and so forth", comments Norman Douglas, "Small wonder, for these eastern regions were in touch with Constantinople from early days, and the spirit of Byzance still lingers." In less flowery language, the Eastern Emperors were nominal rulers here till the twelfth century.

Until the 1960s funeral rites of great antiquity were observed. No one could leave the house for ten days after a relative's death, or attend the burial, food being sent in by neighbours; men stopped shaving for a month and wore black shirts as well as suits, women wailed and tore at their faces with their nails as the coffin was taken away. At marriages a rope of handkerchiefs barred the church door, the bridegroom untying the knots.

Strange superstitions linger, such as a belief in *Laùro*, the mischievous Apulian Puck. As everywhere in Apulia, there is widespread fear of *iettatura*, the evil eye: a tiny piece of coral, silver or horn is worn as protection against it, while a gesture with the first and fourth finger of the right hand can avert it – but only if the *iettatore* sees you make it. Owls are known as 'birds of death', since to hear one hooting means that somebody in your family will die. An eclipse of the sun will be followed by famine or pestilence. There are countless other ill-omens, such as spilling oil. Spilling wine, however, can only bring good luck.

Even now, the people of the Gargano are credited with practising magic, often very unpleasant. Love potions based on menstrual blood are not unknown and spells are sometimes laid to harm enemies, animals being used as proxies; occasionally the hind feet of a living dog are chopped off for this purpose, the fate of a fine Alsatian encountered in San Giovanni Rotondo. It is said that some women continue to wear a dead mouse as a protection against the wiles of the Devil, hanging the mouse from their belt over the part where the Devil is most likely to enter in.

Among the supernatural gifts of Padre Pio, the great saint of modern Apulia, was that of being able to see angels and demons. He warned that the sky over San Giovanni Rotondo (where he lived) was literally black with demons. Even the most sceptical might easily suspect that they fly over many other places in the Gargano.

3

Monte Sant' Angelo

...the cave, down some steps, is hallowed by the miraculous apparition
of the Archangel Michael ... you go in through a metal door: on the
altar behind some iron railings is the statue, covered in flowers and
crowned with jewels, of the celestial spirit who slew the Dragon from
Hell ... It is said that in the silence of the night angels may sometimes
be heard singing, symphonies from paradise.

G B Pacichelli, "Il Regno di Napoli in Prospettiva"

D EVOTION, FIRST PAGAN and then Christian, created the shrine
of Monte Sant' Angelo. The mountain is inland, where the
inhabitants were famous for their secretiveness and savagery, even
among those whom Gregorovius called "the wild men of the Gargano."
The cave of St Michael has an eerie atmosphere, and after his visit here
during the 1680s the Abate Pacichelli wrote of dread mingling with
reverence. In ancient times it was the home of the Oracle Calchas,
once a Greek soothsayer, whose ghost appeared in dreams. Those consulting him slept outside, wrapped in the fleeces of black rams.

In 493 AD a nobleman searching for a lost bull found it hiding in
the cave. The bull refused to emerge, so he shot at it, but the arrow
turned in flight, wounding him. The Bishop of Siponto was informed
and, according to "The Golden Legend", had a visitor soon after. "The
man was hurt on my account", he told the bishop. "I am Michael the
Archangel and I want this place held in reverence. There must be no
more shedding of bull's blood." Michael is commander of the Heav-
enly Host, thrusting down to Hell Satan and all wicked spirits who
wander through the world for the ruin of souls.

The bull in the story is significant. Gregorovius, who rode up here in 1874, suspected that devotion to St Michael had been superimposed on a bull-cult. Ninety years later, a *mithraeum* (caves of worship used by the followers of the ancient religion, Mithraism) was discovered beneath the floor, where once the blood of bulls was sacrificed to the sun-god Mithras.

Not until Michael had been seen three times did Monte Gargano become his shrine. Shortly after his first appearance he came to save the citizens of Siponto from a barbarian army. The third vision was to the bishop at the moment when he was about to consecrate the cave. Michael announced that he had already done so, and an altar was found inside, covered by a vermilion cloth with the archangel's footprint on its altar stone.

The archangel in armour who escorted souls to Heaven through swarms of ravening demons, and frightened even the Devil himself, was venerated throughout medieval times with the dread felt by Pacichelli. Over the shrine's entrance are the words: "*Terribilis est locus iste: hic domus Dei est, et porta coeli*" – "This place is fearsome: here is the house of God, and the gate of Heaven." Even today, you feel in the grotto that you are in the presence of some overwhelming, elemental force.

The Byzantine Emperor Constans II came in 683 with rich gifts, lost after the Emir of Bari sacked the shrine two hundred years later. When the Holy Roman Emperor Henry II prayed here in 1022, not only St Michael but Christ appeared in a blaze of light, the archangel presenting a missal to the Lord. Kissing the book, Christ told Michael to give it to the terrified Henry. Having lifted the emperor up to kiss the missal, the archangel threw him to the ground, laming him for life.

In 867 Bernard the Wise, monk of Mont St Michel in northern France, saw the shrine just before its destruction by Saracens. His own monastery was on a rock, where a bull had been discovered in a cave by a bishop, whom the archangel then ordered (this time in a dream) to build a sanctuary. This very similar story helps explain why Norman pilgrims started coming to Monte Sant' Angelo.

Bernard says that in his day the ground above the shrine was covered by oak trees. In 1274, however, a great white *campanile* (bell tower) was built. After going down fifty-five steps cut in the rock, you are confronted by jade-green doors of bronze inlaid with silver, bearing panels with scenes from the Bible; they were made at

Constantinople in 1076 and paid for by Pantaleone, merchant of Amalfi. Inside the cave church, the names of pilgrims down the centuries are scratched on its walls and floors, some written in the earliest runes known in Italy. During the Crusades, pilgrims often drew a hand or a foot before leaving for the Holy land, vowing to draw its pair on returning safely. Holy water said to cure anything is still distributed in a little silver bucket from a well behind Michael's statue.

Keppel Craven, who came in 1818, writes "The cave … is low but of considerable extent, branching out into various recesses on different levels, so that the steps are frequent, and the surface is rugged, irregular, and very slippery, from the constant dripping of the vaults … A few glass lamps, suspended from the rock, which have replaced the silver ones of richer times, cast a faint glimmer of uncertain light." Even Craven was impressed by the pilgrims moving like shadows in the darkness and the hum of prayer.

"The men walked with the air of conquerors", wrote Janet Ross of the pilgrims who she saw in 1888: "Their dress was jaunty and picturesque – short brown velveteen jackets, brown cloth waistcoats with bright buttons, black velveteen breeches, and black worsted stockings tied under the knee with a bunch of black ribbons; while round their waists were dark blue girdles. This costume was crowned with a dark-blue knitted cap, with a sky-blue floss-silk tassel worn quite on the back of the head."

As for the cavern itself, "When we saw it the irregular rock above the high altar was lit by hundreds of wax candles, whose flickering light seemed to make the statue of St Michael, about three feet high with pink cheeks and flaxen curls, move its large white wings, tipped with gold. A priest told me it was a wonderful work of art; he could not remember whether Donatello, Raphael or Michelangelo made it, but probably the latter, 'because of the name.'"

"A wretched morning was disclosed as I drew open the shutters – gusts of rain and sleet beating again the window-panes", wrote Norman Douglas, recalling how he set out to visit Monte Sant' Angelo from Manfredonia, just before the Great War. "I tried to picture to myself the Norman princes, the emperors, popes, and other ten thousand pilgrims of celebrity crawling up these rocky slopes – barefoot – on such a day as this. It must have tried the patience even of St Francis of Assisi, who pilgrimaged with the rest of them and, according to Pontanus, performed a little miracle here *en passant* [in passing], as was his wont."

No friend to the Catholic religion, he was less than charitable about the shrine and its pilgrims:

> Having entered the portal, you climb down a long stairway amid swarms of pious, foul clustering beggars to a vast cavern, the archangel's abode. It is a natural recess in the rock, illuminated by candles. Here divine service is proceeding to the accompaniment of cheerful operatic airs from an asthmatic organ; the water drops ceaselessly from the rocky vault on to the devout heads of kneeling worshippers that cover the floor, lighted candle in hand, rocking themselves ecstatically and droning and chanting. A weird scene, in truth ... It is hot down here, damply hot, as in an orchid-house. But the aroma cannot be described as a floral emanation: it is the *bouquet*, rather, of thirteen centuries of unwashed and perspiring pilgrims ... in places like these one understands the uses, and possibly the origin, of incense.

Douglas's pilgrims sound little different from those seen by Mrs Ross: "travel-stained old women, understudies for the witch of Endor; dishevelled, anaemic and dazed-looking girls; boys too weak to handle a spade at home, pathetically uncouth, with mouths agape and eyes expressing every grade of uncontrolled emotion – from wildest joy to downright idiocy ... And here they kneel, candle in hand, on the wet flags of this foetid and malodorous cave, gazing in rapture upon the blandly beaming idol, their sensibilities tickled by resplendent priests reciting full-mouthed Latin phrases, while the organ overhead plays wheezy extracts from 'La Forza del Destino.'"

"The way down the great flight of steps was ... lined with the lame, the maimed, and the afflicted, all of whom exhibited their wounds with a dreadful and almost brutal insistence which was more than one could bear", shuddered Edward Hutton in the early 1900s. "But the scene in the church beggars description. The mere noise was incredible. Mass was being sung at the high altar, but all around us other devotions were in progress, litanies and prayers were being chanted, and moans and groans rising on all sides. It was impossible to remain for long. Our curiosity seemed more shameful than any superstition."

None of the travellers really understood why the pilgrims had come. "Their existence is almost bestial in its blankness", was Norman

Douglas's opinion. "For four months in the year they are cooped up in damp dens, not to be called chambers, where an Englishman would deem it infamous to keep a dog – cooped up amid squalor that must to be seen to be believed; for the rest of the time they struggle, in the sweat of their brow, to wrest a few blades of corn from the ungrateful limestone. Their visits to the archangel – these vernal and autumnal picnics – are their sole form of amusement." But this does not tell us what brought them to the shrine.

The pilgrims saw him as intercessor and defender. At his feast-days on 8 May and 29 September the choir sang "Holy archangel Michael, be our shield in battle; so we shall not be lost at the dread Day of Judgement." First among the archangels, he was greater than the saints; after God and the Holy Virgin, they were accustomed to confessing their sins to him when seeking absolution. Night and day he defended them against the onslaught of the Devil and his demons, giving patience to bear trials and sorrows. They also firmly believed that St Michael could save them from natural disasters – from droughts, crop-failures, cattle-murrains and earthquakes, from famine and pestilence. He would protect them too against wicked landlords and their cruel stewards, against brigands and house-breakers; they hung a picture of this ultimate guardian angel in their homes to ward off burglars – many of them still do. And, understandably, in that eerie, awe-inspiring cave they felt closest to him.

During his visit to Monte Sant' Angelo, Norman Douglas discovered the potent local red wine that, two centuries earlier, Pacichelli had called "*vino esquisito*" (exquisite wine), Douglas and his hired coachman getting very drunk indeed. "Gloriously indifferent to our fates, we glided down in vertiginous but masterly *vol-plane* from the somewhat objectionable mountain town." But, whatever Douglas may have thought, it is a most attractive place and must always have been one, even when it was just a mere cluster of shacks or cave dwellings during the Dark Ages. There are some lovely old houses here, especially in the Junno quarter.

From the ramparts of the Tower of Giants on the summit, built by the Norman Robert Guiscard, you have a wonderful view over the Gulf of Manfredonia, or inland, as Norman Douglas says, "of Lesina with its lakes, and Selva Umbra, whose very name is suggestive of dewy glades." During the thirteenth century the Emperor Frederick II enlarged the castle, giving its castellan authority over all others in the area. Frederick bequeathed it to his son Manfred who, until he

Castle of Monte Sant'Angelo – Douglas's "proud aerial ruin"

became king, called himself "Prince of Tàranto and Count of the Honour of Monte Sant' Angelo". The paranoiac King Ferrante added three bastions as a defence against gunfire and a gateway bearing his initials with the date 1493. Sadly, in the early nineteenth century the Prince of Sant' Antimo used it as a quarry, reducing it to Douglas's "proud aerial ruin".

However, Monte Sant' Angelo remains the shrine of the Captain of the Hosts of Heaven, who will one day slay the Antichrist on the Mount of Olives, whose voice will summon the dead to arise. This is the heart of the Gargano, the pilgrims still making their way here in May and September.

4

The Norman Conquest – of Apulia

*On one of these pious visits to the cavern of Mount Garganus in Apulia,
which had been sanctified by the apparition of the archangel Michael,
they were accosted by a stranger ... a mortal foe of the Greek Empire.*

Edward Gibbon, "Decline and Fall of the Roman Empire"

A S THE NORMANS venerated the archangel 'to whom in peril we
pray' at his shrine of Mont St Michel in their homeland, they
naturally made a point of visiting the cave on Monte Gargano whenever they went on a pilgrimage to the Holy Land. The Norman conquest of Apulia began here, a blood-stained epic during which their
exploits became the stuff of legend. "Giants cloven to the saddles;
armies routed by a single warrior; castles and bridges defended by
one person alone; knights travelling over the world in search of kingdoms, princesses and adventures, are no more than the real events of
the lives of William Fierabras, Robert Guiscard, Earl Roger, and their
companions", comments Henry Swinburne.

At the start of the eleventh century, the northern frontier of
Byzantine Italy (which was known as the 'Theme of Italy') ran
from Termoli on the Adriatic to Terracina on the Tyrrhenian Sea.
In practice, apart from acknowledging the suzerainty of the 'Sacred
Emperor' at Constantinople, large areas of the south more or less
ignored his viceroy, the catapan at Bari, so that Imperial rule was
restricted to Calabria, Basilicata and Apulia. Even in Apulia only the
Salento, together with the cities of the eastern coast up to Brìndisi
and the area around Tàranto, was Greek. Elsewhere the population
was predominantly Italian speaking and ruled by the Lombards, even

if by now the originally Germanic Lombards had been completely Latinised except for their personal names and their laws.

Although the *catapan* did his best to rule tactfully, leaving local government as far as possible to the haughty Lombard ruling class and respecting their cherished customs, the Lombards nonetheless developed a deep dislike for the Greeks, resenting the obligation to pay heavy taxes to the Emperor. Bari rebelled against Constantinople in 1009, joined by other cities, but the *catapan* (govenor) Basil Boiannes crushed the rising within a year, apparently without too many reprisals. Nevertheless, the Lombards remained bitterly resentful. In 1016 Melus, the Lombard who had led the rising, accosted a group of Norman pilgrims in the archangel's cave and asked them to help him drive out the Byzantines. They accepted, but two years later they were annihilated by Boiannes at Cannae. Even so, other Normans began coming to Apulia in increasing numbers, as mercenaries.

Despite their defeat by Basil Boiannes, these formidable cavalrymen with their chain-mail, conical helmets and kite-shaped shields, armed with lance and sword, could rout the toughest opposition if they had really good leaders. They found one in the terrible William 'Iron-Arm', eldest of the twelve sons of a small squire in the Cotentin called Tancred of Hauteville. In 1040 'Iron-Arm' seized the castle at Melfi, from where he regularly rode out to raid and plunder. Intending to evict him, in March the following year a large Byzantine army (which included the axe-wielding Varangian Guard) intercepted his entire force near Venosa.

Because he outnumbered the Normans, the then *catapan,* Doceanus, optimistically hoped to frighten them into surrendering and leaving Italy. Instead of attacking, he tried to negotiate. However, to the Greeks' horror, a huge Norman named Hugo Toutebonne rode up to the *catapan's* herald and felled the man's horse to the ground with a single blow of his fist on the animal's head. Next day, he and his comrades cut the entire Byzantine army to pieces. In May Doceanus attacked for a second time, in the plain of Cannae, and once again he was totally defeated. In September the same year the Normans overwhelmed a third Byzantine army no less completely, taking prisoner the new *catapan*, Eustathius.

Within a year, save for Bari and Trani, all Apulia north of the Tàranto-Brìndisi road was in Norman hands. At Melfi in 1042, claiming that the land now belonged to them 'by right of the sword', they swiftly divided the area from Monte Gargano down to

Monopoli into twelve counties, 'Iron-Arm' being elected Count of Apulia. Scores of lesser men acquired rich estates and castles, just as their brothers and cousins were going to do in England.

Still, Bari and the Terra d'Òtranto remained loyal to Constantinople and the conquest would take many years to consolidate. There was no decisive victory comparable to Hastings, but instead countless small-scale campaigns and raids, with the odd siege or minor battle. Merciless robber-barons, the invaders killed and plundered in much the same way that their Viking ancestors had done. As Gibbon puts it, "Every object of desire, a horse, a woman, a garden, tempted and gratified the rapaciousness of the strangers." In the end, like the Lombards before them, they were to intermarry and became indistinguishable from other southern Italians. However, the transformation would not be apparent for well over a century.

They acquired a handsome young giant as their new leader, Robert Guiscard, who replaced the Tower of the Giants on the summit of Monte Gargano (built two hundred years previously by a Lombard Duke of Benevento) with a grim new castle that still stands as a fitting monument to him. The seventh of Tancred of Hauteville's sons, he had arrived in 1046 as a penniless adventurer, but he had become pre-eminent by 1157 and two years later Pope Nicolas II made him Duke of Apulia, Calabria and Sicily. In 1061 he beat off a final Byzantine counter-attack and in 1071 he captured Bari, their capital and the catapan's last bastion. His nickname, 'Guiscard' means weasel or wily yet the epitaph on his tomb is "*terror mundi*" (terror of the world), for in 1082, he defeated the Emperor of the East and in 1084, the Emperor of the West.

It was the youngest Hauteville brother, Count Roger, however, who conquered Moslem Sicily, besides inheriting everything that Guiscard had won in Southern Italy. In 1130 Roger's son, Roger II, was crowned King of Sicily, Duke of Apulia and Prince of Capua. On both sides of the Straits of Messina, despite a French-speaking nobility the Hauteville realm was a staggeringly exotic blend of Latin, Greek and Arab civilization. Known as the Kingdom of Sicily (and later as the Two Sicilies), this new political entity would endure for more than seven centuries. Italians called it the *Regno* or Kingdom since it was the only one in Italy, although sometimes the term meant the mainland alone.

All Apulians, not only the Lombards and the Greeks, had suffered wretchedly during the conquest. Even though commanded to write his chronicle by Count Roger, and allegedly a Norman himself, Geoffrey Malterra says bluntly that "Normans are cunning and revengeful", in his rhymed history of the Hautevilles dating from about the year 1100, in which he also refers to their greed, treachery and ferocity. Yet, he admired their toughness: "Weapons and horses, costly clothes, hunting and hawking, these are what Normans enjoy, but if necessary they show extraordinary stamina on campaign and endure the worst weather, hardships and privation."

As in England, these ruthless conquerors quickly created a completely new society by introducing the feudal system that they had known at home in Normandy, which meant holding their estates in return for military service and riding out to fight for their king or lord whenever they were summoned. The Lombards were expropriated without delay, losing their lands and being reduced to poverty – just like the Anglo-Saxon thanes in England. Too late, they realised that they had made a ghastly but irreparable mistake in calling in the terrible Normans to escape from the far milder government of the Byzantine Emperor.

When the Norman pilgrims first saw the Lombard Melus at the archangel's shrine on Monte Sant' Angelo they had laughed at his turban and flowing Greek robes. No doubt Melus thought that the crop-headed Normans were barbarians. Yet few meetings can ever have had such fateful, long lasting consequences for Apulia as that chance encounter in the eerie grotto church.

5

San Giovanni di Rotondo
and Padre Pio

Do you want to see? Then you shall see.
Padre Pio

I N   T H E   W E S T E R N and northern Gargano, at the foot of the great
mountain where the landscape is less rugged, there are attractive
little cities, some quite big. Among these cities, San Severo was once
capital of the province of the Capitanata, the De Sangro Princes of
San Severo ranking with the *Regno's* greatest magnates. Its vineyards
produce what are among Apulia's best wines, red and white. At Serracapriola the lowering castle of the eponymous Dukes has an octagonal Norman tower. There is another impressive feudal stronghold
at Sannicandro Garganico, built in the fifteenth century by the della
Marra family.

It is San Giovanni Rotondo, however, whose fame has exceeded
all other towns in the region in recent times, now attracting more
pilgrims than Monte Sant' Angelo. It has been a place of veneration
since time began. The baptistery or *rotonda* from which it takes its
name, the Chiesetta di San Giovanni, stands on the site of a temple
of Janus. Reputedly the oldest of Roman gods, double-headed Janus
guarded doorways; his feast was in January, the month named after
him, a day when devotees gave each other sweets and big copper
coins with his two heads on one side and a ship on the other. In
the thirteenth century Emperor Frederick II surrounded the city
with high walls, and during times of trouble it sheltered pilgrims
to St Michael's shrine, fourteen miles further up the mountain. The

amazingly energetic Abate Pacichelli, who came here too, wrongly thought the *rotonda* had been a temple of Apollo, but he was justified in saying it was set "in a pleasant plain amid lush meadows". As usual, he was overawed by the local grandee, in this case, the Duke Cavaniglia. He may well have visited the Capuchin friary of Santa Maria delle Grazie, founded in 1540.

Born into a family of poor peasants at Benevento in 1887, Padre Pio entered the Capuchins as a young man, joining the friary at San Giovanni Rotondo during the Great War and then became seriously ill with tuberculosis. In 1918 he collapsed in choir and was discovered to have the same stigmata as St Francis of Assisi – constantly bleeding wounds in the palms of his hands. He nonetheless managed to live a comparatively normal if invalid existence here for the next fifty years, wearing mittens to hide the wounds on his hands.

'Normal' is not quite the right word. His struggles with the Fiend recall St Anthony in the desert, and in his letters he tells of onslaughts by the Devil and demons from Hell, of a mind filled with hallucinations and despair, of being beaten. Often he thought he would die or go mad, sometimes he was bruised all over, spitting blood. The noise was so loud that it could be heard by other friars passing his cell.

He is said to have told the then Archbishop of Cracow that he would be Pope. Carol Wojtyla had come to San Giovanni Rotondo dressed as a simple priest, but Padre Pio picked him out from among a huge crowd. (The Vatican refuses to confirm or deny the story.) He cured very many people, healing not only physical ailments such as blindness, but alcoholism and personality disorders. Tens of thousands of men and women visited him, while he received 600 letters a day. He had the gift of "bilocation", the ability to be in two places at the same time; when bedridden at San Giovanni Rotondo, he was seen at Rome on five occasions, his explanation being that it was done by "a prolongation of personality." He smelt of roses, violets or incense and, although he died forty years ago, people think he still visits them, recognising the scent. His relics continue to heal.

His most spectacular miracle was for a pilot whose plane blew up at high altitude. The man woke up on a beach near Naples with an unopened parachute – at the time of the explosion his mother had a vision of a bearded friar telling her in dialect not to worry about her son. Usually, however, his interventions were less dramatic, advice full of earthy common sense. A widow asked him whether she should marry again. "So far, you've wept with one eye", he told her. "If you remarry, you'll cry with both."

He raised vast sums of money, sufficient to build not only a new basilica for the pilgrims, flanking the friary's nice little Baroque church, but also a large hospital and a centre for handicapped children. Some people who remember him say he looked "like everybody's favourite grandfather", but others who claim to have seen his ghost in the friary church or the new basilica describe a man of about thirty-five. As a man devoted to poverty, he would have hated the gilded statue of himself that stands outside the basilica.

The nails went through Christ's wrists, not through the palms, and a friar who nursed Padre Pio on his deathbed once told us the wounds began to close within ten minutes of his dying. But this does not detract from his sanctity and it seems strange that it took so long to canonise him. Some have suggested that his "bilocation" encouraged the local witches, inspiring them to attempt similar feats. The real reason, however, is more prosaic: The Vatican needed time to read the letters he had sent to all the men and women who had written to him asking for advice. When his steel coffin was opened, his body was found to be uncorrupted. He was beatified in 1999, the first step towards being made a saint, then canonised in 2002. For several months in 2008, his body – still in a remarkable state of preservation, with a silicone mask round the face – was put on display for veneration in a glass casket at the friary in San Giovanni Rotondo.

This mysterious friar is more like some figure from the Middle Ages than a man who died only in 1968, and many people alive today owe Padre Pio their physical or mental well-being, and sometimes both. With St Michael, he has become part of the Gargano.

6

The Gargano Coast and the Tremiti

Behold me again launched on a small sailing
boat on the waters of the Adriatic.
Crauford Tait Ramage, "The Nooks and By-ways of Italy"

ALTHOUGH EVEN TODAY the Gargano remains secret and
mysterious inland, it has become a very different story on the
coast, where in summer the lonely beaches and the little fishing
towns of former times are now overrun by tourists. Yet these places
too are often very ancient, most of them with colourful and dramatic
histories. If possible, it is best to explore them from a boat, as Crauford Tait Ramage did in 1828.

Manfredonia lies at the foot of Monte Sant' Angelo and is
the most important port in the Gargano. It was founded by King
Manfred in 1260 to replace nearby Siponto, destroyed a few years
before by earthquakes and malaria. After consulting famous astrologers specially imported from Sicily and Milan to advise him when
and where he should lay the foundation stone, according to the
Abate Pacichelli the Hohenstaufen king "provided for it most nobly,
with walls, towers and a castle, and also a jetty that could accommodate any number of big ships." It was said that Manfred had such
enormous quantities of stone, sand, lime and timber brought to the
site that every ox and mule in Apulia was in a state of collapse.

Significantly, despite King Manfred having been overthrown and
killed by the Angevins, who were always infuriated by any reference
to their Hohenstaufen predecessors, the city has kept the name he
gave it. Manfred remains one of Apulia's great heroes, even if he only

became king of the *Regno* by pretending that the real heir to the throne, his half-brother's infant son Conradin, had died in Germany.

The Turks captured Manfredonia in 1620, razing two thirds of the city to the ground. Although Manfred's castle survived and a new cathedral was built in 1680, the city has never really recovered. Most of the travellers found it a dismal little place. In 1818 Keppel Craven was surprised to learn that its women were obsessively house-proud: "I was informed by the commandant ... that they every morning made up their beds with a pair of fine sheets, which again being removed at night, were never destined to be slept in." Ramage thought Manfredonia "not unlike the 'lang toun of Kircaldy', the main thoroughfare being a long and wide street from one gate to the other." He says the inhabitants had a pale, unhealthy appearance, due to malaria.

Janet Ross met a fine old innkeeper here. "He held up the lamp to my face, then put it down, slapped me on the shoulder and said *'Tu mi piace'* (Thou pleasest me). When Signor Cacciavillani asked him to prepare his famous fish soup, he rushed off to give the order, and waited upon us himself at dinner, producing a bottle of good old wine." He insisted on her drinking from a silver mug, and presented an absurdly small bill. Such an establishment was untypical. Twenty years later, Sir George Sitwell was bitten by fleas eighty times on one arm between wrist and elbow during a single night at a Manfredonia inn.

Edward Hutton's experiences in 1914 at "the miserable house in the main street which did duty for an inn" help to explain why there were so few foreign visitors. He describes the hostess as "something between Mrs. Gamp and Juliet's nurse ... so dirty that it was horrible to go near her." When he decided to eat out, he declared "It would be impossible to find in a Tuscan village a place so wretched as the restaurant in Manfredonia ... full of flies, even at night, even in the spring; chairs, tables, plates, glasses, forks, and spoons, all were filthy, and we could scarcely eat anything that it could provide: even the omelette was rancid because of bad oil."

Once, nearby Siponto was the port serving the ancient city of Arpi, and the last safe anchorage before the dangerous waters of the Gargano coast. Hannibal captured it, while the Romans settled a colony of veterans here. King Manfred tore down what was left after a terrible earthquake, using the stone for Manfredonia. "The sea has retired from its old beach and half-wild cattle browse on the site of those lordly quays and palaces," wrote Norman Douglas. "Not a stone is left. Malaria and desolation reign supreme." Since then malaria has been eradicated, and there is now a holiday resort, the Lido di Siponto. One of the two buildings to escape Manfred's demolition, the cathedral of Santa Maria Maggiore, standing forlornly next to the Foggia road, has an air of deep melancholy amid its pine trees. Built over a fifth century church – although Byzantine in proportion and feeling, especially the crypt with columns in the form of a Greek cross – it is nonetheless a Romanesque basilica from the eleventh century. The interior has been restored and tidied; all the votive offerings seen by Augustus Hare went long ago, "women's hair, ball-dresses, and even a wedding-dress, which must have a strange story." Yet you can still see what he meant when he said the interior had "the effect of a mosque."

The other survival from medieval Siponto is the beautiful Romanesque church of San Leonardo, also on the main road to Foggia, with Byzantine vine-leaves on its capitals. It was part of the abbey of San Leonardo, given by King Manfred to the Teutonic Knights. Ferocious warrior-monks, always of German blood, their order was modelled on the Templars and founded in Palestine during the Crusades. So rich were the fourteen Apulian commanderies the Hohenstaufen gave the *Deutschritter* (command) that the revenues enabled them to wage their own Crusade on the Baltic, exterminating the heathen Old Prussians and setting up an independent state. The Iron Cross was modelled on the cross they wore on their white cloaks.

In an area that suffered constantly from raids by North African or Turkish corsairs, there were few ports on the actual coast of the Gargano, notably Rodi, Peschici and Vieste on the north east. Rodi is the most ancient. Cretan in origin, by the eighth century BC it belonged to Rhodes, from where it takes its name. A maze of steep, narrow streets and glaring white, flat-roofed houses, Rodi's greatest attraction lies in the light and the intense blue of the sea at its feet.

Flanked by handsome Aleppo pines, the road from Rodi to Peschici runs beside a long sandy beach, with orange and lemon groves inland, as Pacichelli observed. Life has always been easier here than in the rest of the Gargano, probably than in most of Apulia. A tiny walled town on a cliff, Peschici was founded by Slavs in the tenth century but, apart from being saved by St Elias from a plague of locusts, has little history.

Ramage visited the "miserable village" of Vieste by boat, and describes it as "standing on a kind of peninsula, and washed on three sides by the waters of the Adriatic." It must have changed a good deal since 1828. Although catering increasingly for tourists, the medieval town on its rocky headland is charming, with a Romanesque cathedral and a Hohenstaufen castle. Near the cathedral is the *chianca,* a stone on which the corsair Dragut had several thousand of the inhabitants slaughtered in 1554 before dragging the rest off to slavery.

From the Gargano southwards along the Apulian coast, and along the coastline of the entire *Regno* at intervals of a mile stand squat, square forts which were designed to guard against raids of this sort, and are still called 'Saracen Towers'. Although some of them date from the fifteenth century, most were built in a programme begun in the sixteenth by the Spanish viceroy Don Pedro de Toledo. Machiolated and crenellated, proof against naval gunnery, they offered shelter to anyone in the area, communicating by smoke-signals – when an enemy sail was sighted as far off as Sicily, the authorities at Naples knew within ten minutes.

In classical times the Tremiti Islands, 22 kilometres off the Gargano coast, were named the Diomedean Isles, after one of Homer's heroes, "Diomedes of the Great War Cry", who took eighty black warships to the siege of Troy. Shipwrecked on the coast of Daunia – northern Apulia – he became King of the Daunians. When he died, his companions mourned him so deeply that Zeus changed them into sea-birds – during the sixteenth century local monks told the Duke of Urbino that the birds, apparently great shearwaters, could often be heard talking among themselves. Augustus Caesar confined his granddaughter Julia here because of her notorious promiscuity. When friends tried to intercede for Julia's mother, who was in prison for the same reason, the angry Emperor shouted at them, "May your own daughters be as lecherous and your wives as adulterous!"

According to legend, a church was founded on the largest of the three Tremiti islands, San Nicola, when Diomedes's crown was discovered there in the fourth century after a vision of the Blessed Virgin. Benedictine monks were certainly on the island from the eighth, building the abbey "just like Monte Cassino rising from the sea." Later it passed to Augustinian canons. Since Pacichelli was an Augustinian, he sailed over from the mainland to inspect the abbey. He says that it was heavily fortified, with a garrison of a hundred soldiers under six officers. He tells us too that the famous human birds looked like starlings and, always a gourmet, adds that they were "excellent, boiled or fried."

The canons left in the eighteenth century, when the monastery became a prison. During the Fascist Era Mussolini used the Tremiti as a place of confinement for political opponents. It is hard to believe that somewhere so beautiful should hold such cruel memories.

7

The Heretic from Ischitella

Giannone ... so celebrated for his useful history of Naples.
Voltaire, "Age of Louis XIV"

THE GARGANO has produced heretics as well as saints and holy men. The most famous is Pietro Giannone, author of a book read by many of the eighteenth century travellers to Apulia.

If you turn inland from Rodi and drive a short way up through the orange and lemon groves, you come to Ischitella, a tiny, very pretty hill-town, which has a wonderful view out to sea. After a wistful reference to "the exquisite eels" of Lake Varano nearby, the indefatigable Abate Pacichelli says "it is on a delightful hill looking over the Adriatic, with a sweet climate", but he does not tell us very much else about the town except that it is a principality belonging to the Pinto y Mendoza family. Their palace still stands in the main piazza, a crenellated seventeenth century *palazzo* (a grand urban residence) with a medieval castle for its nucleus.

The only other traveller known to have come here is the young Charles Macfarlane during the 1820s, as a guest of Don Francesco Pinto y Mendoza, Prince of Ischitella. He says the town was on "the edge of a forest, which for extent and wilderness, and the sublime height of its trees, I have never seen surpassed." Although the prince had begun his career fighting for Napoleon, he later became a Borbone general and King Ferdinand II's minister of war. At that time, however, he was distrusted by the court and spent his time improving his estates, building roads and digging much needed wells. He showed his guest another of his great houses, the "half-ruined baronial castle" at Peschici, where Macfarlane met a pardoned brigand in the prince's service, who told him nightmarish stories of bandit life in Borbone Apulia.

The son of a poor chemist, Pietro Giannone was born in Ischitella in 1676, just before Pacichelli's visit. At sixteen he went to Naples to read law at the university, but kept his links with his birthplace, dedicating a book to the then Prince of Ischitella. In 1723, after twenty years research, he published his sensational "Storia Civile del Regno di Napoli", portraying Neapolitan history as a struggle down the centuries between the civil authorities and the Catholic Church, attacking the Inquisition and the ecclesiastical courts, together with the clergy's corruption and greed. He claimed that the Roman Church had destroyed the kingdom's freedom.

The Church reacted furiously, placing the "Storia Civile" on the Index of Forbidden Books. The author was excommunicated by the Archbishop of Naples, hooted in the streets and nearly lynched. Since the Austrians, who then ruled Southern Italy, were far from displeased, he took refuge in Vienna where he was given a pension; here he wrote "Il Triregno", attacking the Papacy even more fiercely. When the Austrians were driven out of Naples and the Borbone monarchy was established in 1734, he lost his pension and moved to Venice, but was expelled within a year. He wandered through Northern Italy under an assumed name, eventually settling in Calvinist Geneva. However, crossing the border into Piedmont in 1736 to visit friends, he was arrested.

Giannone spent the rest of his life in Piedmontese prisons, dying in the citadel at Turin. Although his gaolers allowed him books, pens and paper, even letting him write an autobiography, they forced him to sign a recantation of everything in his books critical of the Catholic Church – he seems to have been threatened with torture.

Europe's intellectuals understandably hailed Giannone as a martyr. His "Storia Civile" was translated into English, French and German, consulted by Edward Gibbon when writing "The Decline and Fall of the Roman Empire", and read by travellers who wanted to find out what had happened in Southern Italy after the barbarian invasion. Nowadays his criticisms of the Church have lost their relevance, but his history remains gripping stuff, especially its lurid accounts of the *Mezzogiorno* in medieval times – of the murder of Queen Giovanna I, of the private lives of King Ladislao and Giovanna II ("two monsters of lust and filthiness"), and of King Ferrante's dreadful banquet for his rebellious barons. The book helps to explain a good deal about Apulia during the earlier centuries.

Life imprisonment, with no hope of release, must have been particularly miserable for a man with so active a mind and such racy humour. He says in his autobiography that he is writing "to assuage in some degree the boredom and tedium." On his deathbed at Turin in 1748, poor Giannone must surely have remembered the orange and lemon groves above the blue Adriatic at Ischitella in the Gargano.

Part II

Hohenstaufen Country

8

"The Wonder of the World"

There has risen from the sea a beast full of blasphemy, that, formed with
the feet of a bear, the mouth of a raging lion and, as it were, a panther in
its other limbs, opens its mouth in blasphemies against God's name ...
this beast is Frederick, the so-called Emperor.

Pope Gregory IX

G OING DOWN FROM THE GARGANO into the Southern Capitanata and the flat Tavoliere that stretches as far as Foggia, you
enter the region most closely associated with the Hohenstaufen
Emperor Frederick II (1194–1250).

He captured the imagination of the thirteenth century English
chronicler Matthew Paris, who called him "Frederick, greatest of
earthly princes, the wonder of the world", and he continues to fas-
cinate. Not even Adolf Hitler was immune to his spell. Among the
travellers, he appealed to Norman Douglas in particular, as a "colossal
shade". For Apulians, "Our Emperor, Federico di Svevia" is beyond
question a Pugliese, by choice if not birth, and there is nobody they
admire more. They remember Hannibal from his elephants and
Bohemond from his tomb at Canosa, but Frederick made his home
among them.

What did he look like, this great Apulian, who terrified both
friends and enemies? All Western chroniclers, even the most hostile,
agree that Frederick was handsome and impressive. The face on his
gold coins shows a fine profile. Yet an Arab who saw him says he was
covered with red hair, bald and myopic, and would have fetched a
poor price in a slave market.

His father, Emperor Henry VI, became King of Sicily and ruler of Apulia by right of his wife, Constance of Hauteville, burning his opponents alive on the day after his coronation, blinding and castrating a seven year old rival for the throne. At Henry's death in 1197 the child Frederick was crowned king. His mother died shortly after, placing her son under the Pope's protection, and he grew up in Palermo, so neglected that he begged for food in the streets. He made Arab friends there, from whom he learned Arabic and an interest in science, while from his Greek subjects he discovered how the Byzantines saw their own emperor as God's representative on earth. His first wife, the Count of Provence's sister, taught him the polished manners of the Provençal court, so that he became famous for his charm.

The '*Puer Apuliae*' (Boy from Apulia) as he was nicknamed, spent his early manhood in Germany, winning all hearts and vanquishing a competitor for the German throne. When crowned King of the Romans at Aix-la-Chapelle he proclaimed a Crusade – something he would live to regret – before returning to Italy in 1220. As he expressed it, "We have chosen our kingdom of Sicily for our very own from among all our other lands, and taken the whole realm for our residence, and although radiant with the glorious title of Caesar, we feel there is nothing ignoble in being called 'a man from Apulia'." He always came back to the plains and marshes of the Tavoliere, the uplands of the Murge and the forests of Monte Vulture.

The chronicler Villani, writing half a century later, tells us Frederick "built strong, rich fortresses in all the chief cities of Sicily and Apulia that still remain; and he made a park for sport in the marsh at Foggia in Apulia, and hunting parks near Gravina and near Melfi in the mountains. In winter he lived at Foggia, in summer in the mountains, to enjoy the sport." One of the reasons the Emperor loved Apulia was the opportunity it gave for hunting and hawking. In those days much of the landscape was covered by dense woodland, containing wolves, wild boar, deer and game birds – he himself introduced pheasants – whilst the marshes were full of wild fowl.

Years after, one of Frederick's sons, King Enzo of Sardinia, by then a prisoner in a cage at Bologna, sang in his *canzonetta* (a popular secular song): "*e vanne in Puglia piana – la magna Capitanata/la dov'è lo mio core notte e dia*" ("go to flat Apulia, to the great Capitanata, where my heart is, night and day"). Enzo was remembering days spent hunting with his father.

As the Emperor drew older, during his unending battle with the Papacy, he became bitter and cruel. Most reports of his savagery date from this period. His enemies claimed that he crucified prisoners of war. They also spread a story that he gave two men under sentence of death a heavy meal, and then sent one out hunting and the other to bed; after several hours both were disembowelled to see who had digested his food better.

Gradually the smear campaign took effect, and Frederick found himself surrounded by friends who had turned into secret enemies. His physician gave him a cup of poison, which Frederick pretended to drink, spilling it down his chest. The dregs were given to a condemned criminal, who promptly died in agony – as did the doctor shortly afterwards.

The Friar Salimbene says of Emperor Frederick: "Of faith in God he had none. He was cunning, deceitful, avaricious, lustful, malicious, hot-tempered, and yet sometimes he could be a most agreeable man, when he would be kind and courteous, full of amusement, cheerful, loving life, with all sorts of imaginative ideas. He knew how to read, write and sing, how to make songs and music. He was handsome and well built, if only of medium height. I have seen him myself, and once I loved him … he could speak many different languages, and, in short, had he been a good Catholic and loved God and his Church, few Emperors could have matched him."

Frederick dazzled and terrified his contemporaries, who credited him with possessing sinister, magic powers. It was not only the Popes who were genuinely convinced that there was something Satanic about the Emperor. Throughout Italy, including Apulia, the Franciscan 'Spirituals', the wandering heretic friars trying to live what they thought was the original Franciscan life, identified him with the Antichrist of the prophecy of Abbot Joachim of Fiore, the fiendish monarch who was going to destroy the Church in its present, corrupt form in 1260. Unfortunately Frederick destroyed the prophecy, by dying ten years too soon. When he died, a monk dreamt that he saw him riding down to Hell with his knights through the flaming lava of Mount Etna.

On the other hand, there is plenty of plausible evidence that the Emperor died a good Christian, while his surviving supporters, who included a fair number of orthodox clerics, were clearly devoted to him. There were even men who believed he would one day return, like King Arthur, and usher in a new golden age.

Frederick of Hohenstaufen was a fascinating enigma during his lifetime, and he has remained one ever since.

Certainly no ruler made a more powerful or more enduring impact on Apulian folk memory. The massive strongholds that he built all over Apulia, and that serve as his monuments, are often said to conceal hoards of gold guarded by his ghost. In Pugliese legend Frederick is still *Stupor Mundi,* "the wonder of the world."

9

Castel del Monte

...on clear days one can see Castel del Monte,
the Hohenstaufen eyrie, shining yonder...
Norman Douglas, "Old Calabria"

A MONG THE MANY HUNTING-BOXES built by Frederick II, the last was Castel del Monte. You come closest to him here. It is the most beautiful and mysterious of all his strongholds.

The Emperor stamped his complex personality and his extraordinarily wide interests on this little castle. His fondness for mathematics could be seen in the plan, his love of nature in the decoration, and his vision of himself as the heir of the Caesars in the classical statues that adorned the rooms. He had a stone head brought from an ancient temple near Andria, with a bronze band fastened around its brow which bore the Greek inscription "on the calends of May at sunrise I shall have a head of gold." He had it placed above the great entrance door that faces east. On the first day of May, the rays of the rising sun gilded this Imperial diadem, in the same way that the heads of Roman emperors had been wreathed in sun-rays on their gold coins.

There are innumerable theories about the design of Castel del Monte, many of them wildly fanciful – even one that it was based on the pyramid of Cheops – but there is general agreement that it was Frederick's own creation. Begun about 1240, after his return from the Holy Land, its octagonal plan is not unlike the Dome of the Rock in Jerusalem. Here, however, the octagon is carried to extremes, each point having an octagonal tower and the central courtyard eight sides. On both floors there are eight rooms (although only five of the towers have rooms, the others containing spiral-staircases) while in the courtyard there was an enormous octagonal bath, cut from a single block of white marble.

Although the plan was eastern, the decoration was French in inspiration. The interior retains Gothic fauns and other sylvan deities on the keystones of its vaulted rooms and windows. It still has white marble columns streaked with lavender and rust, crowned by silver grey capitals carved with vines, ivy and agave. A grey marble frieze linking the tops of the windows and running above the huge fireplace is almost intact. The mosaic that covered the vaults has gone, but traces of the octagonal floor-tiles give some idea of what the decoration must have been like in Frederick's day. The standard of comfort was far in advance of its time. There were flushing water-closets in the towers and even a bathroom where the Emperor took a daily bath, the water coming through lead pipes from a cistern on the roof. Not too big, the rooms would have been well-heated in winter, deliciously cool in summer.

All Frederick's palaces were sumptuously furnished, with a luxury almost undreamed of anywhere else in the Western Europe of his time. Silk hangings woven with gold thread, to clothe the walls and to curtain the windows, always travelled with him, servants going ahead to put them up. Huge cushions softened the stone benches around the walls, while the beds were made with silk or linen sheets. The marble table at which he dined after hunting was laid with a linen cloth and covered with gold and silver plate, and with Chinese porcelain which had been given to him by the Sultan of Cairo. Classical statues stood in niches in the walls; one of them was captured in his baggage at the siege of Parma, giving rise to a silly story that he worshipped idols. The tiled floors were carpeted by oriental rugs, light provided by candles in torcheres of rock crystal or enamelled bronze. There were lecterns for the books stored flat in cupboards along the walls.

Among these books was the "Toledoth Yeshua", a pseudo-biography of Christ written during the eighth century by an anonymous Jew, who claimed that Jesus was a bastard begotten by a Roman soldier on a perfumer's wife, and had learned magic in Egypt before setting out to lead Israel astray; arrested as a sorcerer, he was stoned before being hanged on the Passover – and then went down to hell where he was tormented in boiling mud. Possession of this luridly

Castel del Monte, Frederick II's "spy hole of Apulia"

blasphemous work might seem to confirm the suspicions of some contemporaries that their strange, slightly sinister emperor had ceased to be a Christian, although this was not necessarily the case.

He displayed considerable learning in his own, less controversial book, the elegant "De Arte Venandi cum Avibus" ("The Art of Hunting with Birds"). Based partly on Arab treatises on falconry, but written largely from personal observation, this reveals the author's deep love and understanding of hawks; significantly, the mews that housed them at Castel del Monte could only be reached through his bedroom. Sultans competed to present him with young Arabian birds of prey while he sent all the way to Iceland to buy his favourite gyr-falcons. He was the first European ruler to introduce a close season for game.

Frederick liked to hunt in the woods around Castel del Monte, using hounds or even cheetahs for ground game, although he usually preferred to fly his falcons. He was accompanied by his bastard sons and by scions of royal or noble families from all over Europe and the Middle East. During the winter he did not return until dusk, not stopping to eat since he took only one meal a day. In the evenings, he and his courtiers discussed the nature of the soul and the universe, listened to readings from Aristotle, or sang poems to music of their own composition.

After the death of the Emperor's son, King Manfred, the rulers of the *Regno* seldom if ever came to Castel del Monte, although it was in working order as late as 1459. Then it was abandoned, and the great bronze doors removed. For centuries farmers were allowed to stable their animals there, brigands hiding in the towers. At last the Italian government bought the castle from the Carafa family in 1876 and a trickle of tourists began to visit it, including Augustus Hare and Janet Ross.

"It is a three hours drive (carriage with 3 horses, 20 francs) across the fruit-covered plain, sprinkled with small domed towers, upon which the figs are dried upon tiers of masonry round the domes", reported Hare, who was staying at Trani. "From the point where the carriage-road comes to an end, it is an hour's walk, over a wilderness covered with stones, where the sheep find scant subsistence in the short grass between the great tufts of lilies." But for years few tourists came here.

An old custodian, living in a hut nearby, told Mrs. Ross how delighted he was to see her, "and said his life was very lonely, and that if it were not for Vigilante (his dog) he should not be able to bear it." He dismissed tales of the place being haunted at night by the great Emperor as "only fit for poor peasants."

Even so, "what recalled Frederick II vividly to my mind were the hawks, sailing about and shrieking sharply as they flew in and out of their nests in the walls of the castle", wrote Janet. She admired the view from the roof, where she could see the entire coast from the Gargano down to Monopoli, with the white towns of Barletta, Trani and Bisceglie. Inland, she could see Andria, Corato and Ruvo: "We understood why the peasants call Castle del Monte 'La Spia delle Puglie' (the spy-hole of Puglia)."

Although the Emperor had many other homes in Apulia, Castel del Monte best preserves his brooding, brilliant majesty.

10

The Emperor's Faithful Andria

...her burghers are still proud of the preference shown by the
great Emperor of the middle ages for his faithful town.
Janet Ross, "The Land of Manfred"

IN 1818 THE DISTANT OUTLINE of Andria's three *campanili*
appeared to Keppel Craven "like the minarets of a Turkish
mosque". After a pleasant visit to the city, he included it among the
Apulian cities that were famous for "the hospitable, polished character of their inhabitants". In Roman times it was a staging post on
the Via Traiana. Since it was the nearest important city to Castel del
Monte, only eight miles to the north, Frederick II appears to have
spent a good deal of time at Andria.

Janet Ross drove here from Trani and gives us a vivid idea of what
the neighbouring landscape looked like during the 1880s:

> rich but dull country, teeming with corn, almond trees and
> olives, the large fields divided by rough stone walls. It is singular
> to see such vast stretches of country without any cottages or
> farm-houses. The ground was splendidly tilled, seemingly by
> invisible hands, for it was a holiday, so we saw no peasants about,
> and look in vain for their houses. Large cisterns for collecting
> rain-water were dotted about, and the only living creatures we
> saw were the men engaged in hauling water for their animals
> ... On approaching Andria we crossed a "*Tratturo*", one of the
> broad grass-grown highways which since time immemorial have
> served for the yearly emigration of the immense herds and flocks

of Apulia to their summer pastures in the mountains of Calabria
and Abruzzi.

She goes on to account, accurately enough, for the strange lack of
human habitation:

In former times all this country was subject to perpetual inroads
from the Turks, and the general insecurity was so great that the
peasants were forced to live in large towns. This custom still
prevails, and explains the size of Apulian towns …

The Emperor Frederick was obviously very fond of the elegant
little city, presumably because of its unswerving loyalty. When the
Pope tried to turn Southern Italy against him in 1228, while he was on
crusade in the Holy Land, unlike all too many Apulian cities it stayed
faithful. According to tradition, Andria gave Frederick an emotional
welcome at his triumphant return from Palestine, "five youths of
noble family" chanting verses in his honour. He rewarded the city
with valuable privileges.

The Porta Sant' Andrea, known in Frederick's day as the Porta
Imperatore, still bears the inscription that he ordered to be placed
above it, beginning "*ANDREA FELIX NOSTER*". The Teutonic
Knights, no less loyal than the citizens to the Emperor, built a church
near here, Sant' Agostino, where the remains of beautiful thirteenth
century frescoes have been uncovered from beneath the Baroque
plasterwork.

Somewhere in the crypt of the *duomo* (cathedral church) lie the
coffins of two of Frederick's empresses, Yolande of Jerusalem and Isabella of England. Heiress to the crusader kingdom of Jerusalem and
a queen in her own right, Yolande is said to have been marvellously
beautiful, but she died at only sixteen. Her successor, King John's
daughter and an old maid of twenty when the Emperor married her
by proxy at the palace of Westminster in 1234, pleased him by her wit
and her learning. She too died young, however, after a mere seven
years of marriage. The lives of these two young ladies cannot have
been particularly happy, since both of them must swiftly have disappeared into their husband's harem, described by a contemporary
chronicler in a chilling phrase as "the labyrinth of his Gomorrah."

Unlike Castel del Monte, Andria's importance did not end with
the Hohenstaufen. At the end of the fourteenth century it became a

duchy, created for the del Balzo, who built a castle in the city centre to ensure obedience. During her visit here, Mrs. Ross met one of them when she inspected the church of San Domenico that they had built in 1398:

"An old man who lived in the refectory of the deserted convent asked us whether we had seen the tomb of the Duke, and on our answering in the negative, led us into a chapel out of the picturesque cloister. With pride he pointed to a rudely painted board let into the wall, on which was inscribed '*Hic jacet Corpus Serenissimi ducis Domini Francisci di Baucio fundatoris huius conventus 1482, aet 72*'; and proceeded to unhook it. We then saw a long hole in the wall, in which was placed an open coffin with glass on the side facing us. In this lay a brown mummy, and a few white hairs still remaining on the head, and one leg slightly drawn up as though the Duke had died in great pain. To our horror, the old man laid hold of the mummy, and danced it up and down in the coffin; he was quite disappointed at my refusing to feel how light it was, and explained that this was one of the 'divertimenti' (amusements) that Andria could offer to strangers." (The duke's mummy is still there).

Born in 1410, the Duke had fought for Aragon against Anjou in the struggle for the throne of the Two Sicilies. A family who claimed Visigoth royal blood, the del Balzo's ancestral castle of Les Baux (or Balthasar) in Provence had belonged to them for so long that they were convinced they descended from one of the Three Kings and bore a Star in the East for their coat-of-arms. They first arrived in the *Regno* in 1264 as henchmen of Charles of Anjou.

King Ferrante's second son Federigo, who was to be the last Aragonese ruler of Naples from 1496–1504, originally bore the title of Duke of Andria, since the heir to the throne of the *Regno* was always the Duke of Calabria. The most likeable of his dynasty, Federigo's reign ended in tragedy, his entire kingdom being taken from him by the King of Spain. Cesare Borgia was briefly Duke, but it seems very unlikely that he ever came here.

Like most Apulian cities, Andria was ruled by feudal lords until the Napoleonic invasion, passing in 1525 to a branch of the Carafa family, who besides being Dukes of Andria were Dukes of Noja, Counts of Ruvo and Lords of Corato and Castel del Monte. They built a great palace on the site of the old Del Balzo fortress, which Pacichelli found most congenial; he writes of a luxuriant roof garden and "a noble and numerous ducal court".

In October 1590 Fabrizio Carafa, the handsome young Duke of Andria, was murdered in Venosa, just a day's ride from Andria, in one of sixteenth century Italy's most notorious crimes of passion. He was conducting an affair with the beautiful but neglected Donna Maria d'Avalos, wife of the homosexual Carlo Gesualdo, Prince of Venosa, famous for his eerie motets and madrigals. Returning to Venosa unexpectedly from a hunting trip, Gesualdo was infuriated by the flagrant affront to his honour. He broke down the door of the bed-chamber and killed the pair as they lay in bed, shooting the duke with an arquebus, then finishing him off with a halberd, before stabbing Donna Maria repeatedly with a stiletto. Despite the Carafa family's fury, he escaped scot-free – at this date a full scale military campaign would have been needed to bring an Apulian magnate to justice.

Just outside Andria is the celebrated shrine of Santa Maria dei Miracoli. In 1576 a carpenter from the city, Giannantonio Tucchio, saw the Virgin in a dream, who told him to go to a cave in a ravine and light a candle before her image. An old man, he was nervous about visiting such a desolate place, but after she appeared twice more, went with a young friend, the lawyer Annibale Palombino. They found a picture on a wall and left a lamp burning before it. When they returned a week later, they found the lamp still burning, miraculously refilled with overflowing oil. Then Palombino's mare went lame; every remedy failing, he tried the lamp oil and she was immediately healed. After this, humans began to be cured of diseases and pilgrims came flocking. In 1617 a magnificent Baroque church and a Benedictine monastery were built over the grotto by the great architect Cosimo Fanzago. A tablet records that in 1859 King Ferdinand II, very much at one with his subjects in matters of religion, came here and prayed for a cure. The shrine is now served by friars, crowds still descending the fifty-two steps into the grotto to pray before an ancient fresco on the wall of what was once a Byzantine cave chapel.

Ettore Carafa, Count of Ruvo and heir to the duchy of Andria, can be seen either as a patriot or as a quisling. Visiting Paris during the French Revolution, he became a fanatical revolutionary, wearing a tri-coloured waistcoat and distributing copies of the "Declaration of the Rights of Man" when he went home. As soon as the Neapolitan Republic was proclaimed, he raised a troop of like-minded volunteers to help the French subdue Apulia. In March 1799 he led his men in the storming of Andria, his birthplace. Its citizens, who had erected an enormous crucifix in the main square to protect them, fought desperately, pouring boiling oil from their windows. The besiegers put the city to the sword, and by Carafa's own account the casualties on both sides amounted to 4,000. The usual looting took place; later a dragoon was arrested in Barletta nearby for trying to sell the dress of Andria's statue of the Madonna del Carmine. Ironically, after being captured and condemned to death, Carafa, that enemy of privilege, demanded to be beheaded instead of hanged, as was his privilege as a noble; he also insisted on dying face upward. The King commented, "so the little duke has gone on playing the hard man [*guapo*] till the very end." The request was granted, Ettore's head being removed with a saw in place of the customary axe.

The Carafa palace still stands at Andria, a huge dilapidated building of dingy brick. During the nineteenth century it was refurbished by the Spagnoletti, formerly the ducal stewards, who had bought out their masters; eventually they were to rank among Apulia's biggest landowners and wine-producers, acquiring a papal title. They have long since deserted this forlorn barrack.

The dying King Ferdinand II stayed at Andria in January 1859, apparently in the Carafa palace. He was on his way to Bari, inspecting Apulia for the last time, and came here to see the San Ferdinando agricultural colony. Very much a benevolent despot, the king had established the colony over twenty years before as a refuge for labourers whom he had forcibly evicted from the Barletta saltmarshes, to save them from the lethal malaria. In contrast to Ferdinand's paternal approach, the *Risorgimento* would bring poverty and despair.

"I was told that every morning, at daybreak, over ten thousand labourers leave Andria, many of them mounted on donkeys, mules or horses, as their fields are miles away", Janet Ross recorded after her visit in 1888: "The shepherds drive their flocks of goats and sheep and the herdsmen their cattle through the streets, making sleep impossible." She did not realise that the mounted labourers were going out as sweated labour in work gangs, that many of the city's population were dying of hunger. She was puzzled that there was no inn of any kind here despite the 40,000 inhabitants, and wondered why the very few shops were so poor.

During the year after Mrs. Ross's visit to Andria, Colonel Caracciolo, who commanded the local *carabinieri*, reported, "Entire families have had no food for several days. They wander through the streets and are a horrifying sight. Any description of them might seem to exaggerate. Yet many go so hungry that they cannot stand and have to stay in bed." Eighty per cent of the male population were landless labourers, all too frequently unemployed and totally penniless. They lived in slum-dwellings or 'grottoes', four out of five being illiterate. It was a very long time before their condition improved. In 1914 Edward Hutton observed, "the place is like a vast peasant city, the like of which no other province of Italy knows."

Today, however, Andria is a pleasant, prosperous little city with charming inhabitants. They have regained all their ancient spirit. "Most cultivated and with the finest manners are the Andriesi", commented Pacichelli in the seventeenth century. The modern Andriesi are just as amiable.

Andria is certainly one of the best places to go looking for the Emperor Frederick's ghost, especially its cathedral and the landscape around the city. Together with Castel del Monte, this is the heart of the Hohenstaufen country.

The Land of Manfred

Fair was he, handsome, and of noble air
Dante, "Purgatorio, III"

THE OTHER ROYAL GHOST of Apulia is Frederick's son, Manfred. Like his father, he loved Apulia, where he was born, hunting there whenever possible. "The peasants still speak with pride and affection of 'our great Emperor', and of his son, 'our King Manfred', so that the chivalrous figure of the 'Bello e biondo' (handsome and fair-haired) son of Frederick seemed to haunt me at every turn", Janet Ross wrote. She was obsessed with him, calling her book on Apulia "The Land of Manfred".

He was born in the castle of Venosa in 1231, one of Frederick's bastard children by Bianca Lancia, his father making him Count of Monte Sant'Angelo and Prince of Tàranto. When Frederick lay dying in 1250, he named him regent of the kingdom since his half-brother, Emperor Conrad IV, was away in Germany. When Conrad died four years later – poisoned with powdered diamonds by Manfred, according to his enemies – he seized the throne, even though Conrad had left an heir, the baby Conradin. In 1258 he was crowned King of Sicily, soon controlling not only the *Mezzogiorno* but much of central Italy.

The following year he married a Greek princess, Helena, daughter of Michael Angelus, Despot of Epirus. Her dowry was Corfu together with several towns across the Adriatic. The marriage seems to have been a happy one, and there were three sons and a daughter.

Had Manfred been content with his southern kingdom, he might have founded a lasting dynasty, but he wanted to rule all Italy and the Papacy was implacably hostile, terrified of being hemmed in by the Hohenstaufen north and south. Successive popes did their best to destroy "the sultan of Lucera", offering his crown to a son of Henry III of England, without success. But in 1263 it was accepted by the ruthless Charles of Anjou, brother of the French king, St Louis.

Manfred ignored the threat and spent all his time hunting in Apulia. When the eagle-faced Charles arrived at the head of a French army in February 1266, Manfred met him outside Benevento, with heavily armoured German knights, Saracens and the barons of Apulia. The king sent in his Germans, his crack troops, too soon, their charge was beaten off and the Apulian barons rode away. Manfred, who might have saved himself, died fighting. Pope Clement IV wrote, "Our dear son Charles is in peaceful possession of the whole realm, having in his hands the putrid corpse of that pestilential man, his wife, his children and his treasure."

An Apulian Dominican recorded that "on 28 February news arrived that King Manfred and his army had been routed near Benevento ... After a few days it was learnt that King Manfred had been found dead on the battlefield. Queen Helena, waiting for news at Lucera, fainted from grief. The poor young woman did not know what to do, since all the barons and courtiers left, as they usually do in such cases."

The only people who did not abandon her were some citizens of Trani – Messer Monualdo and his wife and a Messer Amerusio. They advised her to go to their city and sail for Epirus with her children, Amerusio sending a message to get a galley ready. "They reached Trani on the night of 3 March but could not sail because the wind was wrong", continues the friar. "Queen Helena and Amerusio hid in the castle, where they had been warmly welcomed by the castellan." But agents of Pope Clement discovered they were there, forcing the castellan to arrest them and raise the drawbridge. On 7 March King Charles's men-at-arms came for the queen, "and they took her and her four children with all their treasure away by night, no one knows where."

Two years later, Manfred's nephew, Conradin of Hohenstaufen (Emperor Conrad's son) marched down from Germany. Many supporters were waiting for him in Apulia, where Manfred's Saracens still held out at Lucera. But Charles intercepted Conradin's army, capturing and beheading the sixteen year old king.

Meanwhile, Manfred's wife and children had been imprisoned at

Nocera, where Queen Helena died in 1271. The girl was rescued after eighteen years, but the boys remained in prison for the rest of their lives, King Charles's successor considerately ordering their chains to be removed in 1295. One at least was still alive in 1309, the very last Hohenstaufen.

Manfred left a no less abiding memory than Frederick II. *"Biondo era e bello e di gentile aspetto"* ("golden hair, and noble dignity his features show'd"), wrote Dante, born the year before he died, who placed him in Purgatory – with the certainty of going to Heaven after he had purged his sins. This impression of the fair-haired king's good looks and charm was echoed by the Florentine chronicler Giovanni Villani, Dante's near contemporary, although he had some unpleasant things to say about him:

> Manfred was beautiful in person, and very like his father, but even more dissolute in every way; a musician and singer, he loved having jesters, minstrels and beautiful whores around him, and always dressed in green. He was unusually generous, courteous and amiable, and as a result much loved and popular; yet his entire way of life was given up to sensuality, as he cared for neither God nor the saints, only for fleshly pleasures.

It has to be admitted, too, that the king also had a slightly sinister reputation; for instance, that he owned a magic ring that could summon up demons.

You are just as close to King Manfred at Castel del Monte or Andria as you are to the Emperor Frederick, and his name is commemorated all over Apulia, although he built (or rebuilt) fewer castles than his father. Like Frederick, he loved Puglia, whose people have never forgotten him. Janet Ross had every reason to call it "The Land of Manfred."

Part III

The Tavoliere

12

Foggia and the Tavoliere

*In a dry summer at Foggia water costs more than wine; it is brought
by train, and the station is besieged by people with pails, jugs, basins
and bottles, who buy it by the litre.*

Janet Ross, "The Fourth Generation"

WHEN AUGUSTUS HARE visited Apulia early in the 1880s
he came by rail from Naples to Foggia, through the mountains to the Tavoliere. "We have now entered a part of Italy which is
behind-hand in civilisation to a degree which will only be credible to
those who have tried it", he sniffed. *"All* sanitary arrangements after
leaving Foggia are almost unknown. The filth even of the railway stations is indescribable." In those days there was simply not enough
water to clean them properly.

Many travellers remarked on the bare, endless expanse of the flat
Tavoliere, with not a house in sight, the only notable feature being
the giant fennel lining the trackways. Flocks of sheep were everywhere, guarded by milk-white dogs as intelligent as they were fierce
– the beautiful *Abruzzesi*, whose descendants can still be seen.

Nothing could be more different from the mountainous Gargano
than this vast plain in the southern Capitanata, whose centre is
Foggia. The name 'Capitanata' (land of the *catapan*) is a memory of
the Byzantine governors who ruled for the Emperors at Constantinople. Under the Romans the Tavoliere had been farmed by veterans of the Punic Wars, before they and their small-holdings were
displaced by sheep ranches. From the second century AD until the
Risorgimento the land was dominated by sheep, driven up into the

Abruzzi during summer when the Apulian grass was parched, but returning in the autumn.

By Apulian standards Foggia is a late-comer as a city, founded in the eleventh century around a spot where a miraculous icon of the Virgin had been discovered, the "Icona Vetere", now hanging behind a curtain in the cathedral. No other town then existed in the area, only hamlets peopled by refugees from the old city of Arpi, destroyed by Saracens. The Normans fortified Foggia, which became important in the thirteenth century when Frederick II made it his administrative headquarters, because of the good roads to Naples, Bari and Tàranto.

The palace which Frederick built was destroyed by Papal troops, who used its stones to strengthen their entrenchments while fighting Manfred. Contemporary descriptions give some idea of it, "rich in marble, with statues and pillars or verd-antique, with marble lions and basins." Part of the extensive gardens was set aside for aviaries and the Imperial menagerie.

A royal menagerie was fashionable throughout the Middles Ages. Frederick's is the best recorded, perhaps because it always travelled with him and was seen by thousands of his subjects. The Sultan of Cairo sent an elephant, complete with howdah, which led his procession from town to town, and a giraffe – the first in Europe. Hunting leopards and baggage camels came from Tunisia where there was a Sicilian consul. Frederick's hosts must have dreaded his visits. At Padua he spent many months at the monastery of Santa Justina with the elephant, five leopards and twenty-four camels.

Although personally abstemious, the Emperor entertained foreign princes on a lavish scale, both here and at Lucera. A contemporary chronicler gives us this picture of life at court: "Every sort of festive joy was there united. The alternation of choirs, the purple garments of the musicians evoked a festal mood. A number of guests were knighted, other adorned with signs of special honour. The whole day was spent in merriment, and as the darkness fell, flaming torches were kindled here and there and turned night into day for the contests of the players."

The ladies of the court, on the whole excluded from the hunting boxes of Castel del Monte and Gravina, lived a normal life at Foggia. Appropriately for such an Eastern kingdom they dressed very like their sisters across the Adriatic, with Byzantine coronets, and veils to preserve their complexions.

Old Foggia disappeared in an earthquake in 1731, and only the lower part remains of the cathedral where King Manfred married Helena of Epirus. The Baroque church of the Calvary has survived, however, memorable for five domed chapels, once seven, which stand on the path to the church – walking beside them, the faithful were meant to reflect on the Seven Deadly Sins.

After the city centre's restoration in the 1770s, Swinburne described it as having two or three streets and a handsome customs house (the Dogana delle Pecore), "neatly built of white stone". Forty years on, Keppel Craven found Foggia more prosperous than anywhere else in Southern Italy except Naples, while in 1828 Ramage remarked on its handsome, comfortable houses, some of which escaped the bombing in 1943, and its "numerously attended" theatre. The theatre has since changed its name in honour of Foggia's favourite son, Umberto Giordano, composer of "André Chenier" and "Fedora".

There were no trains in Octavian Blewitt's day (1850), but Foggia could be reached by coach, the mail leaving Naples at midnight every Monday, Wednesday and Saturday. The fare was six ducats, a sovereign. The road went through the narrow defile of the Val de Bovino, where until recently brigands had often lain in ambush. En route, Blewitt saw from his coach window the Tavoliere as it was before the *Risorgimento*, covered with sheep in winter and spring, the flocks on their way to the Abruzzi in summer.

In 1865 Juliette Figuier decided that while Foggia might have a theatre, a hospital, a museum and public gardens, it felt like a village. "We didn't see a single *borghese* [noble man or woman]", she tells us. Pigs and chickens roamed the streets while the men wore cloaks slung over their shoulders and wide-brimmed hats with pointed crowns, even when eating their meals – "They could have been mistaken for Moslems." Only some children serving in a restaurant showed any sign of cheerfulness; otherwise people seemed old before their time, weakened by malnutrition. "You can have no idea of the wretchedness, listlessness and apathy of this slothful population", she wrote. But she liked the plays at the theatre, simple, unpretentious comedies.

"We would have quite enjoyed our time at Foggia, it if hadn't been for the uncontrollable revulsion we felt for our *locanda*", explains Mme Figuier. She and her husband slept in what was called the *camera d'onore* [chamber of honour], for which she thought "chamber of horror" would be a good translation. They realised they were lucky not to have to share it. White-washed, furnished with four huge beds and two rickety chairs, it was without curtains, chamberpots or wash stand – save for a small salad-bowl of water in a corner, and they had great difficulty in persuading the servant to replace this precious commodity each morning. The only lighting was a candle-end a centimetre high. It was bitterly cold, yet there was no heating, not even when it snowed. They were kept awake by the chill, and by the noise of mice chewing the straw in their mattresses.

Augustus Hare found Foggia "a handsome town", yet only a little later Janet Ross thought it "dirty and mean, and the dust is worse than Egypt". She was astonished by the lack of water, especially in summer. This was old Apulia's perennial problem and explained why the region often seemed so dirty to the travellers. In Mrs Ross's day bottled water from Venosa was available, for those who could afford it.

"There would be no object in lingering at Foggia if it were not for the excursions", Hare tells us. One of these was a visit to the sanctuary of the Madonna dell' Incoronata, about six miles south of the city: "It is the oak wood in which Manfred, flying from his enemies in 1254, worn out with fatigue, and frozen by icy rain, lighted in terror the fire which he feared would betray him; and where, five years after, as a victorious king, he illuminated the forest with wax lights, and invited 12,000 people to a banquet in commemoration of his escape."

During the Middle Ages, much of the Tavoliere was covered by the same sort of dense woodland you can still see in the Gargano, and Frederick II had extended the Forest of the Incoronata, planting both oak and elm. The Hohenstaufen held some famous hunting parties in this forest, one of King Manfred's continuing for several days and involving fifteen hundred people. Hunting went on here as late as the eighteenth century. "The Puglian sportsmen run down hare with greyhounds, and pursue the wild boar with one large lurcher, and two or three mastiffs", writes Swinburne. "The hunters ride with a lance and a pair of pistols."

Very little of the Hohenstaufen's woodland remains, and nowadays the Incoronata is best known as a place of pilgrimage. In the eleventh century a herdsman discovered a statue of the Virgin in the branches of an oak tree, after his cows had knelt down reverently around it. A chapel was built on the spot and later the original statue was replaced by a thirteenth century one of blackened wood, a Madonna and Child. Janet Ross watched pilgrims dragging themselves towards the altar on their knees. "Some women were flat on their stomachs licking the filthy pavement as they wriggled along", she writes: "Their faces were soon such a mass of dirt that they no longer saw where they were going, and a relation led them by a handkerchief held in one hand. Near the altar the pavement was streaked with blood, and it was revolting to see the swollen, cut tongues of the wretched, panting creatures, sobbing hysterically as they tried to call upon the Madonna to help them."

Today's pilgrims are no less devout, if more restrained. In the past they arrived on foot or in the high-wheeled Apulian carts; now most come by coach or car, although some continue the tradition of walking between Monte Sant' Angelo, Bari and the Incoronata for their respective saint's days, all of which fall in May. The Sanctuary of the Incoronata is now a large modern church, quite unlike that seen by Janet Ross. During the service for the robing of the Virgin and Child the women's ceaseless chanting is led by someone with a peculiarly harsh yet musical voice, their refrain being "Evviva Maria! Evviva Maria!" After an hour or so of chanting, the Madonna and Child appear above the altar to rapturous applause. Slowly the black wooden statue descends on the platform, winched down by a boy feverishly turning a handle at the side. Once safely installed on the altar there is more clapping and renewed shouts of "Evviva Maria!" (the bishop's sermon is applauded with no less enthusiasm). The Virgin and Child are now taken to one side; last year's robes and crowns are removed and the statue is re-dressed in gorgeous new ones. Then, accompanied by civic dignitaries and a police escort, they process slowly round the large church and back to the altar.

The Incoronata preserves something of the Tavoliere of long ago. Augustus Hare claimed that "at all times the place is worth a visit to those who can admire flat scenery, and the ... Cuyp-like effects of the oxen and horses and groups of pilgrims (for some are here always) seen against the delicate aerial mountain distances; and in the beautiful colouring of the plain, pink with asphodel in spring, or golden with fenocchio."

During the Second World War large airfields were built near Foggia, from which the Regia Aeronautica took off to bomb Greece, and then Malta and British shipping in the Mediterranean. When Italy changed sides in 1943 the Luftwaffe operated from here, trying to stem the Allied advance. The German troops on the ground were too few in number to put up much of a defence, however, and the airfields' capture in the autumn of the same year enabled the Allies to bomb not only Austria and Southern Germany but also the vital oil wells of Romania.

Sadly, during the brief German occupation of the airfields the city of Foggia was more heavily bombed than anywhere else in Apulia, losing a good deal of its Baroque architecture. Traces of the damage can be seen even today. Yet it still retains something of its charm and, above all, that glorious cathedral.

13

The Tavoliere: Lucera, Troia and Cerignola

We are on a hill – a mere wave of ground; a kind of spur, rather, rising
up from the south – quite an absurd little hill, but sufficiently high to
dominate the wide Apulian plain.

Norman Douglas, "Old Calabria"

THE WESTERN SIDE of the Tavoliere is bounded by the foot-
hills of the Appenines, on one side of which stands Lucera.
A reasonably important city in ancient times, supposedly founded
by the Homeric hero, Diomedes of the Great War Cry, there was a
temple of Athene Ilias here, guarded by dogs, who, it was claimed,
barked at the barbarous Daunians but fawned on Greeks. The
Romans founded a colony of 20,000 veterans, giving the city a fine
amphitheatre.

Lucera's golden days, however, were in the thirteenth century
under the Hohenstaufen, when Frederick II built the biggest and
most luxurious of his fortress-palaces in the city, its curtain-walls
large enough for a sizeable town, with twenty-four towers. "All round
the outside of those turreted walls (they are nearly a mile in circumference; the enclosure, they say, held sixty thousand people) there
runs a level space", wrote Norman Douglas. "This is my promenade
at all hours of the day. Falcons are fluttering with wild cries overhead;
down below, a long, unimpeded vista of velvety green, flecked by a
few trees and sullen streamlets and white farmhouses –the whole
vision framed in a distant ring of Appenines."

The Emperor installed a colony of 16,000 Saracens from Sicily
in the enclosure and in the ruins of the old Roman town, and they

created a new, Muslim, Lucera with a mosque and a souk. "No monarch has ever had more grateful or more loyal subjects than Frederick's Saracens at Lucera", comments the Prussian Gregorovius. "They formed his Praetorian Guard, his Zouaves, his Turcos, light cavalry with javelins and poisoned arrows, a crack corps." The Emperor's personal bodyguard was exclusively recruited from these Saracens so that enemies nicknamed him 'The Sultan of Lucera'. His Muslim colonists included not only warriors but potters, forgers of Damascus steel, makers of war machines, Greek fire and poisoned arrows – some of their women made carpets, cushions and harnesses, while others were courtesans.

The custodian suspected Norman Douglas of being a treasure-hunter, probably because the Emperor was known to have kept his money at Lucera: "After a shower of compliments and apologies, he gave me to understand that it was his duty, among other things, to see that no one should endeavour to raise the treasure which was hidden under these ruins; several people, he explained, had already made the attempt by night."

It was essential for King Manfred to gain the support of the Lucera garrison when his brother, Emperor Conrad, died in 1254. As soon as he arrived at the city the Saracens cheered him from the battlements, but their commander, John the Moor, "whose heart was as black as his face", had gone off to pay homage to the Pope, leaving orders that the gates must be opened to no one. His lieu-tenant, Marchisio, refused to admit Manfred. The king was about to crawl through a culvert beneath the walls when the entire garrison except for Marchisio rushed to the main gate, threw it open, placed Manfred on a horse and led him into Lucera in triumph.

When the castle surrendered in 1269 to Manfred's supplanter, Charles of Anjou, he left the Saracens in peace. However, in 1300 his son Charles II made them choose between death and conversion to Christianity. Some think that a secret, clannish people who lived at Troia until quite recently, the *Terrazani* (the Earthy Ones), are descended from the Lucera Saracens.

Much of Frederick's palace survived until the eighteenth century, including a great octagonal tower, but then the stones were used to build new law courts at Lucera. When Janet Ross came and admired the castle's "beautiful warm yellow-ochre colour" in the 1880s, she found an old woman, who had come from the Abruzzi for the winter with her family and 800 sheep. They lived in a crude shelter they had

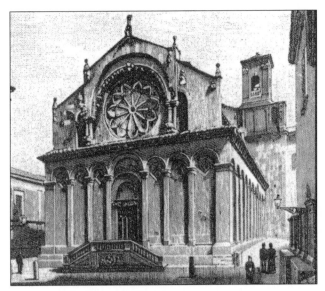

Troia Cathedral before post World War II restoration

made inside the walls, a few planks covered with felt, sleeping on a pile of sheepskins.

On a low hill between Lucera and Torremaggiore lie the scanty ruins of another of the Emperor's fortresses, Castel Fiorentino. Riding to Lucera, he fell ill from dysentery and rested here when too weak to go further. Astrologers had warned him he would die "among flowers" near an iron door, and all his life he had avoided Florence. Learning that there was an iron door behind a curtain near his bed, the Emperor muttered, "This is where, long ago, they said I would die, and God's will must be done." He died on 13 December 1250. His supporters claimed he did so in a monk's habit, his enemies that he expired grinding his teeth with rage and refusing the Sacraments.

"The road ... to Troia (*Inns*, most miserable) passes through a most desolate country which till lately was completely in the hands of brigands", Augustus Hare tells us. "The town is situated on a lofty windstricken eminence, and occupies the site of the ancient Accas or Acca". Utterly destroyed during the barbarian invasions, Aecae lay in ruins till 1018 when Basil Boiannes, *Catapan* of Bari, built a heavily fortified new town, which he filled with Greek settlers but called 'Troy'. Norman Douglas writes of "Troia, wrapped in Byzantine slumber", yet while it is certainly sleepy no one else can see anything remotely Byzantine about it.

Hare thought the Romanesque cathedral, begun in 1093 on the site of a Byzantine church, "the noblest in Apulia", admiring "a great rose-window of marvellous beauty", but adds "The exquisitely beautiful interior has suffered terribly from a recent wholesale 'restoration' at the hands of its bishop, by whom it has been bedaubed with paint and gilding in the worst taste".

However, the city's commanding position over the plain ensured that the cathedral would be heavily bombed in 1943, after which it returned to something like its Norman appearance. Two wonderful green bronze doors with lions, lambs, dogs and dragons, were made in Benevento in 1119.

A few miles south of Troia is the little town of Orsara di Puglia. In the thirteenth century the huge castle was a commandery of the Knights of Calatrava, Spanish warrior monks, but it began as a Norman keep. Later it became a *palazzo baronale* (baronial estate). During an attempt to relieve the besieged fortress in 1462, King Ferrante unexpectedly defeated his Angevin rival, the Duke of Calabria – a decisive victory which saved his crown.

The battle that decided if France or Spain would rule Southern Italy was fought at Cerignola, south-east of Foggia, in April 1503. A French army under the fire-eating Duc de Nemours had been marching towards Troia in search of the Spanish, mistaking giant stalks of fennel for enemy lancers, many dying from thirst because, this being the beginning of the Apulian summer, there was no water in the few rivers or streams. At dusk the French finally located the Spaniards near Cerignola, camped behind a shallow ditch and a bank of earth on a small, vine-covered hillock; they included some of the new arquebusiers. Convinced that his men-at-arms and pikemen could easily storm such a feeble earthwork, Nemours insisted on an immediate assault, which he led in person. Almost at once, he was killed in the ditch by an arquebus bullet through the head, all his officers being shot down with him. Leaderless, the French troops fled across the flat plain, pursued by Spanish light horse, who killed large numbers of them. The military significance of this brief engagement lies in it having been the first really important battle to be decided by small-arms fire.

Under the long and repressive government by viceroys sent from Spain which now began, these three little towns on the Tavoliere became somnolent backwaters. It has been said that the only benefits the Spaniards brought to Apulia were tomatoes and wrought-iron balconies, yet at least they were accompanied by two hundred years of peace.

Although Cerignola is one of the oldest cities in Apulia, it was totally devastated in 1731 by the same earthquake that destroyed Foggia. "To look upon it today one might think it a creation of our own time, even the cathedral being an entirely modern building" is Edward Hutton's ponderous verdict. Designed in a style the guide-book calls *"goticheggiante"* ("gothic"), the neo-gothic cathedral houses the sole survival from the medieval city, a thirteenth century painting of the Virgin, the "Madonna di Ripalta" who is the city's protectress. "The place is scarcely worth a visit, but it bears witness to the transformation of all this country by modern methods of agriculture which are fast turning the better and higher part of this ancient pasture land into vineyards and olive plantations", writes Hutton.

He seems to have had not the slightest inkling that for all too many Apulians the 'transformation' had made life on the Tavoliere very nearly as wretched, painful and lethal as a battlefield.

14

Life on the Old Tavoliere

The northern plains of Apulia are still, as in the time of
Strabo and Pliny, famous for the rearing of sheep…
Augustus Hare, "Cities of Southern Italy and Sicily"

WHEN HARE WROTE this in the early 1880s, sheep farming had
been giving place to wheat on the Tavoliere for nearly twenty
years. The traditional way of life had almost gone for ever, and he was
lucky to see it.

Each autumn the ancient Samnites had brought their flocks down
to the low ground of Apulia, returning to the Abruzzi for the summer
grass. Ramage was told at Ascoli Satriano that "during the later ages
of the Roman Empire a tax was levied on all sorts of cattle and sheep
thus migrating." The system was known to Frederick II, who ordered
compensation for anyone whose trees or crops were damaged by the
animals: his laws were not enforced, resulting in the loss of great
tracts of Apulian woodland, since the trees' self-seeding was annihilated by goats. In 1442, not only did King Alfonso make the shepherds pay tolls for grazing their sheep here, but also for selling their
flocks and skins, wool or cheese, solely at Foggia. Taxes per hundred
sheep had to be paid to the Foggia customs house, the Dogana delle
Pecore, while the king guaranteed protection and drove-roads for the
flocks. Over the centuries the drove-roads, the *tratturi,* came to form
a bewilderingly complex network known as the *Draio.*

Wild animals were attracted by the grazing. When King Ferrante
rode out from Barletta in 1462 to fight the Duke of Calabria, he saw
a cloud of dust so big that he thought it was a huge enemy army and

fled back to Barletta. Later he realised that it had only been a herd of deer.

Landowners were forced to give up land for several months a year, to provide the enormous tracts needed for grazing, expanded as the number of sheep increased. Pasturage eventually included not only the Tavoliere but the Murge, part of the Salento and the lower slopes of the Gargano, causing widespread destruction of arable and the disappearance of whole villages, unable to grow the vegetables that formed their diet. In the fifteenth century there were 600,000 sheep, by the seventeenth four and a half million. The Dogana delle Pecore at Foggia was such a source of wealth that, during the brief period when the French and Spanish divided Southern Italy between them, they agreed to share the Dogana's extremely lucrative revenues from tolls and taxes.

Each flock of sheep was accompanied by a shepherd, a dairyman and a cheese-maker, all dressed in sheepskins, living on coarse bread, oil, salt, sheep's milk and cheese, sleeping on sheepskins in a sheepskin tent. Two white *Abruzzesi* dogs, with spiked collars for protection against wolves, guarded each flock, a mule carrying the tent and the cheese-making utensils. Every flock of three or four hundred was part of a large flock of ten thousand, known as the *punta* that was supervised by a head shepherd, an under-shepherd and a head dairyman. Sometimes the wives stayed in the mountains, spinning or looking after the crops, but very often they and their children came too, on horses and donkeys. François Lenormant compared this once familiar spectacle to a folk migration.

The unusually white-wooled sheep nearly always belonged to a breed known in Apulia as the *pecora gentile*. Some said that the breed had been introduced from Spain by King Alfonso, but more probably it was indigenous. (Tarantine sheep were famous in antiquity and wore coats to keep their white fleeces clean). Shorn twice a year, completely in the spring but only half in the summer, these sheep were particularly valued for their excellent cheese, which made up an important part of the Tavoliere's diet and was worth more than the wool, earning the owners of the flocks a great deal of money.

There was a long-developed art in making the cheeses and an experienced shepherd could tell from their taste on what sort of grass and in which month the sheep had been feeding when milked – a skill that, even now, is not quite extinct at certain *masserie* on the

Murge. In years of drought he would proudly prefer to let his flock die rather than feed it on wheat in place of grass.

The *punte* met annually at the Foggia sheep fair, their shepherds solemnly leading them in a ceremonial review before the chief taxman, '*Il Magnifico Doganiere*', who wore a special robe of office. This splendid dignitary ranked as a magistrate and had his own tribunal. The fair took place in May, when the pilgrims were returning through the city from the feast days of the Madonna, the Archangel Michael and St Nicholas that had replaced the old pagan spring festivals. "On this occasion Foggia becomes a place of great resort and gaiety, even for the Neapolitan nobility", Henry Swinburne observed in 1780. "They come here to exercise their dexterity at play upon the less expert country gentlemen, whom they commonly send home stripped of the savings of a whole year."

Some farmers began to lease more land than they needed for pasture, sowing corn from which they made a hefty profit because of the low price they paid for the lease. In consequence, during the early eighteenth century, a considerable amount of wheat was being grown on the Tavoliere. Such crops were of course technically illegal and in emergencies, Swinburne tells us, the authorities enforced the letter of the law ruthlessly. "In the famine of 1764, instead of encouraging the farmers of Puglia to throw a reasonable supply of corn into Naples by the offer of a good price and speedy payment, the ministry sent soldiers into the province to take it by force, and drive the owners before them, like beasts of burden, laden with their own property. Such as were unwilling to part with it, by compulsion and upon such hard terms, carried their corn up into the hills and buried it. If they were detected in these practises, they were hanged."

This period saw the start of emigration to America, if on a comparatively small scale. Henry Swinburne tells us that Apulian labourers were crossing the Atlantic during the eighteenth century, returning home after a few years. Others found seasonal work in France, Germany and the Low Countries, including musicians, who when not playing their fiddles or bag-pipes, dug ditches. A fair number of these came from the Tavoliere.

Another eighteenth century development was the authorities' concern about the enormous amount of Tavoliere land that belonged to the Church, two thirds of the total and increasing daily. One reason for this was the notorious 'soul-will' or '*testamento dell' anima*', the words "I bequeath my lands to the Church" muttered on a death-bed, that needed no written proof and merely the witness of the priest and his sacristan. Once it belonged to the clergy, land could neither be sold nor taxed. Despite tithes, the abbeys usually had a fairly good relationship with the peasants, and were often model farmers, but the system was costing the Crown large sums in lost revenue. During the 1760s the government made soul-wills illegal, abolished tithes and dissolved several monasteries.

As soon as the French occupation began in 1806, not only were many more monasteries dissolved, but the Dogana delle Pecore and the Apulian System were abolished, causing considerable hardship on the Tavoliere. The nomadic shepherds from the Abruzzi and Basilicata suffered most, since they had nowhere else to take their sheep in winter. Many became brigands. However, the Dogana delle Pecore and pasturage rights returned in 1817 after the restoration of the Borbone monarchy.

Terrible misery would ensue in the wake of the *Risorgimento*, when the new regime sold off the *Regno's* crownlands and the lands of the Church, United Italy's attitude being essentially that of an asset-stripper. The Apulian System came to an abrupt end in 1865, with the auction of vast areas of the Tavoliere. Since by now this included not just the Capitanata but parts of the Terra di Bari and the Terra d'Òtranto, the sales had a disastrous impact on the lives of countless Apulian labourers and their families.

15

Latifondismo

No words descriptive of wretchedness can portray the utter deprivation
of the peasantry in these southern provinces, or the way in which large
families are huddled together, with their pigs and fowls, eternally
unwashed and covered with vermin, to which in time they become
impervious, like the beasts themselves.

Augustus Hare, "Cities of Southern Italy and Sicily"

THE PEASANTS OF THE TAVOLIERE became victims of *latifondismo* (land ownership), a term derived from the Latin word
for the vast estates of Roman times that had been worked by slaves.
Even if the Tavoliere men's life on the former estates of the crown and
the church or on the sheep runs had been wretched enough, it is no
exaggeration to say that now they were reduced to slavery.

The introduction of free trade resulted in the collapse of Southern
Italy's factories and textile mills. Overnight, land became the only safe
investment. Anyone who had any money or could borrow it rushed
to buy when the confiscated estates were sold off, changing the Tavoliere out of recognition. For the first time in centuries it went under
the plough, huge *latifondi* (estates) being created. The province of
Foggia became known as 'The Apulian Texas'. No attempt was made
to form a new class of peasant proprietors, the buyers ranging from
finance companies to tradesmen, many from Northern Italy. The
enormous new farms were let on very short leases, run by *massari*
whose sole concern was to make money as fast as possible, without
worrying about the soil, let alone the workers. Grain yields were
miserably low, wine of the poorest quality. Because the buyers had

exhausted their credit, there was no capital for development, the purchase money going north. Far from "liberating" Apulia, as often claimed, the *Risorgimento* reduced much of it to semi-colonial status, especially the Tavoliere.

Augustus Hare, not the most compassionate of men, was horrified by what he saw. "Much of the misery is due to the immense size of the great farms (*latifondi*), which are worked by gangs under an overseer, and to the absenteeism of landlords ... Their vast domains are managed by *fattori* [farmers] or rented by *mercanti di campagna* [merchants of the campaign], the sole intermediaries between the proprietors and the peasantry, of whom they are often as much the cruel oppressors as the slave owners in South America."

Most Tavoliere labourers worked as diggers, *zappatori,* boys as young as eight spreading fertiliser or killing mice. Hired by the day, before dawn they lined up in the local town's main *piazza* (city square), hoping to be hired by the *massaro's* overseer, many of whom demanded a bribe to take them on. They then walked as far as twelve kilometres, to work from dawn to dusk, after which they walked back; at harvest time they slept in the fields or in dirty sheds. Their food was bread and pasta, broad beans, a little oil and plants picked on the way to work, vegetable plots having vanished with the common land; meat was eaten only at Easter and Christmas. It was a way of life that broke a man by the time he was fifty, when he became unfit for work in the fields. There was no poor relief, the system operated by the Church having disappeared with the monasteries.

There was competition for even this miserable employment, however, from migrant workers like those seen at Foggia by Charles Yriarte in 1876:

> You would have thought the city's entire population sleeps under the stars, when we walked through interminable rows of sleepers wrapped in cloaks on pavements turned into dormitories ...
> Natives told us that these unwanted *lazzaroni* [homeless] had been camping on them for three days; they were all peasants from the Abruzzi, come for the harvest ... I was able to watch them at my leisure, and they were thin and haggard if well built, dark-skinned; many shook with fever and had a greenish hue; their only belongings consisted of a small bag and a big, worn-down sickle with a very thin blade. All day long they wandered listlessly through the streets, their eyes lack-lustre and expressionless.

A small class of skilled workers, the *annaroli,* consisting of ploughmen, vine-dressers, shepherds and carters, were recruited from outside the Tavoliere, so that they would have no kinsmen or friends in the labour gangs, and hired annually instead of daily. They had good pay – an ordinary labourer's wage could not even buy the bare necessities of life – and vegetable plots. From their ranks were recruited the overseers and estate guards, who were mounted, armed with rifles, cudgels and whips, and accompanied by notoriously vicious dogs.

When American wheat began to be imported in large quantities in the late 1870s, many landowners went over to vines. Minute plots were let on twenty-five year leases to day-labourers, who somehow found the money to buy them and time to plant and dress vines – the owner's overseer making sure the conversion was done the way his master wanted. When the lease expired, the land reverted to the owner, turned into a thriving vineyard at no cost to himself. He then had it worked by day-labourers, whose conditions were only marginally better than in the wheat-fields.

A sub-human existence as a day-labourer was the sole occupation open to four out of five Tavoliere men. Not all accepted it tamely. Overseers and estate-guards were knifed as they slept or had their faces slashed with cut-throat razors, many never daring to go out of doors without a revolver. The fortified *masserie* (fortified farms, see chapter 27) were occasionally attacked, the occupants being murdered and the buildings going up in flames. Some labourers became brigands, fighting battles with the *carabinieri* especially peasants known as *'ciccivuzzi'* who had lost their land because of enclosures.

Cerignola at the end of the nineteenth century has been called 'the company town'. Behind the *corso* (main street) on which stood the land-owners *palazzi* were the worst slums in Apulia. The streets were muddy paths that doubled as sewers, giving off a sickening stench, the houses hovels with ten people in a single, filthy, windowless room, often underground. Here lived the labourers who formed the bulk of the city's population, paying exorbitant rents. From December to March, when there was no work, they stayed in bed, the only furniture. Diseases such as malaria, trachoma, syphilis and leprosy flourished. The death rate was the highest in Apulia, the chief causes in 1905 being cholera, enteritis and bronchitis, though tuberculosis took its toll. Starvation was the tenth commonest cause of mortality.

Most of the new landowners were ex-tradesmen, the old Apulian nobles making way for people with titles purchased from the House of Savoy or the Pope. Frank Snowden (in "Violence and Great Estates in Southern Italy") writes, "as parvenu nobility with freshly acquired titles, the Apulian proprietors assumed the grand manner. On the rare inspection tours that owners made of their property, for instance, they insisted that the labourers should bow and kiss their hands." To such men their workers were "wild unwashed people who lived underground with their animals, and spoke an impenetrable dialect. The workers believed in magic and committed savage crimes."

The men in the labour gangs saw the new landlords as thieves who had stolen the common lands where they once grew vegetables and kept a pig or a goat. Enclosures had begun during the French occupation, continuing a little under the restored monarchy, but accelerated drastically under the *Risorgimento*. By 1898 only 6,000 acres remained. "They cannot accept the thought of having been robbed for ever of fields they regard as part of their very being," a journalist observed: "Again and again they revisit them, like some Irish farmer's children brooding over the cabin with a long dead fire from which the family has been evicted."

After decades of bad farming, by 1900 the Tavoliere was producing less and less wheat, a crop fetching lower prices every year. Vineyards were destroyed by phylloxera; what wine was made faced a French tariff war. Employment was harder to find and at Cerignola starving men fell dead in the streets. All over Apulia rioters shouted for work, bread and a guaranteed wage at the start of the day. The first strike took place at Foggia in 1901 and 'peasants leagues' (unions) were founded. Their members, who called themselves "syndicalists", demanded the replacement of landlords by workers' co-operatives. In their few free moments, they tried to look like *borghesi,* wearing tattered frock-coats and battered bowlers instead of the old Apulian folkdress. Yet it was almost impossible for them to air their grievances in the parliament at Rome. Men were given the vote only if they had served in the army or could read and write; most Apulians were too undernourished to be accepted for military service or were illiterate. In any case, the ruling Liberal party was hand in glove with the *latifondisti.*

Even so, emigration was reducing the supply of cheap labour. "The roles are now reversed, and while landlords are impoverished, the rich emigrant buys up the farms or makes his own terms for work to be done, wages being trebled" Norman Douglas wrote with considerable exaggeration. Besides emigration, another escape from life on the Tavoliere was work on building the new Apulian aqueduct, which began in 1906, although contractors paid starvation wages. To some extent, the effects of emigration and the aqueduct were offset by labourers from the Abruzzi and Basilicata.

The new unions' demands meant bankruptcy for the *latifondisti*. They fought back, breaking strikes with hired thugs and calling in troops, 2,000 of whom were needed to crush a rising at Cerignola. They welcomed the outbreak of war in 1915; wheat prices rose dramatically, there were government contracts and subsidies, and it forced into the fields women who could be paid less than men. When Italy was nearly defeated in 1917, they staved off revolution by promising to share out the *latifondi* and restore common rights as soon as the War was over.

The landowners went back on their word in 1918. But Apulian soldiers came home hoping for a Russian-style revolution. Very soon, bands armed with scythes and mattocks were terrorising the Tavoliere, and many other rural areas as well, slaughtering livestock, burning *masserie* and lynching overseers. All workers demanded impossibly high wages.

In 1920, labourers from Cerignola occupied the land of a young ex-army officer, Giuseppe Cardona, burning his grain and smashing his wine vats. In response he set up a Fascist cell, recruiting veterans from the trenches. Union activists were beaten up, forced to drink quarts of castor oil or chained naked to trees while their offices were burned down. The authorities openly supported Cardona and by 1922 he controlled all the provice of Foggia. The unions had been broken. Overseers on the Tavoliere now wore black-shirts and the *latifondi* would survive until Mussolini's land reforms of the later 1920s and the 1930s.

Part IV

The Adriatic Shore

16

Cathedral Cities on the Coast

English travellers nearly always play at follow the leader,
and there are probably not two hundred living who have
explored the characteristic cathedrals of Apulia.

Augustus Hare, "Cities of Southern Italy and Sicily"

ONE OF THE REASONS for Apulia's fascination is the fact that its
landscape has changed so little. Despite motorways and con-
tainer lorries, despite light industry and high-rise flats, in the old city
centres and on the roads between the cities, often you can still see the
same buildings – generally in a much better state of repair – and the
same countryside that the early travellers saw. Sadly this is no longer
true when you are following the shore of the Adriatic southward.
The coast and the hinterland from Barletta down to Bari have one
of the most remarkable concentrations of medieval architecture in
Europe – cathedrals and churches built in a distinctive style known as
Apulian Romanesque, combining the Norman Romanesque of Jumi-
èges and the Burgundian Romanesque of Vézélay, with Byzantine
and even Arab elements – but the countryside, particularly between
Barletta and Trani, has been covered with factories and stone-yards.

Before the Norman conquest, the coastal towns of Apulia were
merchant communes trading very profitably with the Byzantine
Empire and Egypt. Later they prospered spectacularly during the
Crusades, as the ports from which pilgrims, soldiers and supplies
could most quickly reach the Latin Kingdom of Jerusalem. However,
the Black Death caused a crippling fall in their populations, while
political instability put them in the hands of feudal overlords; there

were also attempts to absorb them into the Venetian empire that lasted until the sixteenth century. The long regime of the Spanish viceroys was a period of stagnation and decline, eventually brought to an end by the re-emergence of an independent Southern Italy under the Borbone monarchy in the first half of the eighteenth century.

Going south through the Terra di Bari, the first of these beautiful little cities is Barletta. It became important under the Normans, who gave it a castle and a cathedral. In the seventeenth century Pacichelli described it as "one of those fine cities of the realm which may truly be called royal." Swinburne, who came a hundred years later, gave it qualified if scarcely less flattering praise. "Barletta has, from without, a ruinous aspect; its walls tumbling down, and its ditches filled with rubbish. But the inside of the city is magnificently built, though thinly peopled. It conveys the idea of the capital of some mighty state reduced to the condition of a conquered province, or depopulated by a raging pestilence ... the port is at present a mere labyrinth, consisting of several irregular piers, where ships are moored; but without any shelter from the north wind which sweeps the whole bason [*sic*]". He gives a typically *Pugliese* explanation for Barletta's origin – it had begun "as no more than a tower or drinking house, on the road to Cannae, which had for its sign a barrel, *'barilletta'.* " In 1805 Major Courier found that although it was a port, fish was unobtainable because its fishermen never put to sea, frightened of being kidnapped by North African slavers.

After the *Risorgimento*, Barletta went into a decline and in 1883 Augustus Hare saw "filthy streets" and "innumerable beggars." Six years later, Janet Ross wrote of "another milk-white town whose dirty streets do not correspond to one's first impression of gaiety and brightness." She was very upset by her cabman, who "insisted on taking us to the church of the 'Teatini' to see 'bella roba' (beautiful things), which turned out to be horrible mummified bodies in the crypt." Even so, Hare admired the cathedral, part Romanesque and part Gothic. "Marvellous marble monsters adorn its doors," he tells us, noting its noble *campanile* and twelfth century west front, and the pierced marble windows which he thought "quite Saracenic". The sinister King Ferrante was crowned here in 1459.

The city has another superb medieval church, San Sepolcro, built by the Templars during the thirteenth century, where Crusaders kept vigil on the night before they sailed to the Holy Land. It houses a relic of the True Cross that locals credit with many miracles. Around

"Ari" at Barletta,
probably the Roman
Emperor Valerian
(AD 164–75) and
once at the Imperial
capital of Ravenna

the reliquary hangs a gold chain and a gold medal with a Maltese cross in enamel; both church and relic had been acquired by the Knights of Malta, whose prior gave the medal he wore round his neck to serve as an adornment in 1759, in thanksgiving for a miracle. Pacichelli says that the Knights' Priory at Barletta was particularly opulent and luxurious.

Outside San Sepolcro stands a bronze statue sixteen feet tall, a Roman centurion holding an orb and a cross. Probably the Emperor Valentinian (364–75), it was once thought to be Heraclius, which is why it is known locally as 'Are'. Once considered to have been looted at the sack of Constantinople in 1204, and shipwrecked here on its way to Venice, recent forensic research has proved it was never immersed in sea water. It is now thought to have been sent from Ravenna by Frederick II to be set up at Melfi but arrived after his death in 1250 and remained in Barletta. The hands and feet of the statue were barbarously chopped off, to be recast as bells for a friary in Manfredonia, but were replaced by new ones in 1494.

The castle of Barletta was a favourite residence of King Manfred, who roamed the streets at night, dressed in green and singing to a lute. After holding his coronation banquet here in 1459, Ferrante made it one of the strongest fortresses in Italy. Fearful of Turkish invasion, Emperor Charles V made it even stronger, siting huge rectangular bastions packed with earth at each corner; the gun-turrets inside, with vents for smoke to escape, anticipate those of a dreadnought battleship. There are huge guardrooms, halls, store rooms, cellars and an unusually deep moat. When attacked by Suleiman the Magnificent's fleet in 1537 the castle proved to be impregnable, and it was still able to stand up to shelling by the Austro-Hungarian battleship *Helgoland* during the First World War.

In the Piazza della Disfida is the gloomy Cantina della Disfida, the ground floor of a medieval palace turned into a tavern. This was where the Italians met on 13 February, 1503 before going off to fight in the *Disfida* (Challenge) of Barletta. During the war between France and Spain over who should rule the Two Sicilies, when the Italo-Spanish army under General Gonsalvo de Cordoba was besieged in the city, a French captain, Guy de la Motte was taken prisoner in a sortie. He told his captors scornfully that Italians would never face Frenchmen in open combat. Gonsalvo gave the boast wide circulation, after which thirteen Italian men-at-arms, led by Ettore Fieramosca, met thirteen French men-at-arms led by de la Motte in an olive grove between Barletta and Andria. They had agreed that the vanquished should forfeit horse and armour, besides paying a hundred gold ducats in ransom. Watched by a huge crowd, after six hours they had fought each other to a standstill, the ground being dyed red with blood and littered with broken lances and discarded armour. The sixteenth century historian Guicciardini, who had spoken to eyewitnesses, says the spectators watched in "a wonderful silence." The Italians finally won, killing one of the Frenchmen, which made the others limp off. "It was almost unbelievable how their victory discouraged the French army and put new heart into the Spaniards", comments Guicciardini.

While travelling from Barletta to Trani, Swinburne noticed the huts in nearly every field, built with stones picked out of the soil when digging. "These conical towers serve as watch houses for the persons that attend before vintage, to prevent the depredations of quadruped and biped pilferers; when old and overgrown with climbing weeds and fig-trees, they become very romantic objects, and appear like so many ancient mausolea. The shape of these piles of rude stones, covered with moss and brambles, has deceived a writer of travels [Riedesel] into a belief of their being Roman tombs." Octavian Blewitt tells us that in his day the hut roofs were used to dry figs, "which are arranged on a ledge on the outside, winding round the buildings to the summit." Sadly on this stretch of the road they are no longer visible, hidden by shoe factories and stone-yards, although many remain elsewhere.

Many of the travellers found Trani so interesting, and had so much to say about it, that we have given this elegant city, which lies next along the coast, a chapter to itself.

Bisceglie's medieval streets lead down to a port below the castle. The cathedral is a fine piece of Apulian Romanesque, a basilica with three aisles and a splendid thirteenth century façade. Alfonso d'Aragona, a bastard son of Alfonso II of Naples, was created Duke of Bisceglie and in 1498 married Lucrezia Borgia; despite being a most amiable young man, he fell foul of his brother-in-law, Cesare, who had him garrotted. The Abate Pacichelli called Bisceglie "a joyful city", writing of "a handsome theatre for staging comedies and tragedies in turn, which has not its like in the realm."

Molfetta, on the other hand, in the eyes of the travellers, lacked charm although impressive from a distance. Count de Salis visited it with Archbishop Capecelatro of Tàranto. While admiring its past glories as one of the most important trading ports in Apulia, he found it "filthy, ugly and badly built." It is full of unhappy memories; in 1902, for example, thousands of starving men and women besieged the municipality and the *carabinieri's* (national military police) barracks, then looted the flour mills. To some extent the city is redeemed by the *duomo vecchio,* the former cathedral, begun in 1150 and as much Byzantine as Romanesque, whose twin white towers dominate the harbour.

In the eighteenth century travel by land between these cities was not always easy. According to de Salis, the road between Molfetta and Giovinazzo, the next port, was "the worst I have every traversed in my whole life, so cluttered up with stones, that the mules were obliged to leap like goats, from one heap to the next; so that at a certain point we were obliged to leave the carriage and make our way on foot."

At Giovinazzo, once known as Iuvenis Netium by the Romans, a forgotten mosaic floor from the early Middle Ages slowly emerged before the cathedral's high altar during a recent restoration. "The view of the sea and the symmetry of its architecture, including that of its suburbs, make it delicious" was Pacichelli's flattering opinion of Giovinazzo, whose enthusiasm may have been prompted by admiration for its feudal lord, the Duke Giudice, "noble from the dignity of the purple and splendour of the toga, and from sagacity."

Keppel Craven ate an excellent dinner at Giovinazzo, washed down with a good local red wine. Afterwards he took a stroll, before retiring to a bed at the inn spread with clean linen, entering "possession of it with the prospect of a comfortable night's rest. But in this I greatly erred; for the bed and all its alluring appendages contained 'that within which passeth outward show', a most numerous and lively population." At the end of the nineteenth century, however, Janet Ross did not need to worry so much about bed bugs, although at least one Apulian inn-keeper mistook her travelling bath for "some novel musical instrument."

17

King Ferrante's Coronation at Barletta, 1459

Whether it was his blood or the plots formed against his life by the barons which embittered and darkened his nature, it is certain that he was equalled in ferocity by none among the princes of his time.

Jacob Burckhkardt, "The Civilisation of the Renaissance in Italy"

A S WELL AS the Emperor Frederick and King Manfred another royal ghost haunts this landscape, even if no Pugliese would ever wish to call King Ferrante an Apulian. "Besides hunting," says Burckhardt, "his pleasures were of two kinds: he liked to have his opponents near him, either alive in well-guarded prisons, or dead and embalmed, dressed in the costume they wore in their lifetime. He would chuckle in talking of the captives with his friends, and made no secret whatever of the museum of mummies." He is also credited with feeding prisoners to a pet crocodile, which he kept in a dungeon.

Ferrante's coronation as King of mainland 'Sicily' (Naples) took place in the cathedral at Barletta on 4 February, 1459. In the knowledge that everyone present was aware of his illegitimacy and being challenged for the crown by a rival, he made heralds throw silver coins into the crowd with an inscription stating that his cause was just; they had been minted out of reliquaries stolen from Monte Sant' Angelo. A coronation banquet followed, in the hall of the great Hohenstaufen castle by the sea.

Meanwhile the Neapolitan Wars of the Roses dragged on. Ferrante's father Alfonso of Aragon had routed his rival, Réné of Anjou

Frederick II's castle at Barletta, rebuilt by Emperor Charles V

– but Réné's son, the Duke of Calabria, and the Angevin party remained extremely dangerous. In the circumstances Barletta was a good place for a coronation since it was near the Tavoliere, enabling Ferrante to get his hands on the revenue from the grazing tolls. He needed money desperately. John of Calabria had the support of France, and the French occupied Genoa, controlling its formidable fleet. He knew that the *Regno's* haughty barons despised Ferrante as a young Catalan bastard who was widely rumoured to be the son of a Moorish slave. He also knew that the king's brother-in-law, the Prince of Rossano, hated him for having committed incest with his sister. Even Ferrante's uncle by marriage, the Prince of Tàranto, the greatest magnate in Apulia, was in close touch with the Angevins.

In autumn 1459 the Duke of Calabria landed north of Naples and many barons rose in rebellion. Even so, within a year Ferrante had almost beaten off the challenge, but then his army was unexpectedly defeated at the mouth of the River Sarno near Naples, and he fled with only twenty men-at-arms. He continued the struggle from Apulia, where in 1461 he suffered a fresh disaster, when large numbers of his troops and horses perished from thirst during a dreadful, waterless march across the Gargano. He took refuge in Barletta. Save for Trani, the rest of Apulia belonged to his enemies.

Both sides employed mercenaries, Iacopo Piccinino fighting for the Angevins, Alessandro Sforza for the king. By mid-summer 1461 the Prince of Tàranto occupied Andria, Giovinazzo and even Trani, while the Duke of Calabria held the Gargano. The tide soon turned, however, when Ferrante's ally, George Castriota Skanderbeg, brought 800 tough Albanian veterans from across the Adriatic. In August the king besieged the castle of Orsara di Puglia near Troia. Calabria tried to relieve it, a skirmish turned into a pitched battle and suddenly the Angevins were routed beyond hope of recovery. The barons, including Tàranto and Rossano, changed sides. The rebellion was over.

"No one could ever tell what King Ferrante was thinking", records the French statesman Commynes. "Smiling in a friendly way, he would seize and destroy men ... His kinsmen and close acquaintances have told me he knew neither mercy nor compassion." After a show of reconciliation he had the Prince of Tàranto strangled and flung the Prince of Rossano into a dungeon, to await a nightmare death for a quarter of a century. He lured another old enemy, Iacopo Piccinino, to Naples, welcomed him like a brother, wined and dined him for a month, and then had him murdered – thrown from a window.

"Where money was concerned, he never showed pity or compassion for his people," writes Commynes. He bred horses and pigs on a huge scale, his subjects being made to pasture his horses, lend him stallions and fatten his pigs. In oil-producing areas like Apulia, he bought the oil cheap, then forced the price up and compelled the public to buy it. He used the same method with corn. Loans were ruthlessly extracted from every rich nobleman.

Ferrante's private life was equally swinish, especially after the death of his beautiful, highly intelligent queen, Isabella Chiaramonte. According to Commynes, " he raped several women savagely."

A paranoiac, he became as frightened of Turkish invasion as he was of revolts by his barons, and he added cannon-proof bastions to every castle on the Apulian coast. From his friend Skanderbeg, he realised that what had happened to Serbia and Albania might all too easily happen to Southern Italy, especially after the Turkish occupation of Òtranto in 1480.

The barons were terrified of his heir, the future King Alfonso II, who was even crueller than Ferrante. In 1485 a plot, the famous *Congiura de' Baroni* (conspiracy of the barons), attracted many of the kingdom's great dignitaries; they wanted Ferrante to be succeeded by his second son, the gentle Federigo. There was sporadic fighting during 1485–86, some of it in Apulia, and then the king made a peace which the plotters foolishly took at face-value.

One of the plot's leaders was an Apulian baron, Francesco

Coppolo from Gallipoli, Ferrante's financial adviser, whom he had made Count of Sarno. The king invited several people involved in the plot to the marriage at Naples of Sarno's son Marco to his own grand-daughter. During the celebrations in the Castel Nuovo, all of them were arrested and beheaded soon after. A few months later several other magnates were seized, none of whom was ever seen again; according to Giannone, "it was generally believed that they had been strangled, put in sacks and thrown into the sea." Among the victims were Ferrante's brother-in-law, the Prince of Rossano, who had spent twenty-three years in prison, and Pirro del Balzo, Prince of Altamura.

Surprisingly, King Ferrante died a natural death in his own bed in 1494, after a stroke. He did so knowing that the French were about to invade the *Regno* and that his dynasty was doomed. The Apulians do not care to remember him, even if he was crowned at Barletta.

18

Trani

...the whole town is so gracious in spite of modern improvements that a whole day is not too much to give it, lingering in the old churches, or about the harbour, or lounging in the pretty public gardens by the sea.

Edward Hutton, "Naples and Southern Italy"

MANY PEOPLE THINK TRANI is the most beautiful of all Apulian cities. It has a long history and its famous maritime code, the *Ordinamenta Maris,* dates from 1063 when it was part of the Byzantine Empire. Under the Normans countless Crusaders embarked for the Holy Land from Trani, after a night spent in vigil at the church of Ognissanti.

Facing the sea, its deep moat filled with seawater, Trani Castle is one of the few Hohenstaufen castles to retain its original geometric pattern. The Emperor Frederick, who built it, hanged Pietro Tiepolo, the Doge of Venice's son, from its walls in full view of the Venetian fleet cruising outside, in revenge for Venetian raids on the Apulian coast. The Via Giudea commemorates the Jewish quarter at Trani, to whose community the Emperor gave a monopoly of the city's silk trade, and the little thirteenth century churches of Scuolanuova and Sant' Anna began as synagogues.

It is King Manfred, however, who has the most dramatic associations with Trani. In 1259 an anonymous Dominican chronicler, from the friary next to the harbour, watched the arrival of Manfred's Byzantine queen, Helena Comnena:

On 2 June eight galleys brought to Apulia the bride of
King Manfred, Helena, daughter of the Despot of Epirus,

accompanied by many lords and ladies of our realm and from her father's. She landed at the port of Trani where the King was waiting for her. When the lady landed from her galley, he warmly embraced and kissed her. After leading her all the way through the city to everybody's applause, he took her to the castle where there was feasting and dancing, while during that evening there were so many illuminations, with beacons in every town in the land, that it seemed just like day-time .... the said queen is most agreeable, with a kindly manner, far more beautiful than the King's first wife, and people say that she is only seventeen.

In 1496, King Ferrantino pawned Trani to the Venetians, who remained here for thirteen years. They occupied it again in 1529, but were driven out by the Spaniards. Some *palazzi* have a distinctly Venetian air. The city then declined steadily under Spanish rule, the harbour being deliberately left to silt up, to make it uncompetitive.

When the tireless Abate Pacichelli visited Trani at the end of the seventeenth century, he was distressed to find it so decayed. Many fine houses had been allowed to fall down while its spacious squares were deserted. This was partly due to the plague of 1656, in which "more than a hundred of the best families had been extinguished." He noticed and, uncharacteristically, queried an inscription over a gate, claiming that the name Trani combined those of Diomedes's son Tyr-rhenius, who founded it, and of the Emperor Trajan who restored it.

Bishop Berkeley enjoyed the wine here in 1734. "N.B. The muscat of Trani excellent," he recorded. As usual, his notes are as vivid as they are terse: "This city, as Barletta, paved and built almost entirely out of white marble; noble cathedral, Gothic, of white marble ... port stopped and choked." He adds "piracies of the Turks make it unsafe travelling by night." By "Turks" he meant North Africans or Albani-ans, who generally arrived in fast boats, abducted a few women and animals, and then vanished as swiftly as they had come. The last raid of this sort on Apulia took place in 1836.

During the mid-eighteenth century Charles VII briefly made Trani the political and administrative centre of Apulia, siting all the law courts here. He dredged the harbour, enabling its merchants to export wool, grain and olive oil. However, it soon silted up again.

Swinburne had a low opinion of the wine, and of the cathedral too– "in very mean taste, the ornament preposterous." The interior had suffered from Baroque "improvements". Nor did this dour Northumbrian care much for the inhabitants:

> Our evening was spent with the archbishop, a worthy conversable prelate. He told us he had taken great pains to introduce a taste for study and literature into his diocese, but hitherto without much success as the Tranians were a very merry race, *gente molto allegra*, but unfortunately born with an unconquerable antipathy to application. The collegians, though under his immediate inspection, were above his hand, and often, when he thought the whole seminary buried in silence, wrapped up in studious contemplation, or lucubrations, he had been surprised, on entering the quadrangle, to find all ring again, with gigs and tarantellas. We were satisfied that he spoke without exaggeration, for never did we hear such incessant chattering, and so stunning a din as was kept up the whole day under our windows. It is a rule established by the custom of time immemorial, that no work shall be done in Trani during dinner; the whole afternoon is to be spent in dozing, chattering or sauntering: we could not prevail upon the blacksmith to shoe one of our horses in the evening.

The ancient custom of the siesta still infuriates Northern tourists in Apulia. Even the most famous churches are firmly shut in the afternoon. According to J.J. Blunt, writing in his book of 1823, "Vestiges of Ancient Manners and Customs discoverable in Modern Italy and Sicily", this comes from the old pagan practice of closing temples at noon for several hours so that the gods may sleep. "Hence the goatherd in Theocritus ventures not to play upon his pipe at noon, for fear of awakening Pan."

In 1799, the common people of Trani rose for the King when the municipality proclaimed the Neapolitan Republic, hoisting the white Borbone standard and taking control of the administration. Sailors, fishermen and labourers, they defended the city heroically for several days against the troops of General Broussier and Ettore Carafa, the revolutionary Count of Ruvo. In the end, the besiegers stormed it at the point of the bayonet, reducing the buildings to ruins and the population to mounds of corpses.

During the nineteenth century, Ferdinand II was so proud of the city that he made his second son Count of Trani. He dredged the harbour once again, this time for good, finally restoring prosperity. The depots near the cathedral, inscribed "AMSTERDAM", "DANIMARCO", "LONDON" AND "SVEZZIA", all date from his reign.

In 1865 Mme. Figuier and her husband, eager to escape from the *chambre d'horreur* and the *restaurant nauséabond* at Foggia, looked forward to seeing Trani. They expected to eat better, even if they prudently brought a basket with a cold chicken and a bottle of wine. When they arrived in the rain, however, they both thought the town uglier and unhealthier than Foggia, with dark, narrow, winding streets, badly paved and crowded by wretched looking houses, although the population of sailors and traders seemed bustling by comparison. Out of the seething mob that fought for their custom at the station, they hired a driver and his assistant: "One was a peevish old man with red eyes and hair like a hedgehog, only half-dressed in tatters, and the other was a squat, one-eyed youth in rags." These two drove them in search of a room. In the first *locanda* they tried, they were puzzled at seeing six pillows on each of the four beds in the *camera d'onore* till informed that six persons slept in a bed – one being reserved for women. The next hostelry was a complex of huge passages opening into each other, windowless and doorless, faintly lit by night-lights. The beds were smaller, flanked by jars of foul-smelling oil. There was a knife on every bed. "My *locanda* is for merchants who carry a lot of money when they come here", the proprietress explained proudly. "So they like to sleep with a knife handy." She suggested the couple might lodge with her sister, the widow of a sea-faring man, where they could have a proper *chambre bourgeoise.*

The rain had stopped, so after arriving at the sister's house, they went out onto the balcony to admire the view of the harbour. Going back into the room, Juliette Figuier found their hostess raiding their trunk. "The old woman had a hard, glaring stare, pale lips and a false, cruel face." She ran up to Mme Figuier, raised her veil and cried with a hideous laugh, "What no earrings, no necklace, no jewels? My sister must be mad. Here's a guest who's not worth strangling, not even worth the price of the cord."

Juliette was so frightened that she ran out into the street, to see dark blotches on the paving stones which she fancied were bloodstains. Telling the cabmen to retrieve their trunk, she and M. Figuier just managed to catch the 3.00 pm train back to Foggia, the last that day. On the journey they tried to eat the chicken, unsuccessfully, deciding that when a fowl was killed in Apulia it was always the oldest member of the flock.

Twenty years later, no one tried to strangle the formidable Janet Ross when she arrived with her timid protégé, the painter Carlo Orsi. She was amused by the ill-feeling between Trani and Andria. "At Trani they told us that the people of Andria were all thieves and assassins, uncivil to strangers, and perfect savages; while at Andria we were informed that Trani was a nest of robbers, and its inhabitants *'maleducati e gente di nessuna fede'* (ill-bred and untrustworthy)". There were certainly some unusual members of the medical profession in Trani. In a dirty back street Janet Ross found an advertisement posted up outside the house of a Professor Rica:

> The said Professor Rica will buy, for making his salves, live
> snakes and big serpents, wolves, bears, monkeys, marmots,
> weasels, and may other kinds of wild animal, alive and in good
> condition.

But Mrs. Ross met only politeness in the town, even if the people were amazed by her courage in walking about alone. They were equally astonished at her wearing a hat instead of a shawl over her head. "'Are you a man that you wear a hat?' asked a small boy. Some nice-looking young men at once reproved him and asked me to excuse the bad manners of an *ignorante* [uneducated]. They then offered to show us the way to the cathedral and made way for us through the crowd." To be fair to the little boy, there was clearly something unmistakably masculine about Janet Ross, judging from photographs.

The cathedral, with its tall *campanile* and its magic setting by the sea, was largely built between 1159 and 1186 although only completed in the thirteenth century. A recent restoration has removed the Baroque ornament disliked by Swinburne, revamping the interior in twilight twentieth century style. The effect is unspeakably bleak, that of a soulless barn, even the local clergy comparing the bishop's new throne to a dentist's chair.

On the evening of Holy Saturday, Mrs. Ross returned to the cathedral, to find out just what was meant by the *abbavescio di Cristo*:

> As the clock struck eleven a great curtain which hid the high
> altar fell, and the noise which followed was frightful. The whole
> congregation shouted, knocked their sticks on the pavement

Trani cathedral

and dashed chairs against the walls, while the bells rang all over the town. This was the *abbavescio* which I discovered meant the resurrection of Christ ... The noise outside was even worse. Crackers, paper bombs and rockets were exploding all over the place, and on the pavement in front of every house were lines of little brown-paper parcels full of gunpowder, which went off with a deafening effect. This was the *batteria di Gesù* (the battery of Jesus), a demonstration of joy at His rising from the tomb.

What she did not appreciate was that the *abbavescio* was a survival from Byzantine Apulia, from the Greek Orthodox celebration of Easter.

She thought the public gardens "wildly picturesque", and her description shows that they still remain much as they were a century ago. They are next to the seawall, adjoining the little semi-circular harbour, which reminded her of Venice.

Part V

Bari

19

The *Catapans*

It was at Bari that the Byzantine troops made their last stand; it was
Bari that remained capital of the Theme of Italy until the very end.

Jules Gay, "L'Italie méridionale et l'empire byzantine"

IN 1071 THE LAST *CATAPAN*, Stephen Pateranos, was freed by the
Normans and allowed to sail home to Constantinople. He had
been taken prisoner when Bari fell to Robert Guiscard after a siege
of nearly three years. Besides trying to assassinate Guiscard (with a
poisoned javelin as he sat at dinner in his tent), the Byzantines had
made desperate attempts to relieve the doomed city – only that
winter Stephen had slipped in through the Norman blockade on his
return from the Imperial capital, where he had gone to make a frantic
appeal for more troops. In April, however, weakened by treachery,
the garrison surrendered. Stephen's departure meant the end of Byzantine Italy.

Originally Bari was Peucetian, then Greek and then Roman.
However the city was unimportant in ancient times. Horace enjoyed
the fish here, seemingly the sole distinction to be recorded in classical literature.

Bari's Byzantine period began in the mid-sixth century, when it
was one of the first places recaptured from the Goths for Justinian.
Shortly after the Emperor's death it was occupied by Lombards and,
together with most of Apulia, governed by the Lombard Dukes of
Benevento under Byzantine suzerainty. What was left of Imperial
Apulia, the Salento, was administered by a *Strategos* (general) at
Òtranto, who took his orders from the Emperor's viceroy in Italy,

the exarch of Ravenna further up the Adriatic coast. They kept in touch by sea, until Ravenna fell to the Lombards in 752, after which the *Strategos* received his instructions direct from Constantinople.

Despite the Lombard occupation, one can safely assume that Bari kept its links with Byzantium, the greatest trading centre in the world, the last bastion of classical civilization and the only source of luxuries.

During the early ninth century Italy began to be attacked by Saracens, Berber Aghlabids from North Africa, who sacked Rome and conquered Sicily. In 847 Bari was captured by Khalfun, once a mercenary in the service of the Lombard prince Radelchis. He evicted its Lombard governor Siconolfo and established the first and only fullyfledged Moslem state in mainland Italy. By 860, Khalfun and his successors – Mufarrag ibn-Sallam and Sawdan – had added Orta and Matera to their territory, using them as forward bases from which to plunder far and wide, and sending countless Apulian men, women and children to the African slave markets.

According to Bernard the Monk their city was defended by a double wall, while they gave it mosques and minarets. Despite being a great sacker of monasteries, Sawdan, the third emir, was no mere pirate but a scholar who obtained formal recognition of his emirate from the Caliph of Baghdad. Up to a point, he even tolerated Christians. In 867, on his pilgrimage to Jerusalem, Bernard had no difficulty in obtaining a passport at Bari and finding a passage to Egypt – although he saw shiploads of Christian slaves bound for Africa. However, in 871 the Western Emperor Louis II retook the city, capturing Sawdan.

After Louis' death in 875 the Carolingians were too busy with troubles in France and Germany to intervene in Italy, and three years later the *Strategos* Gregorios marched up from Òtranto to reoccupy Bari in the Eastern Emperor's name. It should be realised, however, that outside the Salentine peninsula which was governed from Òtranto, held by Constantinople since the sixth century, there was no continuous Byzantine presence. Even after Greek settlers began arriving at the end of the ninth century, most Byzantines in Apulia were soldiers or officials – apart from a handful of monks, who had first arrived a hundred years before, fleeing from iconoclastic persecution.

In 975 the Byzantines commenced a long campaign of reconquest. Bari replaced Òtranto as their Italian capital while the *Stratagos* was given the new title of *Catapan*, which meant becoming a viceroy with full military and civil powers over the 'Theme of Lombardy'. In 1011 the *Catapan* Basil Mesonardonites built a *kastron* (town) here. After Basil Boiannes – ablest of the *catapans* – had established Imperial rule over all Apulia, Greek settlers poured into Apulia, most of whose rock-churches date from this time. Had another brilliant Emperor followed Basil II (the 'Bulgar Slayer'), who died in 1025, the Byzantines might have succeeded in re-creating Magna Graecia.

"Among the many perverse notions of which we are now ridding ourselves is this – that Byzantinism in south Italy was a period of decay and torpid dreamings", wrote Norman Douglas with considerable justice in 1915. "There was no lethargy in their social and political ambitions, in their military achievements, which held the land against overwhelming numbers of Saracens, Lombards and other intruders."

Yet only in the Salento were Apulia's Greeks in a majority and only there was Greek universally spoken. North of Brindisi, the population in most coastal cities as well as inland was dominated by 'Lombards'. Latin speaking by now despite their Germanic names, intermarriage had turned them into a caste rather than a race, a caste which differed from its neighbours merely in laws and customs. Chronically short of men and money yet having to extract taxes and raise troops, the catapans handled the Lombards with Byzantine subtlety, carefully respecting their customs and allowing them to live under their own laws with their own magistrates.

Nonetheless, the Byzantine Emperors set the utmost value on Bari. Ever since the Moslem period the city on the promontory had been so well fortified that its possession was vital for control of the southern Adriatic. As in other Apulian ports, its inhabitants were an exotic mixture of Lombards, Latins, Greeks, Armenians, Jews and Moslems, governed by Byzantine officials. The city grew rich from importing the gold, spices, silks and luxury goods that could only be obtained at Constantinople, in return exporting oil, almonds, wine, salted fish and slaves. Prosperous citizens enjoyed luxuries unknown in most of Western Europe, Lombard nobles dressing like Byzantines in silk robes and fantastic head-dresses.

Even so, the Baresi resented having to pay taxes to Constantinople, and serve in the *catapan's* levies. In consequence there were several rebellions such as that of Melus, the Normans' first Apulian ally. Basil Boioannes had no difficulty in putting down opposition of this sort, but he was recalled to Constantinople in 1027 and the catapans who followed him were mediocrities.

When the *Catapan* Eustathius was released from Norman captivity after the crushing defeat at Melfi, in true Byzantine style he took care to flatter the Lombard magistrate of Bari, Bisantius. He thanked him warmly for his steadfastness against the 'Franks' (Normans), and rewarded him with a large area of land, permission to bring in settlers and tax them. He also confirmed his powers to judge all crimes according to Lombard law – save for plots against the *catapan* or the 'Sacred Emperor'.

But flattery and bribery were no match for Normans at a time when an overstretched Imperial army was fighting Turkish invaders on the far side of the Empire. The situation deteriorated steadily. When Tàranto fell in 1063 the Lombards decided that the Normans were bound to win, and the surrender of Bari was due to a Lombard traitor, Argirizzo, who let them into a key bastion. What made the city's loss final was a disastrous Byzantine defeat in Anatolia, only a few weeks later.

The early Norman period was chaotic and during the first quarter of the next century the new regime almost fell apart. From 1123 Bari, with its large population, was autonomous under Prince Grimoald Alferanites, and for a short time it seemed as if the rich city might become a merchant republic like Venice, a 'Republic of St Nicholas'. But Roger II stormed it in 1144, hanging Grimoald's successor, Jaquintus.

The Baresi had learned to regret the loss of the catapans, particularly resenting a new Norman castle that had been built to cow them. When they rebelled in 1155 they asked the Byzantines to return and an expedition arrived from Constantinople, demolishing the castle. However, King William I ('William the Bad') soon recaptured the city. He gave the Baresi only two days to leave before he destroyed every building in it – saying that since they had pulled his house down he was doing the same to them.

20

Old Bari

...a noble mart for all the Adriatic Sea...
Paolo Giovio, "Vitae Illustrium Virorum"

O LD BARI was not only the capital of the Terra di Bari, but a microcosm of Apulia. No doubt its inhabitants were distrusted by other Apulians because of a Greek subtlety and Levantine flair for business they did not share. Even so, the Old Baresi had more in common with the wildest woodman from the Gargano or shepherd from the Alta Murgia than with anyone from outside Apulia.

Every spring the people of Old and New Bari commemorate the arrival of St Nicholas's bones 900 years ago. The celebrations last for days, with processions and pageants. Pilgrims come from all over the world, especially from the Abruzzi, many walking for a week behind their parish banners. Some carry pilgrim-staffs decorated with pine cones, olive flowers or feathers, singing their ancient prayer to San Nicola in an archaic, hypnotic chant that haunts those who hear it long after. The culmination is when a life-size Baroque statue of the saint has been carried through the crowded streets to the harbour by fishermen and sailors. The Archbishop says Mass on the mole, finally throwing a flask of St Nicholas's oil into the waves, and then, escorted by an armada of small craft, the statue is taken out to sea in a fishing boat. As it crosses the harbour, sirens shriek and rockets burst, while the Baresi consume the nuts, olives and dried beans without which no Apulian holiday is complete. When night falls and the statue goes home to its shrine, the sky is lit by fireworks.

San Nicola, the shrine of St Nicholas of Bari

In 1087, sixty Baresi landed at Myra in Asia Minor, smashed open the tomb of St Nicholas and stole his bones. A fourth century bishop, his fame is due to the miracles listed in the pilgrim's prayer: "The sick are healed by his oil, and those in danger of shipwreck are saved ... he raised a dead man to life by the roadside, baptised a Jew after finding his money for him, recovered a vase from the bottom of the sea, and a lost child ..." Listening to the pilgrims crying their thanks on the quay, you realise that he still works miracles. The original Santa Claus, his gifts to some young girls won them husbands when their fathers could not afford dowries. He became the patron of small boys after reassembling and bringing to life three who had been chopped and pickled "to make tunny-fish". This idea is quite possible; as late as the seventeenth century a consignment of so-called 'tunny' from North Africa turned out to be human flesh from the corpses of the fallen in a local war. Like the three boys, it had been salted and put in barrels.

A shrine was built, the first Apulian Romanesque basilica and the largest, completed in 1105. San Nicola stands where the Cata-pan's palace stood, the tower known as the Torre del Catapano being almost certainly Byzantine, while the carvings – lions, elephants, eagles – are Lombard, Byzantine and Saracen. Nicholas is buried in the crypt, which was consecrated by Pope Urban II, preacher of the

First Crusade. His bones exude the colourless "St Nicholas's Oil", bottled as a cure for many ailments.

Frederick II rebuilt the Norman castle by the sea. In 1220 he gave an audience here to Francis of Assisi, and then put a beautiful whore in his bed, but Francis lay down on the fire and invited her to join him, to the consternation of the whore and also of the emperor – watching through a keyhole. Frederick did not trust the Baresi, ostentatiously erecting a personal gallows in the city. After they deserted him for the Pope but were brought to heel, he placed an inscription over a gate: "The faithless Baresi are full of promises but then break them. Cherish in your noble heart, I pray you, this warning: 'Be on your guard against a Barese as you would against a drawn sword', and if he cries 'hail', then beware of an enemy."

The grim Charles of Anjou was no less cynical, despite an enthusiastic welcome, but his son Charles II – *Lo Zoppo* (The Lame) – became a devotee of St Nicholas, lavishing treasure on the shrine, one gift being a tooth of Mary Magdalene. Meanwhile the city grew richer and richer. The Latin conquest of Constantinople in 1204 brought even more trade with the East, since Bari was a staging post on the route from Venice to the Golden Horn.

However, due to wars between rival dynasties and as a consequence of becoming a duchy, the fourteenth and fifteenth centuries were a wretched period for the Baresi. One fifteenth century duke was Gianantonio del Balzo Orsini, Prince of Tàranto, who had the lucrative right of exporting foodstuffs from his estates free of duty; his flocks amounted to 31,000 animals. When he died in 1463, probably murdered by King Ferrante's agents, the duchy was given to the Sforza of Milan, Ferrante's allies in the war against the Angevins.

From 1500–24 Bari was ruled by the Duchess Isabella Sforza, who was the daughter of Alfonso II of Naples and the widow of Gian Galeazzo II of Milan. She hated the French for chasing the Sforza out of Milan and for taking her young son by Galeazzo a prisoner to France, where they forced him into becoming a monk. She never saw him again, signing herself "Isabella, unique in misfortune." A poetess and an accomplished musician, she lived in splendour at the castle, devoting herself to her daughter Bona. But in 1517, in a dress of blue studded with golden bees, Bona was married by proxy to King Sigismund of Poland.

After Isabella's death, Bona governed Bari from Poland. When Sigismund died in 1548, she took a lover, her luxurious court at

Cracow corrupting even the clergy. She was on bad terms with her son, Sigismund II, hating her daughters-in-law; the first died in childbirth, the second within days of being crowned, and it was widely believed that Bona had poisoned them. After a final quarrel with her son, in 1555 she returned to Bari, taking so much treasure with her that, at their coronation, future Kings of Poland had to swear to recover it. She died two years later.

Bona may have brought one or two Protestants with her from tolerant Poland, for during the latter half of the sixteenth century, "a foreigner from a distant land" appeared in Bari, teaching philosophy. When it was discovered that he was "a perfidious Calvinist", who cast doubt on the doctrine of Transubstantiation, Archbishop Puteo ordered his arrest. He fled to Trani, but was caught and sent to Rome, where he was burned at the stake.

Since the Turkish conquest of the Balkans, the city had been increasingly threatened by Muslim pirates, Baresi notables being captured and held to ransom on their way to greet Bona at Venice when she was returning from Poland. The situation became so serious that the *duomo*'s bell-tower was used as a look-out post, a permanent watch being kept for the sails of Turkish or North African raiders. Inland, brigands frequently intercepted wagon-loads of food en route to Bari.

In 1579 Camillo Porzio wrote of the Terra di Bari, "this province is famous for corn, oil, cotton, wine, saffron and ... whole woods of almond trees." Rich Baresi often owned a *masseria* in the country or a share in one, where olives were pressed, but many of the city's *palazzi* contained presses that could handle several hundred-weight. Grapes were pressed in the country, the must brought in to the *palazzi* to ferment. A *palazzo* generally had two storeys and a roof-terrace, the owner's apartments being on the first floor, store-rooms and cisterns on the ground floor; if more storage space was needed the courtyard would be covered with sail-cloth. Five hundred Venetian merchants came regularly to buy wine and wheat.

As elsewhere, savage taxation caused a popular rising in 1647. Plague broke out in 1656, killing 12,000 Baresi out of 15,000. Brigandage grew even worse, pirates more active, so that the walls had to be rebuilt at great expense. With not enough labour to work them, the price of arable land, olive groves and vineyards slumped; by the 1670s they were almost unsaleable. There was famine in 1672, another outbreak of plague in 1690–92.

Yet the Abate Pacichelli, visiting Bari in the 1680s, calls it the "Crown of the Province and Jewel of Cities". He liked the people, whom he says are good looking, fine men of business, honest, hardworking and kind-hearted, and make good soldiers – *Arditi nelle Guerre.*

As a result of the War of the Spanish Succession, Austrian rule replaced Spanish from 1707 to 1738. In his journal George Berkeley describes Bari at this time. It "hath inhabitants 18,000; moles old and new, port shallow, not admitting ships of any burden." He says of two friaries outside the walls, "pleasantly situated, cool cloisters, orange and lemon groves in them, fine views, delicious living." He adds that the outskirts abound in cornfields, vineyards and orchards, and admires the extremely delightful small white houses. But he also tells us, "The gentry of Bari dare not lie during summer in their villas for fear of the Turk."

In 1738 the kingdom of the Two Sicilies became independent once more under Charles VII of Bourbon, the first of the Borbone dynasty, who revived Southern Italy's prosperity, building countless roads. In 1740 he spent three days at Bari to thank St Nicholas for the birth of a son and heir, presenting the basilica with a silver *baldacchino* (canopy of state).

The composer Nicolo Piccini was born here in 1728. His first success was at Naples; the opera "*La Cecchina: la Buona figliuola*", with a plot inspired by Richardson's novel "Pamela" about the trials of a virtuous servant girl. Piccini later went to Paris, to become the unwilling rival of Gluck. When he died in 1800, he had written more than 150 long forgotten operas. "*La Cecchina*" was revived some years ago, at the Val d' Itria festival.

Henry Swinburne visited Bari at the end of the 1770s, finding its streets "narrow, crooked and dirty", but enjoyed the prospect from the harbour wall – "at every turn you catch a different view of the sea and the coast, stretching from the mountains of Garganus to the hills of Ostuni." His reaction to the shrine of St Nicholas was typical of his period: "a dirty, dark, subterranean chapel ... Underneath its altar is a hole through which devout and curious persons thrust their heads, to behold a bone or two swimming below in water; this liquid is drawn up by the priests in a silver bucket, and distributed under the name of Manna, as an infallible cure for sore eyes and disordered stomachs."

In 1798 Ferdinand IV gave the city's *borghesi* equality with its nobles. By then everyone agreed that Bari should be expanded.

Huddling behind crumbling walls, it still covered no more ground than in medieval times, with too many ruinous houses and horribly inadequate sewage. Already, in 1790 two engineers, Viti and Palenzia, had produced a plan for a new city. But the plan had to be postponed, although King Ferdinand had approved it.

At the beginning of 1799 the French invaded Southern Italy, chasing out King Ferdinand and inviting their sympathisers to set up the "Parthenopean (Neapolitan) Republic". In February the Baresi joined it, planting a Tree of Liberty in their city with great ceremony. Early in the summer, however, Bari was reoccupied by Borbone troops. Later, the *Risorgimento* would canonise the Southern Revolutionaries as "Patriots of '99", although their regime was incapable of surviving without foreign bayonets. It was not a good moment to begin rebuilding.

When the French invaded the *Regno* again in 1806, Napoleon's parasitical brother, Joseph Bonaparte, was placed on the throne of Naples as 'King Giuseppe Napoleone I'. Remembering how pro-French Bari had been in 1799, the new monarch decided to make it the Apulian capital. The royal favour continued when in turn the Emperor's flamboyant brother-in-law, Marshal Joachim Murat, became "King Gioacchino Napoleone I". He gave his regal approval to Viti and Palenzia's plan for Bari, the first stone of the New City being laid in April, 1813.

21

Bari, 1647 – Revolution

...an unequivocal social revolution, from which the reactionary class
of seigneurs emerged triumphant. The nobility had won for years to
come...

Fernand Braudel, "Le Méditerranée et le monde méditerranéen"

SURPRISINGLY, THE CITY had experienced a genuine people's
revolt well over a hundred years before the French Revolution.
Admittedly, it did not begin there. But in 1647 the initially successful
rising at Naples led by Masaniello, the 'Fisherman King', had spread
like wildfire all over Apulia, inspiring popular anti-Spanish and anti-
feudal revolts of the same sort. They included a particularly serious
one at Bari.

As the seventeenth century went by, life had become increasingly
difficult for the Baresi of every class, especially for the poor. Like the rest
of the Mediterranean, trade was suffering from Atlantic competition
while at the same time there was a long running agricultural depression.
All this was made worse by Spanish taxation. Fighting to keep their
dominion over Western Europe, the Spaniards had run out of money
and were draining dry what should have been the richest kingdom in
their empire. During the later stages of the Thirty Years' War Spanish
troops were paid almost entirely from Southern Italian revenues.

The *Regno's* public debt was astronomical, and everybody in Bari
was in debt too: city, nobility and *borghesi*. So were the barons in the
countryside of the Terra di Bari. The value of agricultural land, a large
part of the capital of even Baresi merchants, fell steadily. However,
the burden of taxation was born by the poorer classes.

The little city was governed by its nobles from the Palazzo dei Sedile in Piazza Maggiore. The sociable Abate Pacichelli carefully records some of their names: Affaitati, Boccapianoli, Cassamassimi, Doppoli, Gerundi, Izzinosi and Taurisani, *"& altri"*. They were largely exempt from taxation or service in the Spanish army, and often owned their own bakeries, avoiding the levies on public bakeries. Despite the recession, life cannot have been too bad for most of them in their small but imposing *palazzi* – there were excellent shops where they could buy luxuries.

In contrast, crushing taxation on food was making life almost intolerable for the poor. An added misery was the press-ganging of young men for the Spanish armies while, at the same time, there was constant friction with the castle's underpaid Spanish garrison, always prone to rob and rape. In 1641 riots had broken out in Bari against conscription, followed by riots against the price of food, mobs marching through the narrow streets and assaulting the better off. During the summer of 1647 it became clear that there was going to be a very bad harvest, which meant still higher prices for bread, at a moment when new taxes on food had just been introduced.

Even a hundred and fifty years later, the poorer Baresi normally lived in a single, smoke-filled basement room dug out of the rock, whose only light came from a small window at street level or from the door through which one stepped down, a dwelling shared with hens and a pig or sheep, sometimes with a horse or donkey as well. It was people inhabiting dens like these who bore most of the tax burden. The majority worked in the surrounding countryside beyond the walls, but this was becoming a very dangerous place indeed, since the barons were employing brigands as enforcers, and they were getting out of hand, robbing all and sundry.

To a limited extent the Baresi poor looked to the *borghesi,* who also had to pay swingeing taxes, for leadership. The *borghesi* had their own *piazza* or assembly of commoners, who argued endlessly with the nobles in Piazza Maggiore. But the nobles stayed in control of the city – for the moment. Meanwhile, the viceroy's authority was collapsing. Some of the great magnates toyed with the idea of inviting the French to invade the *Regno* and free them from the by now detested Spanish regime. But then, sparked off by yet another new tax, on fruit, Masaniello's rebellion broke out at Naples in July 1647.

Within days, a revolt had broken out at Bari. Led by a sailor called Paolo di Ribeco, mobs surged through the streets, attacking the *palazzi* of nobles and rich merchants, looting and setting fire to them. The Spanish garrison did nothing and within a short time Ribeco and the people were masters of the entire city save for the castle. They insisted on being represented in the assemblies of nobles and *borghesi,* and on the abolition of the most hated taxes. Although, as at Naples, the revolt was as much against the nobles and their privileges as against the Spaniards, the attack on Bari's nobility seems to have been fairly restrained. It was different outside the city walls. There, the collapse of authority came just after an explosion of brigandage throughout the Terra di Bari and the peasants, driven beyond endurance, rose up savagely against brigands and barons.

In response, the Apulian nobles quickly forgot their resentment of Spanish rule, rallying to the viceroy. They were lucky in possessing two formidable soldiers in Giangirolamo, Count of Conversano and Fra' Giovan Battista Caracciolo, Prior of the Knights of Malta at Bari. Within weeks their army of Spanish troops and baronial levies routed the main body of Apulian rebels near Foggia, though not without some vicious fighting. Meanwhile, *borghesi* who had supported the revolt at Bari lost their nerve amid the anarchy and bloodshed, surrendering the city to government forces as soon as they heard of the defeat at Foggia. Paolo di Ribeco died on the gallows.

Not much is known about what really happened inside Bari during the revolt (despite the efforts of that magnificent historian Rosario Villari). Even so, it seems obvious that the revolt never had any hope of succeeding. What we know for certain is that taxes were re-imposed at the old level, and that the city's nobles regained their privileges.

The story of Paolo di Ribeco and his forgotten rising ought to be remembered by anyone who wants to understand the Baresi. They have always been rebels by temperament, as they would show again and again, not just in 1799, but in 1922 and in 1943.

22

New Bari

Bari, not long ago, consisted of a dark and tortuous old town…
It now has its glaring New Quarter.
Norman Douglas, "Old Calabria"

NEW BARI'S CITIZENS are said to have inherited all the distinctive qualities of the Old Baresi. They are no less wily and money-minded than their ancestors. At least, that is what every Apulian who comes from outside the city will insist on telling you.

Little change could be seen when Keppel Craven visited Bari during the spring of 1818, although he conceded that trade with Trieste and the Dalmatian ports gave "an appearance of animation, ease and opulence." But the first house had already been built in 1816 in what is still the New City's main street, the Corso Ferdinando (later renamed Corso Vittorio Emmanuele). The public buildings were begun in the 1820s, the entire New City being paved in 1830. Soon there was a railway station, and work started on a new harbour. An opera house, the Teatro Piccini, opened in 1854 with Donizetti's *Poliuto*. This pioneer phase coincided with the last days of the Borbone monarchy.

Ferdinand II and the royal family came to Bari in 1859, to greet Maria Sophia of Wittelsbach, who had just married by proxy the heir to the throne, the Duke of Calabria. A cheering mob dragged the King's carriage through the streets to the castle. Harold Acton describes the occasion:

On February 3, a spring like day, the bride's approach was

Maria-Sofia (1841–1925), wife of Francis II and the last queen consort of the Kingdom of the Two Sicilies

announced by repeated cannon fire at ten in the morning. The Queen as well as the Duke of Calabria climbed on board the frigate which had brought her from Trieste, and there was a rapid exchange of greetings and embraces. The Duke clasped both his bride's hands and kissed her forehead; they spoke to each other in halting French, she a little pale from the sea voyage, he abashed by the beauty of his Bavarian bride.

Already a dying man, King Ferdinand burst into tears when she visited him in his bedroom. Yet on the same day he found enough strength to approve a plan "to encourage the city's growth, prestige and dignity." They were to be two huge new squares, a state boarding school and a nautical institute.

Ferdinand died in May. An abler man than his nervous young successor, Francis II, was needed to save the tottering *Regno*. First Garibaldi and then the Piedmontese invaded the Two Sicilies, the last Borbone king sailing into exile early in 1861.

The handful of Apulians who fought for the *Risorgimento* cannot have foreseen its consequences. Peasants left the land in droves to escape from speculators' work-gangs; in 1861 the population of Bari was 23,000 while ten years later it was nearly 51,000. Augustus Hare thought the city had "all the characteristics of the meanest part of Naples – flat roofs, dilapidated, whitewashed houses, and a swarming, noisy, begging, brutalised population. Two modern streets intersect with formal dismalness the labyrinths of old houses and narrow alleys", "Begging is unfortunately still a national industry" says *Murray's Handbook for Travellers in Southern Italy* of 1878: "The best way to get rid of the nuisance is to give it a very minute coin." The "nuisance" included middle-aged men too broken by work to toil on in the fields, monks and nuns thrown out of their convents, and the rank and file of the former Borbone army turned off without pensions.

During the economic crisis that afflicted Europe in the 1870s, the situation was made worse by protectionist measures designed for the North. If it helped new industries in Piedmont and Lombardy, the tariff of 1878 on mechanical products and textiles caused many bankruptcies, driving capital northwards and encouraging the flight from the land. All this made life still more miserable in Bari – as it did in every other Apulian city.

Old Bari, more ruinous than ever, was packed with unemployed labourers, crammed into dirty rookeries and cellars, riddled with tuberculosis, pneumonia, arthritis and syphilis, even leprosy. Murder was commonplace in both the Old and the New Towns; "A betrayed husband generally kills", observed the chairman of Bari's Chamber of Labour. In 1898 cholera and famine led to savage riots; a mob trying to storm the municipality was dispersed by troops with much bloodshed. In 1903 deaths in the province of Bari were 29.30 per thousand, the second highest rate in Italy and nearly twice that in England and Wales. A large proportion of the deaths were in Bari itself, which seethed with discontent and class hatred. Understandably, there was massive emigration, mostly to the United States, Argentina or Venezuela, or to Libya after its acquisition by Italy in 1912.

New Bari continued to grow remorselessly, buildings going up every year. Another opera house was built in 1903, the Petruzzelli – affectionately known as *La Perla di Bari* (the pearl of Bari)– which saw many memorable productions. (In 1991 it was completely destroyed during a fire started by rival claques, but was eventually restored and re-opened in 2008.) The expansion surged on until the Great War of 1915.

Inflation went up by fifty per cent in 1918–20, unemployment rocketing as men came home from the Front. In the 'Red Years' after the War, Bari seemed to be on the brink of a Russian-style revolution. There were countless strikes and demonstrations, well-dressed people were jostled, army officers booed. The Left was encouraged by news from all over Apulia of riots, of town-halls stormed and police stations stoned. But at the end of 1920 Giuseppe Caradonna set up a Fascist cell at Cerignola which was so effective that it earned him the name 'Duke of Cerignola'. Soon Fascist *squadristi* (blackshirts) were smashing labour unions and breaking strikes throughout the province. The blackshirts made ready to stem "the rising Bolshevik tide". Organised by the firebrand Giuseppe di Vittorio, the Left bought as many ex-army rifles and revolvers as it could. On 1 August, 1922, it rose in a carefully planned revolt, a vicious struggle raging between armed workers on one side and troops, *carabinieri* and blackshirts on the other. Women threw stones or burning oil. But after three days the Red Baresi were broken and would give no more trouble.

Accounts of what happened in Bari during the Fascist Era are often deliberately confused, but clearly Mussolini found more than a few supporters when he was seen to be firmly in power. Economic expansion revived, an annual trade-fair, the *Fiera del Levante* being established in 1930 to encourage trade between Italy and the Middle East, a university was founded and emigration continued, many Baresi settling in Abyssinia when it was an Italian colony. Little was done, however, for the slum-dwellers of Old Bari.

In 1939, the invasions of Albania and Greece were launched from Bari and Brìndisi. The following year, however, Bari seemed to be in real danger when the Italian offensive in Greece collapsed; for a time there were fears that the Greeks were going to invade Apulia. The Fascist Era ended with considerable bloodshed in July 1943, after which the city became the headquarters of Marshal Badoglio's anti-Axis government. When the Germans attacked in force in September, General Bellomo counter-attacked, taking many German prisoners and saving the port for the Allies.

Allied troops did not behave well at Bari, requisitioning houses and evicting their owners without any warning. In a sad little book, "Il Regno del Sud", Agostino degli Espinosa tells of famished children flocking round the city's restaurants and cafés, reserved for British or American personnel, and begging for the scraps left on their plates. The only way to avoid starving to death was to buy stolen army rations.

Evelyn Waugh came here and (in "Unconditional Surrender") says less compassionately that there was an agile and ingenious criminal class consisting chiefly of small boys. Yet he comments, too, that the city regained the "comsopolitan martial stir" which it had enjoyed during the Crusades. Allies soldiers crowded the streets and the harbour was full of small naval vessels. For in late autumn 1943 Bari became one of the three main ports of the "British Italy Base".

Waugh adds that the city "achieved the unique, unsought distinction of being the only place in the Second World War to suffer from gas." On the evening of 2 December a hundred German planes from Foggia attacked the harbour, sinking seventeen ships. Among those that blew up was the USS *John Hervey* with a secret cargo of mustard-bombs; over 600 Allied personnel were gas casualties besides those killed by German bombs, together with all too many Baresi. 'Many of the inhabitants complained of sore throats, sore eyes and blisters', says Waugh: "They were told it was an unfamiliar, mild, epidemic disease of short duration." Even now, you meet aged Baresi whose respiratory problems are due to mustard-gas. Old Bari was further damaged in 1945 when the American ammunition ship *Henderson* exploded in its harbour.

Part VI

The Murge

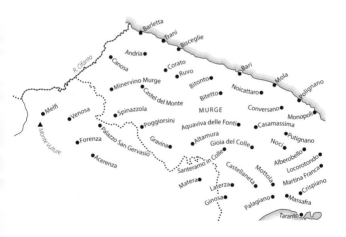

23

The Murge

...an arid region, not unlike parts of northern Africa.

Norman Douglas, "Old Calabria"

NORMAN DOUGLAS decided he did not care for the Murge, which he dismissed as "that shapeless and dismal range of limestone hills." He never saw them properly, however, only glimpsing the western Murgia from the train, on a wretched journey by night from Venosa to Tàranto.

The Murge form the plateaux seventy miles by ten that covers most of the Terra di Bari. From the coast it rises almost imperceptibly till in the south-west it is a good 1,500 feet above sea level. In the north east, where the limestone has been heavily eroded, the rich red soil is very fertile indeed; inland from Bari vines are grown, while climbing towards Gioia del Colle, olives and fruit trees take over. By contrast, in the south-west the Alta Murgia is bleak, rocky downland, providing only a small amount of poor quality arable and some scanty grazing, a landscape that was known in Roman times as Apulia Petrosa. Partly because they were unafflicted by malaria, from the eighteenth century until the *Risorgimento* the Murge's little cities were generally much more flourishing than those on the Adriatic coast, although they seem to have been visited by comparatively few of the early travellers.

The River Òfanto marks the boundary between the Capitanata and Terra di Bari. In the mountains behind Melfi, which the poet Horace knew well, this can be a boiling torrent in winter, but here the Òfanto is no more than a sluggish trickle, almost dry in summer, the "stagnant Aufidus" of the ancient writers. The last river in Apulia as you go south, it is a reminder of just how little water there was until recent times.

In February 1817 the eighteen-year-old Charles Macfarlane explored the banks of the Òfanto, to see the battlefield of Cannae where Hannibal had defeated the Romans: "I had no companion, except the Calabrian pony that carried me, and a rough haired Scotch terrier." Whatever scholarly conclusions Macfarlane may have reached about the battle, he has left us a fascinating glimpse of a long vanished way of life that had been lived on the desolate uplands of the Murge for centuries before the coming of the Romans.

The young traveller met some shepherds, who invited him to spend the night in their *tugurio,* a long, low hut, where he was given a meal; an omelette, fat bacon, maize bread and ricotta, with a glass of rough wine.

> When all the pastoral society was assembled, the patriarchal chief shepherd taking the lead, they repeated aloud, and with well modulated cadences, the evening prayers, or the Catholic service of "Ave Maria". A boy then lit a massy old brass lamp, that looked as it if had been dug out of Pompeii, and on producing it said "Santa notte a tutta la compagnia" (a holy night to all the company). The shepherds then took their supper, which was very frugal, consisting principally of Indian corn-bread and raw onions with a little wine....

The hut was just a single room with no chimney, smoke finding its way out through crannies in the roof. The beds were made of sheep-skins and dried maize leaves.

> Several of the huge dogs lay dreaming with their faces to the fire ... Soon, however, the flames died on the hearth, the embers merely smouldered, and all was darkness, but not all silence, for the men snored most sonorously; the wind, that swept across the wide open plain, howled round the house, and occasionally the dogs joined in the chorus.

Macfarlane says that the shepherds were going to stay here until the middle of the spring, when they would slowly make their way to the Abruzzi, returning to the Pianura di Puglia at the approach of winter.

Some of the olive trees that cover mile upon mile of Apulia

Even in the bleak south-west, however, most of the Murge's peasants lived a very different sort of existence, going out daily from the little cities to scratch a living from the stony soil, ploughing with oxen if they were lucky but more often using mattocks or digging-sticks, by night sheltering their beasts from brigands near some fortified *masseria*. Life was still more dissimilar in the fertile north-eastern Murge, a rich land of olive groves, vineyards, and almond and cherry orchards, that in autumn swarmed with huge gangs of fruit-pickers, men and women who camped in the *masserie's* courtyards. There were also dense forests, more than one of whose clearings contained a famous horse-stud.

The roads of the north-eastern Murge frequently go for miles through grove upon grove of olive trees, their gaunt branches trimmed in the Italian way as opposed to the Greek method used in the Salento, reaching up to the sky in a witches' ballet. "They are pruned into the form of a cup, by cutting out the centric upright branches, in the same manner as gardeners trim gooseberry bushes", noted the ever observant Swinburne. "This treatment lets in an equal share of the sun and ventilation to every part, and brings on a universal maturity."

The absence of tall trees throughout the Murge dates only from the late nineteenth century. Formerly whole areas were thickly wooded, very like the Forest Umbra in the Gargano. Full of game, these had been the primeval forests through which Frederick II had once hunted with such pleasure. After the *Risorgimento*, however, laws specifically designed for clearing useless dwarf oak and chestnut from the lower slopes of Piedmont's mountains, were cynically distorted on behalf of the new, ruthless speculator landowners. They systematically cut down all the great oak and beech trees, stripping the entire Murge of its woodland, and transforming its landscape.

24

Cities of the Murge

*The Apulians ... are strong bodied with fine complexions and white
skins, energetic in matters of business, faithful, highly intelligent,
and very kind hearted.*

G.B. Pacichelli, "Il Regno di Napoli in Prospettiva"

O NE REASON WHY early travellers seldom visited the Murge was
that there were no mail-coaches. Carriages had to be engaged
by the day, the worst in Italy, according to Octavian Blewitt in 1850. If
they were unavailable you had to hire horses instead, "one of which, as
the sumpter horse, will carry portmanteaus, and enable the padrone,
who generally travels on foot, to get a lift occasionally." Yet Blewitt
was impressed by the roads, built "by the present King Ferdinand II,
who has done more in twenty years to improve the internal commu-
nications of the kingdom than his ancestors in many centuries." After
the fall of the Borbone monarchy, no new major roads were built in
Apulia for nearly another hundred years.

Canosa attracted travellers, being close to Cannae. A Greek
colony founded by Diomedes of the Great War Cry, its coins bore
Greek inscriptions while its people remained bilingual until the time
of Augustus. The oldest diocese in Apulia, founded in the fourth
century, then wrecked by the Goths, it recovered only to be sacked
by the Saracens, after which the Byzantines moved the archbishopric
to Bari. In 1734 Bishop Berkeley thought Canosa "a poor town on
a low hill", although he was intrigued by its pre-Christian tombs. A
century later Ramage echoed Horace's grumble that its bread was full
of sand. "I find that the traveller still has the same complaint to make,

The tomb at Canosa of Bohemond de Hauteville, Prince of Antioch and a hero of the First Crusade

owing to the soft nature of the rock from which their millstones are made." Today modern Canosa has bound the medieval town in a ring of high-rise flats.

The body of the Norman hero Bohemond lies at Canosa in a tomb reminiscent of an Arab *turbeh* (mausoleum). During his colourful career he twice defeated the Byzantine emperor and played a key role in the First Crusade, becoming Prince of Antioch. He then spent two years as a Saracen prisoner before being ransomed, returning to Europe and marrying the King of France's daughter. The Byzantine chronicler Anna Comnena says that Bohemond was just like his father, Robert Guiscard, and she had met both, "Father and son resembled locusts, Robert's child devouring anything missed by his father." His tomb just outside the cathedral is a small, square building of white marble with an octagonal cupola, an inscription on its Byzantine bronze and silver doors telling of his bravery. Inside, a flagstone bears a single word in Lombardic script:

BOAMUNDUS

In 1712 Canosa was acquired as a principality by the Capece

Minutolo. Their ancestors may have known Bohemond, who died in 1111, since they were at the coronation of the first Norman king, just a few years later. Their name was originally 'Caca Pece', pitch-shitter, from having thrown pitch at enemies besieging their castle; each branch of the Capece took an extra name, Minutolo meaning dwarf. The most famous Capece Minutolo was Prince Antonio, Minister of Police in 1821, who had the Carbonari revolutionaries flogged. "He regarded the French Revolution as the fatal result of renouncing medieval institutions and beliefs, which could still, if revived, produce a generation of Galahads", writes Sir Harold Acton. But the Prince of Canosa's private life was not quite that of a Galahad – he fathered three bastards by a rag-picker's daughter.

First settled by Peucetians, Ruvo di Puglia became a staging-post on the Via Traiana, Horace's Rubi. An attractive little town, perched on the edge of the Murge 732 feet above sea-level, its few visitors are charmed by an exquisite Apulian-Romanesque cathedral on top of a Paleo-Christian predecessor, itself over a Roman house-church. The *campanile* is a Byzantine watch-tower, while Frederick II built the castle of which only a solitary, crumbling bastion survives.

Ruvo's other attraction is the Museo Jatta, containing Greek and Apulian ceramics dating from the 6th to the 3rd century BC Giovanni Jatta bought vast estates round Ruvo from the Carafa family in 1806 and began to collect Attic and Apulian artefacts discovered in graves on his land. The city had had close links with Greece in the 5th century BC, importing quantities of kraters, vases and cups and then in the following century Greek artisans to found a factory. This local ware, admittedly of far less beauty then the Attic, was usually destroyed when found, until the beginning of the nineteenth century when it suddenly became immensely sought after. His son became an archaeologist, adding to what would become one of the greatest collections of Apulian ware in Italy.

Janet Ross tried to see the Museo Jatta in 1889, without success. "Signor Jatta has gone to Bari, bearing the keys of the museum in his pocket", she was told. "Some of the streets are exceeding picturesque; all are dirty", observed Mrs. Ross. "The people were very civil, but evidently unused to strangers." No one explained to her what had paid for the kraters. It was sweated labour, most of the town's male population being day labourers on the enormous *latifondi* owned by the Jatta and Cotugno families. In 1907 a general strike was broken by 200 armed peasants from the Jatta estates, who fought a pitched battle with the strikers, hunting them through the streets with knives and guns.

Bitonto was once an important Roman city on the Via Traiana, retaken for Byzantium in 975 by the Catapan Zacharias. In a purple-draped litter, Frederick II's body passed through in 1250 on its way to Tàranto to take ship for Sicily, escorted by barons in black and weeping Saracen bodyguards. The citizens are unlikely to have wept – the Emperor had put an inscription over their main gate reading *"Gens bitutina, totia bestia et assinina"* (the people of Bitonto are all beasts and fools).

The castle's round towers date from Bitonto's expansion in the fourteenth century. Unlike Apulian ports, it prospered under the Spaniards, famous for its oil, still the best in Apulia. In 1734, Charles of Bourbon routed the Austrians outside the city, restoring the *Regno's* independence and founding the Borbone monarchy. Augustus Hare calls Bitonto's cathedral "the noblest in Southern Italy". The ultimate example of Apulian Romanesque, inspired by the church of San Nicola at Bari, it dates from the first half of the thirteenth century and was built with unusual speed, probably within twenty-five years, so in style it is all of a piece. A white marble pulpit dated 1229 has a panel portraying Frederick II and three of his sons, with the name of the priest who carved it, "*Nicolaus sacerdos et magister*" (Nicholas priest and teacher).

Swinburne thought Bitonto's inhabitants "more polished and improved in their manners than those that dwell along the coast", commenting on "an air of affluence". Yet, Hare says it was impossible for him to sketch in Bitonto because of "the violence of the half savage crowd in every lowest stage of beggary and filth." Decline had set in, partly due to large scale planting of vines during the 1870s and 1890s, followed by the ravages of phylloxera which appeared in the Salento in 1889 and had almost destroyed the entire Apulian wine industry by 1919. There were bloody riots in 1920, the town hall being stormed and food shops looted. A few years before, Edward Hutton had sensed the misery here, writing of "a curiously lonely city".

Although undistinguished at first sight, the little city of Gioia del Colle has a certain charm. Significantly, on certain Sundays since time immemorial, generations of Gioiesi have picnicked together on a low hill to the north-east, Monte Sannace, the site of the city of their Peucetian ancestors. Gioia became an important Norman fief in 1089, its first lord being Robert Guiscard's brother, Richard the Seneschal, who built the castle. The Emperor Frederick II rebuilt it when he returned from Jerusalem, giving it an appearance that is half Teutonic and half Arab. A Gioiese legend claims his bastard son Manfred was born in the castle, together with his other chidren by Bianca Lancia. The castle was a key Hohenstaufen fortress, guarding the road across the "heel of Italy" from Bari to Tàranto. Trapezoidal in plan, it has two huge square towers, the Torre de Rossi and the Torre Imperatrice. Frederick II used it as a hunting-lodge since in his time, and for long after, Gioia was surrounded by dense woodland. Pacichelli calls it "a sumptuous and ornate palace with a gallery of choice pictures and a theatre", adding reverently that the Princes of Acquaviva often stayed here, accompanied by their court. Made into a county, during the seventeenth century Gioia del Colle was bought, together with the principality of Acquaviva nearby, by the Genoese moneylender Carlo De Mari, who henceforward referred to his *"stato di Acquaviva e Gioia"* (state of Acquaviva and Gioia). His tombstone at Gioia styles him "Prince of Acquaviva, Patrician of Genoa and Knight of Naples", but he began his career behind a counter. The castle was lived in until not so very long ago, by Donna Maria Emanuela Carafa from 1806–68, and by Marchese Luca De Resta into the twentieth century. It now houses the Museum.

"Nothing else worth seeing remains in this busy city of peasants", says Edward Hutton, yet the Baroque façade of the Franciscan friary that dominates the main square, built in 1633 at public expense, surely deserves at least a glance. So does the little neo-Classical Teatro Rossini, built in 1832, bombed during the Second War but triumphantly brought back into use in 1997, and also the seventeenth century Dominican monastery which houses the *Municipio* (town hall).

During the spring of 1809 the brigand Antonio Mirabella informed the commune of Gioia that he was "Prince Leopoldo di Borbone" and had surrounded the city with 1,500 Calabrians equipped with cannon. Terrified, the commune let him into the city, and after a *Te Deum* (hymn of praise) in the *chiesa madre* (mother church) to celebrate the restoration of Borbone authority, he and his army were given a banquet in the friary. When they sat down, however, the 'Prince' looked suspiciously unregal while his 'troops' were a mere handful of ragamuffins, clearly intent on getting drunk as quickly as possible. Armed men were called in and several brigands were killed, but Mirabella escaped to the woods.

The friary was later turned into a police barracks, part being set aside as the *Unione,* a club for the city's élite. Nicola De Bellis of unhappy memory once held court here. During the agricultural disturbances of the early 1900s, Gioia suffered miserably, De Bellis, who was its mayor as well as its deputy, ensuring that the landlords' overseers had police help in breaking strikes. At elections no-one dared to vote against the "King, Tsar and God of Gioia del Colle", police and gangsters with revolvers patrolling the streets to see that the hostile or uncommitted stayed at home. On one occasion the city voted unanimously for De Bellis. In 1920 mounted estate guards rode down a hundred striking field-hands just outside the city, killing ten labourers and wounding another thirty.

Until quite recently, after funerals at Gioia the coffins were taken from the church-door to the graveyard on a hearse drawn by black-plumed, red-hooded horses. This could often be seen en route, sometimes bound for a funeral in Massafra, Noci or Santeramo, or returning at night to Gioia. Once there was an accident in the dark, a car killing two of the lead horses, but the service was soon resumed, to meet popular demand.

Gioia del Colle acquired a brief notoriety in 1999 during the Kosovo war, when planes flew from a NATO aerodrome outside the city to drop bombs from a safe altitude onto the Serbs, and pound them into submission.

There is not much to bring a sightseeing traveller to San Michele, apart from the Museum of Country Life in an otherwise uninteresting castle. This has a fine collection of ploughs, olive-wood presses for wine or oil, pruning-knives for olive-trees, short-handled mattocks that deformed a man before he was fifty and yokes for the oxen that were used until the Second World War. What look like lacrosse-sticks were nets for catching small birds by night. Preserved in jars of wine and bay-leaves for feast days, these birds were often the only meat ever tasted by labourers and their families.

At Capurso the Royal Basilica of the Madonna of the Well houses yet another miraculous icon. Together with the gigantic Franciscan friary that once served it, the basilica was built by King Charles VII in 1740, his son Ferdinand IV adding its majestic Baroque façade thirty years later. Rooms at the side contain ex-votos (trusses, corsets, sticks, splints, crutches, wooden limbs, wedding-dresses and baby-clothes) while a gallery of crude paintings shows the Madonna saving suppliant donors. In 1705 she appeared in a vision to a priest of Capurso,

Don Domenico Tanzella, who had been diagnosed as incurably ill, and told him to drink the water from a nearby cistern. After being completely cured, he explored the cistern and found the icon. Pilgrims still toil down the long stairs below the basilica to drink the healing water.

The cistern here began as a grotto chapel for Basilian monks, who painted a fresco of the Virgin on the rockface – the icon. Like so many other Apulian shrines, Capurso is Byzantine in origin.

25

The Battle of Cannae, 216 BC

Nearly the whole army met their death here...
Livy, "The History of Rome"

H ANNIBAL'S TRIUMPH over the Romans at Cannae is one of the world's great victories. A foreign army consisting mainly of mercenaries annihilated a well-led, well-equipped, much bigger force fighting for its homeland. Down the centuries soldiers have been fascinated by the battle and, even if Apulia were known for nothing else, it would still be famous because of Cannae.

Hannibal's strategy was to beat the Romans so often that their allies in the Roman Confederation would eventually abandon them as a lost cause. He had already destroyed two Roman armies, in 218 BC at the River Trebia and in 217 at Lake Trasimene. Nevertheless, the Romans remained convinced that their legions were invincible.

He had wintered his troops in Apulia, at Gereonium near Lucera, and during the summer seized the town of Cannae to provide himself with a base from where he could devastate all Southern Italy. The Romans decided that they had to engage and eliminate him at all costs.

The battle took place on 2 August not far from Cannae, at the foot of the Murge and on the banks of the River Aufidus, today known as the Òfanto. The consuls Emilius Paulus and Terentius Varro, one cautious and the other rash, who according to custom commanded on alternate days, had 80,000 infantry and 6,000 cavalry. Hannibal had 40,000 foot-soldiers, Gaulish and Spanish swordsmen, Libyan spearmen and Balearic slingers, together with 10,000 Gaulish, Spanish and Numidian cavalry. It was the turn of Varro, the rash consul, to command and despite their inferiority in cavalry, the Romans marched across the flat Apulian plain to attack Hannibal.

On his right, next to the river, Varro placed his armoured horsemen, volunteer Roman citizens, putting the more effective allied cavalry on his left towards the plain. His infantry was in the centre, legionaries in armour with shields, short swords and javelins. They marched in unusually deep formation, to give them maximum impact so that they would smash through the opposing centre. A screen of light troops, archers, slingers and javelin men ran ahead of the legionaries as they advanced.

When the Romans got near, they saw that Hannibal's infantry in the centre was in a very odd formation, his swordsmen bowed outwards in an arc, with the Libyan spearmen on their flanks. More conventionally, on his left, next to the river and facing the Roman heavy cavalry, he had put his own heavy cavalry, while on his right the Numidian horsemen were placed opposite the Roman allies' horse.

As the Romans grew closer, Hannibal's screen of Balearic slingers, the best in the Mediterranean, opened fire. Their sling-shots inflicted many casualties, smashing the arm of one of the Roman consuls, Emilius Paulus. Then Hasdrubal, Hannibal's chief engineer, led his mounted Celts in a charge against the Roman heavy cavalry, routing them, after which he brought his men across the field to help the Numidians break the allied cavalry. But about 500 Numidians surrendered, throwing down their shields and javelins, and were taken to the Romans' rear.

Meanwhile, in the centre the Roman legions were pressing forward steadily, pushing back the Gaulish and Spanish swordsmen so that the arc-shaped formation was reversed, becoming concave. But as the closely packed Romans advanced, the Libyan spearmen began to outflank them, attacking from each side. Suddenly the Numidian 'prisoners' behind drew swords from beneath their cloaks, picked up shields from the fallen and started slashing the Romans' backs and legs. Having sent the other Numidians in pursuit of the Roman and allied cavalry, to ensure it did not return, Hasdrubal now brought his horsemen back and charged the Roman legions from the rear.

Surrounded on all sides, they were annihilated. By the end of the day, out of 86,000 Romans, 70,000 had been killed and another 4,500 taken prisoner. The dead included the consul Emilius Paulus, twenty-nine tribunes and eighty senators. Among the few who escaped, fleeing to Canosa or Lucera, was the consul Varro. Many thought that this shattering defeat meant the end of the Republic.

Despite centuries of passionate debate, it is not possible to reconstruct the battle with complete accuracy, since the River Òfanto has altered course. Livy says the Romans were defeated as much by Hannibal's brilliant use of ground as by his troops: "a wind that got up, locally known as the 'Volturnus', hampered the Romans by throwing dust in their eyes." Ramage asked his guide "if he had ever seen this phenomenon, and he said that it was not uncommon in autumn, after the stubble had been burnt, and the land exposed to the air, for clouds of dust to be driven along the plain."

Like Ramage, most of the travellers had been brought up to read Livy, and in consequence Cannae was a place of pilgrimage for them, one of the main reasons for visiting Apulia.

Not only early travellers were fascinated by the battle. At the end of the nineteenth century, Cannae became an obsession with the chief of the German Imperial General Staff, Count Alfred von Schlieffen, who wrote a book about it – Hannibal's tactics inspiring his plan for the next war against France. He hoped to tempt the French into invading Germany and then attack their flank with overwhelming strength through Belgium. In 1914, however, the infallible Schlieffen Plan went off at half-cock because the German commander, Field-Marshal von Moltke, lost his nerve when the Russians advanced with unexpected speed into East Prussia, and brought too many troops back to Germany.

26

Maundy Thursday at Noicattaro

Whosoever doth not bear his cross and come after me,
cannot be my disciple...
"Gospel of St John"

MOST MODERN VISITORS TO APULIA, seduced by the blue of the Adriatic, confine themselves to the beautiful cities of the coast or the Baroque splendour of Lecce. If they bother to adventure inland into the Murge, it is usually to inspect such showpieces as Ruvo or Alberobello, or to wander over the battlefield of Cannae. They miss a lot that is well worth seeing.

Noicattaro is among the Murge's quieter little cities, and at first sight does not look very interesting, save for a good Romanesque *chiesa madre* from the thirteenth century. Formerly its name was Noja, only becoming Noicattaro in 1863. All that Pacichelli could find to say about the city was that it was "the seat of the Duchy of Noja of the Lords Carafa, set amid fertile fields". And full of "commodious houses, palaces and convents."

The *abate* does not mention an incident that occurred some years before his visit. In 1676 a servant of the Count of Conversano was caught poaching in the forest which then surrounded the city and resisted arrest so violently that the Duke of Noja sent him home minus ears and nose. Shortly after, Count Giulio Acquaviva came to Noja at dead of night with 300 armed men, broke into the ducal *palazzo*, dragged the duke out of bed, bound him and threatened to amputate his features in the same way. Only the tears of his duchess and of his mother the dowager saved the Lord Carafa.

As has been seen, there was a bloodthirsty streak in this branch of the Carafa family who were also Dukes of Andria, and the unfortunate citizens had to put up with some occasionally savage misrule. Adjoining the main piazza at Noicattaro are the battered remnants of what was once the Carafa's palace, where a heartfelt inscription on a worn tablet hails "the breaking of the feudal yoke."

In November 1815 bubonic plague broke out at Noja, probably imported from Albania. For a month the citizens refused to believe it. Then the entire city was put into quarantine for a year, three trenches being dug around the walls and cannon mounted at the gates, to prevent anybody leaving; if a man tried to jump over the trenches, he was shot by the guard of the *cordon sanitaire* (quarantine barrier). Three bored soldiers who used a pack of cards thrown to them by someone inside the city went in front of a firing squad. The carnival became a Dance of Death, when out of fifty celebrating the days before Ash Wednesday forty-five were dead within a week. No less than two thirds of the population died of the plague, the last in June 1816.

When Keppel Craven came two years later, he found a ghost town: "The whole was untenanted, the habitations having been unroofed at the time that the general purification took place; this consisted in repeatedly burning all suspected clothes, goods and furniture, and in renewed ablutions and fumigations, followed by a scraping of the walls and universal white-washing." The *chiesa madre* was white-washed too, when the first victims were buried there in a communal tomb inscribed:

Sepolcro di Appestati
Pena di morte a chi osa aprirlo
(Tomb of the plague-stricken
Who dares open does so on pain of death)

Most, however, were buried in a plague-pit next to the Augustinian priory on the edge of the city, which had been converted into a plague-hospital.

The drama of Maundy Thursday at Noicattaro rivals anything that takes place in Italy during Holy Week. After a white-hooded confraternity, a doleful band and finally the *sindaco* (mayor) in tri-coloured sash have passed, there seems little point in staying. Then, dimly lit by small red lamps on every balcony, people are seen to be gazing intently at something outside one of the lesser churches. Suddenly a huge cross rises from the ground, borne by a figure in black, shrouded from hooded head to ankles, hands black-gloved, feet bare; an iron chain with links an inch thick is tied to one ankle.

In the dusk, carrying the great cross, the faceless penitent staggers down the road, preceded by boys cracking wooden rattles and followed by a growing crowd. There is no sound other than rattles and dragging chain. The figure falls heavily three times, in memory of Christ's Passion. It leaves the cross at the main door of the *chiesa madre,* to kneel at the high altar; a dull, repeated thudding is heard, the penitent scourging itself with the chain. Rising from its knees, it goes out into the moonlight to pick up the cross (which weighs 60 kgs) and slowly continues its painful way down the road to the church of the Carmine. Again, it falls heavily three times. The silent crowd follows. Now and then, someone runs forward to touch the cross. A further scourging takes place before the high altar of the Carmine, above which hangs a text:

AS THE PELICAN IN THE DESERT WOUNDS HERSELF AND
DIES SO THAT HER BROOD MAY ENDURE AND LIVE, SO
CHRIST GAVE HIS BODY AND BLOOD FOR OUR SALVATION
THAT WE MIGHT LIVE.

The rapt crowd has entered the church in the penitent's wake, watching mutely. Suddenly, a second figure in black appears, crawling up the aisle on its knees. On reaching the altar, it gives itself another thirty blows with its chain. Some of the community of brown-habited Carmelite friars, sitting mummified in the crypt below, have heard similar blows every Lent for over two hundred years.

On that Maundy Thursday night you will see at least a dozen other hooded figures in black carrying huge crosses to every church in Noicattaro. Despite bleeding feet they will go on doing so until dawn breaks. They are the confraternity of the *Addolorato*, men and women whose identities are known only to the confraternity's chaplain, doing penance not just for their sins but for those of the entire community.

On Good Friday, in almost every Apulian city a black-robed statue of the Madonna Dolorosa, a silver dagger piercing her heart, is borne through the streets, escorted by a mournful town band, hooded confraternities and hundreds of women in black. At Molfetta a nineteenth century Neapolitan statue of Christ in the garden of Gethsemane is carried on the shoulders of the oldest confraternity in Apulia, the *Arciconfraternità di Santo Stefano;* at His feet lies a reliquary containing a fragment of the True Cross. At San Marco in Lamis the sorrowful Madonna is preceded by *fracchie,* huge wooden cones that are drawn at the head of the procession and then set on fire.

On Easter Sunday, together with a life-sized statue of the Risen Christ, a doll representing Lent is paraded in some places. Stuffed with fireworks, the doll is thrown onto a flaming bonfire while the crowd cheers. These ancient processions derive from the old pagan spring festivals but the form they take is a legacy of Spanish rule, and Apulians from all walks of life take part in them.

27

The *Masserie*

The word is not rendered by 'farm house', which gives but an
inadequate idea of the masseria.
Charles Macfarlane, "The Lives and Exploits of Banditti and Robbers"

ON THE MURGE you never see a house of any antiquity outside
the cities, apart from the odd castle or *masseria*. One or two
of the *masserie* have been converted into small hotels whose guests
wrongly assume that they were manor houses, but in reality the
nobles who owned them preferred to inhabit a castle or a *palazzo*
in the local city, rarely visiting the *masseria* and then merely to hunt.
They were not so much farmhouses as fortified depots for agricultural produce that at certain times of the year – lambing, sowing,
reaping, pruning, fruit-picking, wine-making, etc – took on the role
of villages. Strongholds with battlements and cannon, defended by
armed guards, they sheltered communities of farm workers who otherwise lived in the cities.

Built as protection against slave-raiders or brigands, the surviving
masserie (which are not confined to the Murge) generally date from
between the sixteenth century and the first half of the nineteenth,
although their origin is far older. Sometimes they have rueful names,
for example *Spina, Petrose, Scaserba, Campi Distrutti* or *della Femina
Morta**, that hint at the harsh existence of the old Apulian countryside. Most are deserted, crumbling into ruin; bleak monuments to a
way of life that ended only a little over seventy years ago and is still

---

*"Thorn", "Stony Ground", "Grassless", "Ruined Fields", "Dead Woman"

Masseria del Duca – not a farmhouse or a manor, a masseria was a fortified depot for agricultural produce and residence of the massero (estate manager)

remembered by a handful of very aged men and women. A few have been modernised, serving as ordinary farm houses.

The construction of *masserie* all over Apulia from the late Middle Ages onward reflected not just a need to protect peasants but the increasing importance of olive farming, each *masseria* being equipped with a press and countless oil jars. A feature of Apulian life since the Messapian period, olive trees had begun to be grown commercially during the early thirteenth century, at first by the monasteries. Then the feudal lords copied the monks, so that eventually every big estate had its *masseria* and olive groves.

Since wine was another staple of Apulian agriculture, there were vineyards as well as olive groves near every *masseria*, which always contained a wine-press. In some places the *masserie* stood among seemingly endless almond groves while those around Conversano, Monopoli and Putignano were encircled by no less beautiful cherry orchards. Cherries were preserved in grappa as early as the eighteenth century. With fewer olives and vines, *masserie* on the otherwise treeless sheep runs of the Alta Murgia or the northern Tavoliere specialised in cheese and butter, employing professional dairy men to process the ewes' milk.

Charles Macfarlane, who came to Apulia in 1817 and knew it better than any other early traveller save Pacichelli, has an unusually helpful description. "The *masserie* in Apulia and the provinces of Bari, Òtranto and Tàranto, are all built on the same plan", he tells us:

A square wall of enclosure, sufficiently high and solid, generally surrounds the dwelling-house, built against one side, and containing three or four large habitable rooms, and sometimes a small chapel. The vast stables, granaries, and out-houses, within the walls, form a right-angle with this dwelling-house, but without touching it. In the midst of the enclosure, at some distance from the surrounding walls, rises a round or square tower of two storeys, standing quite alone. The ascent to the upper storey is either by stone steps, inserted in the tower, or by a drawbridge, or by a ladder easily drawn up into the tower.

General Sir Richard Church was also in Apulia in 1817, hunting down brigands. He too describes a *masseria*, "a very good specimen of its class", when prepared for a sudden attack by horsemen, the Masseria del Duca:

Its thick walls dated from the middle ages, and were loopholed and protected by great solid gates and an avenue of trees, which was now effectually blocked up by carts with the wheels taken off, and logs and tree-trunks laid crosswise. At one corner of the enclosure rose a square tower, from the top of which you might overlook the great plain, dotted with white towns and villages, patched with brown leafless vineyards, green meads, silver-grey olive-orchards, and bounded by the shining sea.

The general recalled what he found here, "in a very large room, comfortably furnished after the manner of these Apulian *masserie*", obviously, the quarters of the *massaro,* the steward who ran the estate for its absentee landowner.' At this date, few proprietors ever dared to visit such a dangerous countryside, not even for the hunting.

Great chests, some for holding meal, some for holding clothes and linen, a heavy oaken table, some stools and benches, were on the floor; jars of olives, figs and raisins, stood upon a shelf against the smoke-dried wall; strings of onions, sausages, and dried fish dangled from the rafters. Cheeses were there too, and huge jars of olive-oil, and half-a-dozen demi-johns (great stone bottles), stoppered with oiled cotton, and containing the wine of the country, stood under the table.

Externally, the Masseria del Duca, at the foot of the little hills just south of Martina Franca, still looks much as it must have done in General Church's day, with *caciocavallo* cheeses hanging up under the eaves to mature, even if its outbuildings house battery hens and a very modern dairy.

Although deserted, the vast Masseria Jesce between Altamura and Laterza, in the Murgia Catena on the border with Basilicata, is a particularly impressive example, almost a castle. Built of tufa, on the ground floor there were stalls for oxen and horses, with store-rooms; on the floor above, more store-rooms and living accommodation; sheep-pens ran along the walls outside. Small look-out towers projected at roof level. The lower part dates from the sixteenth century, the upper from half-way through the seventeenth, added by the de Mari family, Princes of Gioia del Colle, who were lords of Altamura nearby. The de Mari also restored a medieval chapel underground, building a passage down to it. Far inland and intended as a defence against brigands and starving peasants rather than North Africans, this gigantic *masseria* is an eloquent monument to the chronic insecurity and dangers of life in the remoter areas of the Apulian Murge.

Nearer the sea, further south, there was another scourge. "The *Masserie,* or farmhouses, in this part of Apulia are generally built on elevated ground, to avoid the malaria", wrote Janet Ross, after a visit to the *masseria* of Leucaspide between Massafra and Tàranto. She continues:

> Round the large courtyard are high walls, and one side is occupied by a vaulted ox-shed, built of stone, with a manger running all round, divided off for each animal ... At one end an archway leads into a vaulted room with stone benches all round, on which the shepherds sleep, and in the middle is a huge slab of stone on which olive branches smoulder, and where the *massara* prepares the meals for the men.

She tells us too that "The hoeing, weeding corn, &c., is all done by gangs of women, who come from the nearest towns, chiefly from those on the *Murgie* hills, sometimes twenty miles off, and stay for six weeks or two months, sleeping all together in a big vaulted room on the ground floor."

Life at a *masseria* was very much that of a community:

On Sundays and saints' days a priest with a small boy came together, on a donkey, from Massafra to say mass in the wee chapel near the threshing floor at Leucaspide ... The fervour with which the labourers beat their breasts when they said "mea culpa", was most edifying, but must have been very painful. Vito Anton, the guard, always served mass with an immense pistol stuck into his belt behind, and was quite the most important person of the ceremony.

On rare occasions they celebrated, dancing a local dance, the *Pizzica-Pizzica*. Mrs. Ross describes the orchestra at a *masseria* party:

a guitar, a fiddle and a guitar *battente*, which has only five thin wire strings, and is a wild, queer, inspiriting instrument which would "make a buffalo dance", as they say; a tambourine, and a *cupa-cupa*, a large earthenware tube, with a piece of sheepskin stretched tight over the top, and a stick forced through a hole in the centre. The player begins by spitting two or three times into his hand, and then moves the stick up and down as fast as he can; this makes an odd, droning sound, rather like a bag-pipe in the far distance.

The result reminded her of "Arab music".

Life was just the same at *masserie* on the Murge or the Tavoliere until almost the Second World War.

28

The Via Appia

The Appian Way is less tiresome ...
Horace, "A Journey from Rome to Brundisium"

THE VIA APPIA, most celebrated of the great Roman roads, was the main route between ancient Rome and Southern Italy. Begun by Appius Claudius Caecus in 312 BC, originally ending at Capua, it was extended through Benevento, Venosa, Tàranto and Oria to Brìndisi – a length of 350 miles. A road for all weathers, it provided fast and easy transport to Rome, bringing more trade with the East and prosperity for the Apulians. Before Tàranto the road went through some of Roman Apulia's most beautiful country-side, and even now you can imagine what it was like when Horace lived at Venosa and Cicero owned a villa there. With the decline of Tàranto, however, and the creation of the Via Traiana linking the cities of the Adriatic coast, the Via Appia lost much of its impor-tance. Eighteenth century travellers preferred the Via Traiana, anxious not to risk meeting brigands for longer than absolutely necessary.

A map of the borders of Apulia and Basilicata can be deceptive. A quick glance shows hilly, even mountainous country, but this is not what you experience. A gently rolling landscape is broken up by small hills, yet the ground rises so gradually and imperceptibly that until reaching Monte Vulture, which for miles can be seen towering above the plateau, you are not aware of being at any height. It is easy to understand why it held such attraction for Horace, the Normans and the Emperor Frederick II, who spent the last summer of his life at

Melfi and Castel Lagopesole. Melfi and Venosa figure so prominently in the story of Hautevilles and Hohenstaufen that modern boundaries mean little – spiritually, they are still part of Apulia.

Venosa was sacked by the Emir of Bari, rebuilt by the Frankish Emperor Louis II and won back for the Eastern Empire by Basil the Bulgar Slayer. Beneath its walls the Normans won their first crushing victory over the Byzantines. All that remains of the medieval city is the ancient abbey of La Trinità. Robert Guiscard, greatest of the pioneer Norman leaders, founded its church in 1065 on the site of several earlier churches, beneath which lay a temple of Hymen. His tomb disappeared long ago, his bones being thrown with those of his brothers – William Bras-de-Fer, Humphrey and Drogo – into a simple marble sarcophagus. Visiting Venosa in 1848, Edward Lear saw "a single column, around which, according to the local superstition, if you go hand in hand with any person, the two circumambulants are certain to remain friends for life."

After Lear's visit there was a terrible earthquake. Part of the hill north of the abbey fell into the valley below, revealing Jewish catacombs. There were Jews in Apulia from the fourth century until their final expulsion in the seventeenth, who followed the Palestinian practice of using grottoes as cemeteries. Those at Venosa were wealthy landowners and supplied several mayors. Frederick II saw that they were left in peace, but vicious persecution broke out when the Hohenstaufen were replaced by the Angevins. Lenormant found inscriptions in Latin, Greek and Hebrew, some in a strange bastardised Italian written in Hebrew characters.

Lear stayed with Don Nicola Rapolla in a large rambling mansion at the end of the square in which there is a statue of Horace. They dined with Don Nicola's brother, discussing Shakespeare, Milton and "*quel autore adorabile, Valter Scott*" (that adorable author, Walter Scott). Lear found everything delightful, food, wine ("superexcellent"), beds and furnishings – which, with the cleanliness of the paved streets, came as a surprise in the depths of the South. One wonders what his hosts made of this very odd Englishman, with his simian features and green glasses. They probably sneered at his watercolours. But he had those letters of introduction that were all important in the old *Regno*.

In Lear's day the fifteenth century castle had not yet become the squalid rooming house seen by Norman Douglas. Built by Pirro del Balzo, Prince of Altamura, on top of the old Norman fortress, the walls of its dungeons were still covered with mournful inscriptions by prisoners.

Melfi's name is associated with Frederick II's "Constitutions" of 1231, the first written law in Western Europe since Roman times. In his own words, "we do not wish to make distinctions in our judgements but to be fair. Whether a plaintiff or a defendant is Frank, Roman or Lombard, we want him to have justice". Women could inherit property and widows were entitled to free legal advice. Rape, even of a prostitute (so long as she had put up a good fight), was a capital offence. Pimps were sentenced to slavery.

During the sixteenth century Apulians preferred Spaniards to Frenchmen, and Melfi would never have fallen to Lautrec in 1530 had not a traitor opened its gates. Lautrec sacked the city, killing many of its citizens. The Spaniards swiftly retook it, slaughtering the French garrison. In the *municipio* courtyard there is a stone pillar with a ring, said to have been the Spanish 'gallows' – presumably they used the garrotte.

Little remains of old Melfi, whose great castle over a precipice was considered "perfectly Poussinesque" by Edward Lear. "One of the towers of Roger de Hauteville still exists, but the great hall, where Normans and Popes held councils in bygone days, is now a theatre." Lear found Melfi attractive, with its clear streams and pretty valleys scattered with walnut trees, black goats clustering on the crags or lying outside the valley's many caves. There were innumerable sleepy convents and pretty wayside shrines. He may well have been the last Englishman to see Melfi like this. On 13 September, 1851, the *Athenaeum Journal* printed the following report:

> The morning of the 14th of August was very sultry, and a leaden atmosphere prevailed. It was remarked that an unusual silence appeared to extend over the animal world. The hum of insects ceased, the feathered tribes were mute, not a breath of wind moved the arid vegetation. At about half-past two o'clock the town of Melfi rocked for about sixty seconds, and nearly every building fell in.

The castle, especially the modern part where Lear had stayed, was badly damaged, convents and churches obliterated. The houses of the poor ceased to exist, the *campanile* collapsed, and a new inn with 62 customers and 25 horses inside became a heap of rubble. In all 840 people were killed. King Ferdinand came to direct the relief operations, spending a night of torrential rain in a hut. Next morning he toured the ruins, handing out money. He pardoned prisoners who had helped dig people out from under the rubble, and sacked the mayor for stealing most of the funds sent by charities.

The woods of Monte Vulture were the haunt of brigands until the late 1860s. An expensive safe conduct was essential for a traveller who wished to avoid being held to ransom; unless it was paid immediately, reminders in the form of an ear or a nose were sent to the victim's family. When the brigands were finally routed, their place in the woods was taken by wolves returning to their old home. They had always been a problem in these remote upland forests, Frederick II ordering poison to be laid for them around his hunting lodge of Lagopesole. Some of the woodland still remains, but the wolves have disappeared.

29

Horace, the Apulian

I, born by sounding Aufidus ...
Horace, "Odes"

ONE OF APULIA'S GLORIES is to have given birth to Quintus Horatius Flaccus. You have to know Latin fairly well to read Horace properly, which is a pity, since his poetry is so beautiful. He has been compared to Bach varying a theme or Chopin developing a cadence, and his verse has lasted down the centuries, its devoted admirers including the Emperor Augustus, Milton, King Louis XVIII and Rudyard Kipling. "No ancient writer has been at once so familiarly known and so generally appreciated", a Horatian addict wrote in the 1880s. "We seem to know his tastes and his habits, and almost to catch the tones of his conversation." Nowadays, most people read him in translation –although almost impossible to translate – yet he still casts a spell.

Horace was born on 8 December 65 BC, at Venosa, then a staging post of the Via Appia and the largest *colonia* (colony) of veteran soldiers in the Roman world, with a population of 20,000. Although he left for Rome when he was about twelve, and spent most of his life there or in the villa given to him by Maecenas, he never lost his love of the country around Venosa. The River Aufidus is mentioned in many of the "Satires" and the "Odes" – as in the prophetic "Exegi monumentum":

> I have achieved a monument more lasting
> than bronze, and loftier than the pyramids of kings ...
> I shall be renewed and flourish in further praise,

where churning Aufidus resounds, where Daunus
poor in water governed his rustic people ...

His father, a freed slave, had settled at Venosa, becoming a tax-
collector and auctioneer. He prospered, buying a small farm, sending
his son to Rome and to Athens for his education. In 42 AD Horace
joined the Roman republican army at Athens and, despite his being
an insignificant young man, small and plump with a paunch, Brutus
gave him command of a legion; he fought at Philippi against Octavian and Mark Antony, throwing away his shield and fleeing during
the subsequent rout. Pardoned and given a post in the treasury at
Rome, his wonderful verses soon gained him patrons.

In 37 BC he travelled to Brìndisi with Virgil and his patron Mae-
cenas, who, as a friend and adviser of Octavian – afterwards the
Emperor Augustus – was hoping to negotiate a reconciliation with
Mark Antony. Horace immortalised the journey in the "Satires".

A staging post whose name he does not give, because the water
he bought there was "the worst in the world", may have been Venosa
where the road forked to join the future Via Traiana. At Canosa the
bread was so vile that he thought the bakers must have mixed sand
with the flour. No doubt he consoled himself with the excellent
Canosan wine, afterwards much admired by Pliny the Elder. (Good
even today, and getting better all the time.) Perhaps it was on this
journey, too, that he heard of a miracle in a temple at Egnatia on the
coast, when incense was said to have liquefied without being burned,
a story that made him laugh.

Horace's lifelong affection for Apulia stemmed from his love of its
countryside, not of its inns, which sound on a par with those experienced by later travellers. The landscape around Venosa has apparently changed comparatively little during the last two thousand
years. There are fewer of the woods that the poet loved, but it is still
agricultural, with little or no industry. The beautiful, extinct volcano
of Monte Vulture now has a road up to the lake in its crater, yet even
now Horace would feel at home here, perhaps more than anywhere
else in Italy. This is rolling, upland country, very different from the
Murge, with pretty valleys and small towns perched on crags. This
was where he had spent his childhood:

On pathless Vultur, beyond the threshold
of my nurse Apulia, when I was exhausted

with play and oppressed with sleep,
legendary wood-doves once wove for me
new fallen leaves, to be
a marvel to all who lodge in lofty
Acherontia's eyrie and Bantia's woodlands
and the rich valley farms of Forentum.

Crauford Tait Ramage, one of the few travellers to visit Venosa during the last century, describes the area as thickly wooded in 1828: "you cannot stroll through such a country as this without feeling that its poets develop a rich and animated conception of the life of nature." The farms Horace knew had been given over to sheep from the Abruzzi and the hills of Basilicata, but today the farms have come back.

A famous link with Horace may lie a few miles to the east of Venosa, at Palazzo San Gervasio, possibly his "*Fons Bandusiae*" ("Spring of Bandusia"). Although most think that the spring is near the poet's villa at Tivoli, as late as the twelfth century the district round Palazzo San Gervasio was called Bandusino Fonte. Two fountains claim to be the spring, the Fontana del Fico and the Fontana Grande. Norman Douglas preferred one of the many springs on the northern edge of the hill on which the village stands, suspecting that the terrain had been altered by earthquakes. Certainly, it would be pleasant to think of the shade of Horace coming here every October, to sacrifice a kid in celebration of the Fontinalia at the "Bandusian spring more brilliant than glass, worthy of flowers and classic wine."

For once, however, Norman Douglas sounds a note of caution. "But whether this at San Gervasio is the actual fountain hymned by Horace – ah, that is quite another affair. Few poets have clung more tenaciously to the memories of their childhood than did he and Virgil ... and yet, the whole scene may be a figment of his imagination ... Here at San Gervasio I prefer to think only of the Roman singer, so sanely jovial, and of these waters as they flowed limpid and cool."

30

Life at Altamura

Situated among gentle hills, surrounded by strong high walls...
G B Pacichelli, "Il Regno di Napoli in Prospettiva"

ALTAMURA IS ANOTHER CITY on the Appian Way, 1500 feet above sea level, among the hills of the Murge. Its name, derived from its "high walls", has taken on a new and unpleasing significance in recent times, because of the bleak grey apartment blocks that have arisen on the outskirts.

Called Sub Lupatia under the Romans, Altamura was destroyed by the Saracens and lay deserted for centuries before Frederick II re-founded it in 1230, specifying that its inhabitants must include Catholics, Greeks and Jews in equal numbers. The Greek rite survived at the church of San Nicola dei Greci until 1601 and a synagogue till the sixteenth century. He gave the city a castle, and also a cathedral that King Robert the Wise began to rebuild in 1316, placing his coat-of-arms over the main doorway; heavily restored in the 19th century, it lacks charm. The castle, a typical Hohenstaufen fortress, together with the high city walls, was demolished during the nineteenth century. It stood in what is now Piazza Metteoti.

In the 1360s one of the naughty Giovanna I's four husbands, the faithful Otto, Duke of Brunswick, was imprisoned at Altamura by the enemies who later murdered her. During the same century Giovanni Pipino, Count of Minervino and Lord of Altamura, was considered so intolerably overbearing that he suffered the ultimate indignity of being hanged from the city walls by his own vassals.

In 1463 the fabulously rich Gianantonio del Balzo Orsini, having grown very old, was secretly done to death in the castle by royal command. Prince of Tàranto and Altamura, most of Gianantonio's life had been spent in civil war and king-making.

In 1482 another over-mighty magnate, Pirro del Balzo, was created Grand Constable of the *Regno* and Prince of Altamura, only to perish miserably a few years after. During King Ferrante's gruesome reprisals for the 'Barons' Plot', del Balzo was strangled in a Neapolitan dungeon and his body thrown into the sea in a sack. The doomed Federigo of Aragon, last of his dynasty, was briefly Prince of Altamura before becoming King of Naples in 1496, but the French and Spaniards soon came and conquered his kingdom.

During the eighteenth century the city become very prosperous, with a population of 24,000. It established a short lived 'studio' or university and called itself the 'Athens of Apulia'. Unfortunately for the Altamuresi, its academics adopted the ideas of the French Revolution.

Early in 1799, the dons at the university rallied Altamura to the new Neapolitan Republic. However, Cardinal Fabrizio Ruffo landed in Calabria, raising a royalist army from his family's tenants. The *Sanfedisti* (Christian Army of the Holy Faith) included not just loyal gentry but a number of brigands who killed and plundered as they went. When they reached Altamura on 9 May, its citizens ran out of ammunition after only a day. They fled the same night, the men going first, followed by the women and children, to hide in the dank grottoes of the Murgia like their ancestors. Entering Altamura, the *Sanfedisti* found a vault full of dead royalists, some buried alive, and any citizens who had stayed were massacred and the houses sacked. Men from Matera and Gioia del Colle joined in, bringing carts, while every sheep and cow, every horse, pig and chicken in the surrounding countryside was stolen, the Gioiesi alone making off with 3000 sheep. After a fortnight the *Sanfedisti* allowed the starving Altamuresi to creep back from the ravines into a city where their goods were still being sold in the market place. They had to ask permission to enter their own houses and 130 were arrested as known Jacobins. It took decades for Altamura to recover.

George Berkeley had commented on the openness of the country in the region between Altamura and Gravina, and on the vast flocks of sheep:

> not a tree in view; some corn, some scrub, much the greater part
> stony pasture; a small brook, no cattle or houses, except one or two

cottages, occur in this simple space; sheep fed here in winter, in the
summer in the Abruzzo, grass here being dried up in the summer,
and a fresh crop in September ... those who own the sheep
mentioned are men of the Abruzzo, many of them, very rich, and
drive a great trade, sending their wool to Manfredonia, and so by
sea to Venice; their cheese to Naples, and elsewhere up and down
the kingdom; they nevertheless live meanly like other peasants,
and many with bags of money shan't have a coat worth a groat.

But this sort of sheep ranching created a landscape like the Scot-
tish Highlands after the clearances, driving many peasants to despair.
Some joined the brigands, others forced their daughters into prosti-
tution in the towns. Sons with good voices were castrated and sold to
choirs – if discovered, their parents claimed that the boy had fallen
asleep in the fields and a pig had bitten off his testicles. The Risorg-
imeno brought even more misery.

Just as on the Tavoliere, the sheep runs of the western Terra di Bari
became *latifondi*. Shepherds and dairymen were thrown out of work
and common land was ruthlessly enclosed. By the late 1860s, it was
said at Altamura that there were only two sorts of people, carriage
folk and the rest. An Altamuran bureaucrat reported how the masses
"openly display their hatred for landlords and officials". Their distrust
of officialdom was justified, corruption being rampant and every
charity maladministered. Former Borbone soldiers turned brigand,
establishing hideouts in the region called the Graviscella, full of small
ravines and caves, from where they emerged at night to find food and
money at gun-point. More than a few landowners or priests sheltered
them out of dislike for the new Northern regime and for its alien,
arrogant Piedmontese troops and administrators.

Most Altamuresi, however, had no stomach for an outlaw's
hunted life, accepting an equally lethal if less dramatic sub-existence
in a labour gang. By 1901 eighty per cent were day labourers whose
misery was aggravated by the uncertainty of being employed at all.
In 1920, when drought made the ground too hard to dig, one in five
went without employment, the lucky seldom working a three day
week. There were government hand-outs of flour, but it was mouldy
or adulterated; the officials at Altamura would only give women
ration-tickets in exchange for sexual favours. With such widespread
resentment, the situation was explosive, kept in check solely by fear
of a nearby Fascist cell at Minervino Murge.

When the Germans abandoned Bari in the autumn of 1943, they established a new headquarters base at Altamura. Up in the Murge, it was ideally placed for directing a stand against the Allies. However, Field Marshal Kesselring – 'Smiling Albert' as his soldiers called him – needed every man he could find, to try and beat back the Allied landing at Salerno, and simply did not have enough troops to hold Apulia. No doubt, his decision to withdraw was helped by the all pervading misery of life in the little city in those days.

Horace must have driven along the Via Appia through Altamura – or, at any rate, Sub-Lupatia – on his way to Tàranto. Nearly two millenia after he had passed by here so cheerfully, most of its inhabitants were worse off under King Victor Emmanuel III than their Roman ancestors had been under the Emperor Augustus.

Part VII

The Cave Dwellers

31

The Cave Dwellers

Remember, O Lord, those in the deserts and mountains,
and in dens and caves of the earth...
"The Greek Liturgy"

O NE OF THE STRANGEST FEATURES of the old Apulian land-scape was the cave-city, originally a hiding-place from Goths and Saracens, but lasting long after the danger had ceased. Whereas grotto-churches existed almost everywhere, Apulia's cave-cities were restricted to an area bounded by Grottaglie in the east, and by Gravina-in-Puglia and Tàranto in the north and west. The major-ity were abandoned during the late Middle Ages, although Mrs Ross saw people living in grottoes at Massafra and Statte during the late nineteenth century, while the underground cities at Gravina-in-Puglia and Matera (the latter now in Basilicata) were inhabited until the 1950s. Matera is the best known, thanks to Carlo Levi's "Christ Stopped at Eboli".

The plateau of the Murge, especially at the edges, is divided by ravines (*gravine*), formed by long-vanished rivers slicing through the tufa. The Apulians either moved into caves already existing in a ravine, some of which had been occupied in prehistoric times, or carved out new ones, their animals living with them. From even a short distance away, in wooded country, many cave-cities were invis-ible, the caves frequently concealed by dense vegetation and their access ladders pulled up each night.

A cave-house was generally divided into a living room and a bedroom, the beds being skins on platforms cut in the rock. At one side there was a tiny kitchen, with a ring carved in the ceiling to hang a cooking pot and a hole to let out smoke. Cisterns were dug in the floor, with channels for collecting rain-water; others covered by wooden trapdoors contained corn or oil, and niches in the walls held provisions and household implements. Where an underground city survived into the sixteenth century, as at Gravina-in-Puglia or Matera, the caves were often disguised by a façade of dressed stone so that outside they looked like proper houses.

Grotto-churches are known technically as rupestrian churches, meaning hollowed into a bank – from the Latin word for a cliff, *rupis*. These eerie places of worship resembled the better-known rock-chapels of Cappadocia, even if the terrain was totally different. Although sometimes no more than a chapel with an altar, frequently they were complete churches with pillars, aisles and apses. Occasionally, they were even full scale monasteries on several floors, possessing not only a chapel, but a dormitory, refectory and library. Their most attractive feature was the Byzantine frescoes that the monks painted on the plastered rock-face. Tragically neglected, these must rank among the most haunting and least appreciated art-treasures in Western Europe.

None of the travellers seem to have visited any of the smaller under-ground cities, such as Laterza and Ginosa. In both places the cave dwellings, including one or two churches containing faded remnants of frescoes, were abandoned long ago. The ravine at Laterza is very impressive, but the most interesting church here is not a grotto in its steep sides, but one dug out of the floor. Now the crypt of the Santuario della Mater Domini, this has some fine twelfth century frescoes, especially a beautiful Santa Ciriaca, who has the long, thin nose and enormous eyes of a true Byzantine saint. There is a fifteenth century marble fountain at the bottom of the ravine where, as in the cave-dwellers' time, flocks still drink in the evening and clothes are washed in water gushing from the mouths of grotesques.

Ginosa has little to offer sightseers, except on the night of Holy Saturday when a Passion play is staged in its ravine, a thoroughly effective revival that makes admirable use of microphones and modern lighting. Before it starts, city dignitaries and religious confraternities escort the cast of actors and children in a procession through the city and along the ravine, which is brightly lit by flares. The audience follows, trooping down the dark, twisting streets to a natural amphitheatre opposite the old cave settlement. They sit on

Entrance to the church of San Nicola at Mottola. The rupestrian cave churches of Apulia contain Byzantine frescoes that are among Europe's least known art treasures

the ground, hissing and booing when Judas betrays Christ, and cheering when he hangs himself from a wild fig-tree.

An ugly incident at Ginosa in 1908 reminds one that, even after the inhabitants had left their caves, they still lacked water. During one of the worse droughts in living memory, a large band of parched and starving children went to the church, shouting at the priest that he must pray for rain. Instead of praying, he threw two buckets of precious water over the children, two of whom were trampled to death in the ensuing panic. A thousand labourers returning from the fields rushed to the church to lynch the priest, who was saved by the *carabinieri* only just in time.

Inspired by Lenormant, who was the first to recognise the merit of Apulia's Byzantine frescoes, Charles Diehl visited Mottola. Perched on top of a hill, the little city has a splendid view of the plain beneath, of the sea, and of the mountains of Basilicata and Calabria. It has been inhabited since prehistoric times and in 274 BC King Pyrrhus of Epirus was routed by the Romans in a skirmish just below the city. Sacked by the Saracens in 846, it was re-fortified by the Byzantines, but those inhabitants who had not been slaughtered or dragged off into slavery preferred to live in the deep ravine that lies to the south, as did their descendants for several centuries.

You cannot see the ravine from the road, only the tops of a line of tall Aleppo pines marking where the land suddenly drops for hundreds of feet. Choked by vegetation, a narrow path leads down to the bottom, joining the caves to each other. A landslide has destroyed part of the settlement, including the main church, yet even so, it remains possible to gain a vivid impression of what an underground Apulian city must have looked like during the early Middle Ages.

Among the cave churches around Mottola is San Nicola, dug discreetly into the side of a secluded *lama* or miniature ravine, filled with prickly pear, acanthus and loquats. Here are some of the best twelfth and thirteenth century frescoes in Apulia. Despite an iron gate to protect them from vandals, on one occasion thieves broke in and cut out the heads, removing the Child from the Virgin's lap. The head of the Archangel Michael was found in the *lama* while the Child and the heads of St Parasceva and other saints were recovered at Castellaneta.

Not far from San Nicola, at the Masseria Casalrotto, is the grotto chapel of Santa Margherita. Originally Byzantine, as can be seen from the frescoes of St Demetrius and the Archangel Michael, it was repainted in a Latin style during the fourteenth century, when the Greek rite was going out of favour. The Archangel escaped repainting through being on the far side of a pillar and less in view of the congregation.

Massafra, teetering on the extreme edge of the Murgia and divided into an old town and a new by a handsome ravine, was visited by Janet Ross in 1888. She found it "very dirty and extraordinarily picturesque", the poor living in "prehistoric cave dwellings". She watched the *festa* (festival) of the Madonna della Scala, brought in procession from the great church at the far end of the ravine to the Benedictine convent that is the statue's home for the rest of the year. The Madonna, clad in gold-embroidered white robes, ready to be hung with jewels on her feast day, is kept in a glass case at the convent.

The story of the discovery of Massafra's miraculous icon, which hangs over the high altar in the church of the Madonna della Scala, seems to change with every sacristan. In 1888 it was said that a simple peasant, lured on by unearthly music and a mysterious light, had dug it up in the ravine. A century later we are told a far more colourful tale; a huntsman had seen it in a dream, on the antlers of a deer that ran down a ladder into a cave. Out with his hounds next morning, he saw a stag disappear down a rough flight of steps into a grotto and, chasing after it, found the icon. Beside the church is the partially destroyed cave chapel of the Buona Nuova, the original home of the Madonna who, after her finding, was reverently cut out from the wall and taken into the new church. As with other Apulian "icons", she must have begun as a fresco painted by a Greek hermit.

The Madonna della Scala has performed many miracles. The most dramatic was for a poor girl who gathered herbs in the ravine by night; she was going to be burned as a witch when the Madonna appeared to her terrified tormentors and saved her life. In gratitude, the girl carved out a flight of steps from the church to the top of the ravine, the *scala*.

Mrs Ross also inspected another rock-hewn church here, Santa Maria della Candalora, "well worth the climb down into the *gravina*." Charles Diehl considered it to be the most important Byzantine church in Massafra, and it contains a superb fresco of the Presentation in the Temple, with a wonderful white-bearded St Simeon. This part of the ravine is full of grottoes once used as cells by a hermit community. Here too, is "The Dispensary of the Sorcerer Gregorius", a complex of inaccessible caves where the hermits kept their medicines and potions.

32

Gravina-in-Puglia

It is built on caves that can be lived in...
G B Pachicelli, "Il Regno di Napoli in Prospettiva"

T HE CITY OF GRAVINA-IN-PUGLIA lies on the undulating plateau
of Apulia Petrosa, the stony Alta Murgia of western Apulia, not
far from the border with Basilicata. Its dramatic setting, on the edge
of the giant ravine from which it derives its name, is very impressive.
When the Roman city here was destroyed in the fifth century during
the Barbarian invasions, its citizens took refuge in the ravine, exca-
vating a troglodyte town with grotto churches, while attempting to
rebuild their city on the surface. Four hundred years later, they tried
to hide in it from the Saracens, but in 983 the Infidels massacred over
a thousand of them. The victims' bones may still be seen in the cave
church of San Michele dei Grotti, once the *chiesa madre* of Gravina,
where Mass continues to be said on the feast-days of St Michael.

Eventually the Gravinesi emerged from their caverns for good and
built their present city. Although clearly a prosperous commercial
town with a population of over 40,000 and possessing some fine
buildings – Gothic, Renaissance, Baroque, Neo-Classical – whole
streets in its medieval quarter are deserted, especially those that
lead down into the ravine. From above, you can see the entrances to
countless caves, nearly all difficult to reach, as was intended by those
who dug them.

A Greek bishopric dependent on Òtranto, Gravina fell to the
Normans in 1042, becoming a county held by Humphrey of Hauteville. It was acquired by the Aleramo family during the twelfth century

and then by the De Say. A cathedral above ground was begun in 1092, while Frederick II built a luxurious hunting lodge a mile away from the city, which became the counts' residence.

John, Count of Gravina (d. 1335) was a younger brother of King Robert and of Philip, Prince of Tàranto – titular Latin Emperor of the East – and in 1318 married Mahaut of Hainault, Princess of Achaea (the Peloponnese). Finding she had secretly married an obscure knight, he divorced Mahaut, imprisoning her for life, but was invested as Prince of Achaea. After a single, futile campaign against the Byzantines, he went home to Gravina, exchanging Achaea for the Duchy of Durazzo on the Albanian coast, and the empty title of King of Albania. However ineffectual it may have been, his career illustrates Apulia's indestructible ties with the far side of the Adriatic.

The Romanesque cathedral was burned down in the fifteenth century and the present *duomo*, from a comparatively rare period in Apulian architecture – yet among the region's loveliest – dates from 1482.

After Gravina had been briefly held by Raimondello del Balzo Orsini, Queen Giovanna II gave it to his kinsman Francesco Orsini, Prefect of Rome, the county being made into a duchy. One of the great Roman princely houses – a family that produced two Popes – the Orsini held the Duchy of Gravina for four centuries, although not always with ease. At the end of the fifteenth century Duke Francesco vainly sought the hand of Lucrezia Borgia. In 1502 he rashly opposed her sinister brother's ambitions, whereupon he and his friends were lured into visiting Cesare Borgia, separated from their troops and arrested. Next year Francesco was discreetly strangled. The story is told by Machiavelli in "The Prince". His son, Duke Ferdinando, built the magnificent Palazzo Gravina at Naples.

When at home in Apulia the Dukes of Gravina lived no less opulently, in contrast to their subjects underground. Ferdinando III (1645–58) was the most interesting because of his taste and patronage, well supported by his Apulian wife, Giovanna Frangipane della Tolfa, the Count of Grumo's daughter. Abandoning the Hohenstaufen *castello*, they built a small but elegant palace in the centre of the city, today a ramshackle tenement divided into flats.

The church of Santa Maria dei Morti, renamed the Purgatorio, which they began building in 1644 has two horrible stone skeletons grinning over its main door. Many Apulian churches built between the mid-seventeenth century and the 1730s are dedicated to Purgatory, the plagues of 1656 and 1730 having made men more aware of mortality. Inside there are some fine paintings by Francesco Guarino, an "Assumption" and a "Madonna among the Holy Souls in Purgatory".

Bernardo De Dominici, chronicler of the artists of Baroque Naples, says Guarino made "ornaments and pictures" for the ducal palace at Gravina. Unfortunately, Guarino fell in love with a beautiful lady of the city whose husband told her to respond, then murdered her. The painter literally pined away, dying of self-starvation in 1654 at the age of thirty-nine "to the great displeasure of the Duke", and was buried in the cathedral.

His patron survived him by four years, to be killed at Naples by the plague. The Duchess erected a life-sized statue of her husband in the Purgatorio, with an epitaph describing him as "A most cultivated spouse with a heart inclined to love", and went on adding to their collection – including works by Caravaggio, Ribera, Carlo Rosa, Olivieri, Altobello, Fracanzano and Miglionico. The collection, by then famous, was broken up at the start of the eighteenth century. During a visit to Venice when he was still only sixteen, her eldest son Pier Francesco II, ran away to become a Dominican friar, renouncing the duchy in favour of his brother, Domenico. As Cardinal Orsini, he gave Gravina's cathedral its splendid *campanile*.

Elected Pope in 1724 and taking the name Benedict XIII, Domenico turned out to be a disaster as pontiff. Leaving all business to his corrupt secretary, Niccolò Coscia, he lived like some village *abate* in a tiny white-washed room in the Vatican, visiting the sick, sitting for hours on end in the confessional, teaching the catechism to children and trying – unsuccessfully – to revive public penance for adulterers, while Coscia busily sold offices and benefices to the highest bidder. There is a ludicrously incongruous statue of Papa Orsini dressed as a Roman Emperor in the Cortile del Belvedere at Rome.

Pacichelli liked what he saw of the city in the last quarter of the seventeenth century: "Its streets are wide if ill-paved, and its houses are commodious, among them the palace of the Duke Orsini." He was struck by the number of mules and horses, also of storks. He comments on the local pottery "majolica in the fashion of faience". Above all, he was amused by a punning inscription over the main gate, "*Grana dat, et Vina clara Vrbs Gravina*" ("Gravina gives Grain and fine Wine").

Sadly, when Papa Orsini's young nephew, Filippo Beruado I, became Duke in 1705, he turned out to be obsessed with hunting, taking little interest in his city. At the same time, relations between the Orsini and the Gravinesi grew unpleasantly strained because of the wrangling over taxes and feudal dues that bedevilled every Apulian magnate.

George Berkeley arrived at Gravina from Matera on 2 June 1734. "Vines left, corn, pasture", he noted: "The same hilly country continued in the night; a world of shining flies." Although a careful traveller, he had somehow taken the wrong road. "Lost our way; arrived after much wandering afoot at a Franciscan convent without the walls of Gravina at 11 in the night, dark." It was still a walled city and, because of the danger from brigands, the gates were shut at dusk until well into the nineteenth century.

Berkeley was let in next morning, his impression being "well paved with white marble; situated among naked green hills; 5 convents of men and 3 of women; unhealthy air in wet weather." He adds, "Duke a wretch; princes obliged by del Carpio to give their own or the heads of the banditti with whom they went sharers." This is a reference to a former Spanish Viceroy's attempt to destroy the secret understanding between magnates and brigands. The Austrians, whose rule was about to end, governed no less firmly. "Bishop of Gravina dead these two years, since which no bishop in the town, the Viceroy not admitting the person made bishop by the Pope as being a foreigner", we learn from Berkeley's journal.

After only a few hours, Berkeley left Gravina. In his staccato yet extraordinarily vivid prose he preserves, as if in a snapshot, a landscape which even today is almost unchanged:

> open green fields and hills mostly covered with corn backwarder than in the plain; corn the commodity of the country. Here and there rocky; some trees on our right thinly scattered; a small brook; pasture and little corn. 11[am], great scene opening, long chain of barren mountains about 3 miles on the right, thistles left; for half an hour passed a green vale of pasture bounded with green risings right between our road and the stony mountains. 11. 40, vast plain, corn, the greater part pasture between ridges of mountains; Appenine on the left, old Vultur on the right; hardly a mountain. 1.20[pm], a deep vale, diversified with rising hills reaching to the mountains on left. 1.25 Poggio Ursini

12th century fresco of The Presentation at the Temple. Crypta di S.Biagio, San Vito dei Normanni

[Poggiorsini], where we dined; chaplain lent us his chamber in the Duke of Gravina's masseria; dirty; the Duke spends some time there in hunting.

When the ducal "wretch" died the following year, his son moved to Rome. The Orsini connection with Gravina was almost severed, but did not end till Duke Filippo Beru_aldo II formally renounced his feudal rights in 1816. However, the family still use the title "Duke of Gravina."

Gravina interested de Salis as a source of saltpetre, among the *Regno's* most important products. He found few inhabitable houses when he came in 1789, most of the population of 10,000 living in "subterranean hovels." The streets and the people on them were filthy, only the clergy seeming to thrive. Every 20 April there was a livestock fair, "little more salubrious than a swamp; and as the concourse of strangers is immense, all the convents become hotels." Jewellers came from Naples to sell shoddy trinkets to the "half-savage beauties who flock down from the surrounding mountains, and who then return in triumph to their nests hidden in the rocks, to arouse the envy of their poorer friends and relations."

"The city is surrounded with strong walls and towers, probably

12th century fresco of The Flight into Egypt. Crypta di S.Biagio, San Vito dei Normanni

not older than the 16th century", recorded Octavian Blewitt in 1853. He adds, "It is a dirty place although it is remarkable for the number of its fountains." He also noted that "the common people live ... in caverns excavated in the tufa."

After the *Risorgimento,* Gravina had to endure the horrors of *latifondismo,* with labour gangs and almost total corruption. An official report of 1888 admits to "the crudest and most squalid poverty." The "shelter for the homeless" consisted of some foul cellars whose occupants were starving, while the orphanage served as a source of recruitment for brothels.

Gravinesi were known to feed and shelter brigands. Even the clergy were suspected of being hand-in-hand with the *banditi* (bandits), like a chaplain at the Purgatorio, Don Matteo Abruzzese, who in the 1860s was charged with helping to kidnap a local landowner's son. A local historian, Don Carlo Caputo, one of Gravina's parish priests, wrote that "Banditry became a normal weapon in the vendetta against [Northern] oppressors."

In September 1943 during a raid on German headquarters at Gravina, Colonel Penkovsky, who commanded a reconnaissance force operating behind the enemy lines, captured a document that listed German troop dispositions in southern Apulia. There were 3,500 in total, including 92 officers and 755 men at Gioia del Colle, 83 officers and 629 men at Altamura, and 75 officers and 140 men at Gravina. However, very few of them were fighting troops, most being administrative personnel hastily evacuated from the coast after the Allied landing.

Many of the rock churches here, Gravina's most interesting feature, have crumbled away, their frescoes lost for ever. Decay has been compounded by vandalism. The beauty of the frescoes in the grotto chapel of San Vito Vecchio deeply impressed Henri Berthaux when he saw them at the end of the nineteenth century. Fortunately these were removed from the ravine in 1956 and taken to Rome for restoration. They returned to Gravina in 1968, to be displayed in a replica of San Vito Vecchio, built on the ground floor of the Museo Pomarici Santomasi. Dating from the end of the thirteenth century, it is thought they are by an Apulian artist who had worked in either Cyprus or Palestine. They are certainly among the best surviving examples of Byzantine art in Apulia.

33

Matera

No one has come to this land except as an enemy, a conqueror,
or a visitor devoid of understanding.
Carlo Levi, "Christ Stopped at Eboli"

ALTHOUGH TECHNICALLY IN BASILICATA, Matera was once part of Apulia. We have included it not only for this reason, however, but also because its caves were inhabited and in working order until the 1950s, and shed an invaluable light on life in the Apulian cave cities.

While scarcely any frescoes survive in the grotto churches of Gravina-in-Puglia, Matera retains a fair number since far more churches were tunnelled into the rock, over a hundred in and around the great ravines known as the *Sassi* that sheltered the old troglodyte community. After the destruction by the Saracens of a large city above ground towards the end of the ninth century, its people returned to the ravines, where they carved out new dwellings for themselves on a more ambitious scale than anywhere else in Apulia. Matera fell to the Normans in 1042, but never the less remained a city completely beneath the earth until the thirteenth century, when the cathedral and the church of San Giovanni were built on top. Other buildings followed, yet even today the place's fascination lies underground.

As in many Apulian ravines, besides hermits, there were several flourishing communities of Basilian monks. Some of them were founded soon after the terrible devastation that accompanied Belisarius's reconquest of Italy from the Goths for the Emperor Justinian and Byzantium. It was the monks of these communities who were mainly responsible for constructing Matera's underground churches. The churches date from the sixth century to the thirteenth, their frescoes from the twelfth to the sixteenth. The most important frescoes are in the Sasso Caveoso and the Sasso Barisano; in the churches of Santa Lucia alle Malve, Madonna della Croce, Santa Barbara and Madonna della Virtù. There are also entire monasteries, the largest *Laura* being the Convicinio di Sant' Antonio which has four chapels dating from the late twelfth century, cells with beds carved out of the tufa, and even tufa wine-presses.

Most of the grottoes at the top of the ravine opposite Matera were oratories and never served a monastic community. Some are still places of pilgrimage but any medieval frescoes they may have contained were obliterated by others who painted over them during the seventeenth and eighteenth centuries.

Diehl records a legend told to him at Matera, an explanation, he believes, for much of the vandalism suffered by grotto churches. After being defeated by the Saracens, Frederick Barbarossa fled with his treasure to Matera where he hid in one of the grottoes, which closed over him. "He is still seen today", says Diehl, "and the mountain shepherds, whose greed is aroused by the treasure of the Swabian monarch, have more than once known the emperor emerge and chase them along the ravine when they went too near his eternal abode." In 1880 memories of this story set off a species of gold rush after a grave containing a hoard of Venetian coins was discovered in San Nicola at Palagianello.

Over the underground city stands the imposing but unfinished castle built by the hated Count Tramontana, Lord of Matera, who was murdered by the cave dwellers in 1514. The city was part of the Terra d'Òtranto from 1500 to 1633, but then became the capital of Basilicata until it lost its status to Potenza in 1806. Still, there are other fine buildings above ground in the upper town from the days when Matera was a provincial capital.

Viewed from the far side of the ravine, Matera does not look like a troglodyte city. The caves are faced with stone walls that have windows and doors, many with extensions under tiled roofs, all of which gives the appearance of a normal town. But a closer inspection reveals the sheer squalor of the caves, crawling with vermin when they were lived in. Often the inhabitants ran the risk of falling to their deaths, according to de Salis:

I visited many of the grottoes, and not without danger, because at the least false step, I could have fallen from the precipice and dashed myself on the rocks below; and in clambering up I could not but tremble at the thought that thousands and thousands of people for many, many years were exposed to a similar danger.

He paints a picture of unutterable degradation, of hideous, filthy savages, the women so liable to commit crimes that the prisons were always overflowing. He attributes it to bad landlords, bad government, bad roads, bad sanitation – and bad health. Under-nourished and deformed, crazy enough to believe unquestioningly in were-wolves and incubi, they were completely under the thumb of the ignorant clergy whom they thought could protect them from such horrors, and led a life no better than the animals with whom they shared their cave. Often it was an abandoned *laura* – Diehl describes the Cripta di Cascione as being used as a stable.

"It is not difficult to see in the summer many men and women, so-called *Tarantolati,* covered with wine-shoots and red ribbons, dancing continuously in the street with no one to stop them," de Salis comments, citing other forms of madness at Matera:

All these illnesses are usually preceded by profound melancholy, and are caused not so much by the hot climate as by the way of life and the normal diet in these villages. The excessive consumption of rancid salt pork, the absolute lack of cleanliness in the habitations, a life spent in dark and damp caverns, the continuous evaporation of open sewers, and the mountains of dung and filth left to decay in the streets, are the actual causes of these disorders and sad illnesses, which usually end in the most horrible manner.

Werewolves were a common phenomenon in these mountain districts. De Salis describes them as howling like wolves, "rolling in the mud and filth, and hurling themselves upon anyone unfortunate enough to find himself in their path." "So wild and barbarous are many of the inhabitants of the caverns in the valley that they have obtained by their howlings at night and the desperate nature of their attacks, the name of Lupi Mannari", wrote Octavian Blewitt. Taken for granted by other peasants, men known to change into wolves at night were treated with respect. Although, they were never seen in such a shape by their womenfolk. Carlo Levi was told by his house-keeper – a witch – that when a husband of this sort came home it was essential to keep the door locked, not only to give him time to regain his human form, but for him to forget he had been with his lupine brethren.

According to Carlo Levi, things had not improved by the Second World War. His sister Luisa, a doctor, visited the city in 1936 and described it to him. She had never met with poverty like this before, nor illnesses such as trachoma and what she took to be black fever, normally confined to Africa. Some caves had no proper entrance, merely a hole in the ground with a trapdoor and ladder. Children lay on filthy rags, their teeth chattering from fever, sharing their dens with dogs, sheep, goats and pigs:

> I saw children with the faces of wizened old men, their bodies reduced by starvation almost to skeletons, their heads crawling with lice and covered with scabs. Most of them had enormous, dilated stomachs, and faces yellow and worn with malaria.

During the 1950s the Sassi's inhabitants were rehoused on the plateau above, although a few stuck stubbornly to their old homes in the ravine.

Today these once verminous lairs have been re-invented as a tourist attraction and at least half-a-dozen have been converted into high-priced hotels. There have been plans to build an underground car park – supposedly adapting modern ways to old, but in practice undermining many of the old dwellings. Even so, the place has kept enough of its menacing atmosphere for Mel Gibson to use it as Jerusalem in his film, "The Passion of the Christ". In 2004, locusts devoured every crop in the area, a plague that affected only a handful of farmers, but which, in former times, would have meant death by starvation for the entire population.

Part VIII

Trulli and the *Difesa di Malta*

34

Trulli

One sees a great number of dry-stone cabins made of limestone or tufa, scattered over the countryside. They are called trulli ... lodgings for beasts and country people.

Galanti, "Della descrizione geographica e politica delle Sicilie"

THE MURGIA DEI TRULLI is famous for strange, bee-hive shaped houses, the *trulli,* and for horses. Despite the area's lush appearance, it has a bitter history of poverty and outlawry, thankfully long over.

Alberobello, which takes its name from *Sylva Arboris Belli* (the wood of fine trees) has over a thousand *trulli* in the old quarter. They also appear around Ceglie Messapico, Cisternino, Martina Franca and Locorotondo, each district having its own version of the basic design – a cone of stones built without mortar. The historian Guelfo Civinino claims that *trulli* are identical to the *specchie* of the Messapians which, besides being burial chambers, were used for religious rites.

The Murgia dei Trulli was once heavily forested, an ideal refuge for brigands, which may explain why early travellers avoided the area. The woods were not cleared until the twentieth century, to make way for vineyards and orchards. Nowadays the Val d' Itria is like a garden, with an unmistakable air of prosperity, but it was very different a hundred years ago. "Their poverty may be imagined by the food of the day labourers, polenta made of boiled beans" says Mrs. Ross, describing the *trulli* people.

A typical Apulian 'trullo' – as a family grew, more cones were added

The inhabitants of some of the towns on the Murge eat "*la farinella*" (pounded maize, peas, chestnuts, &c., which have first been roasted in ovens), which they eat just as it is, never attempting to cook it. These towns, Noci, Albaribello &c., are called by the others "*Paese di Farinella*", to indicate their poverty.

Even if overrun by trippers, Alberobello is well worth seeing. Selva, as it was first called, was given to the Counts of Conversano in the fifteenth century as a reward for fighting the Turks, and became part of estates that stretched from Putignano to within five miles of Martina Franca. Since Selva was uninhabited and uncultivated, the Counts encouraged labourers to settle there, living in rough wooden huts. In 1550 Count Giovanni Antonio gave them leave to build in stone, for protection against the wind, but without mortar. This meant that each house could be quickly pulled down before a tax collector arrived to count the dwellings – and quickly rebuilt after his departure. In 1635, when enough trees had been cleared and sufficient land cultivated, a town was founded by the fearsome Count Giangirolamo II, who built an inn, a mill and a communal oven for the labourers, charging them heavily for the compulsory use of these facilities.

The first *trulli* were very like the stone huts called *caselle* that are seen in every olive grove. Without any windows or chimneys, they had square bases and conical roofs, and often a spiralling outside staircase. According to Civinino, this was the ladder Messapian priests climbed to worship the stars. The only light came through the open door. In many ways such houses were less sophisticated than the cave dwellings of the ravines, but they were very much healthier; dry all the year round, cool in summer and warm in winter. Probably they did not improve in design until the end of feudalism at Selva in 1797, since with a constant threat of demolition there was too little incentive.

Then the *trulli* gradually became much more elaborate, with a small window and a tall chimney. As a family grew, more cones were added. The walls were white-washed inside and out, but the roofs were usually left unpainted, save for a large cross, swastika or heart, magic charms to ward off evil. A cistern was dug for rain-water coming off the roof, the sole water supply. Beds were placed in alcoves round the main living room, while an attic reached by a ladder held flour, dried pulses, fruit and firewood.

Conventional houses began to be built with mortar after 1797, but many peasants still preferred the *trulli* either because they were poor or simply because "what was good enough for my father is good enough for me." As late as the 1920s a church was built at Alberobello in the *trulli* style.

The original church here, a tiny edifice built by the peasants on land given to them by the Count, was served by a priest from Martina Franca, who rode out on his donkey to celebrate Mass each Sunday. Giangirolamo II endowed an oratory next to a house he had built for his visits to the town, placing in it a painting of the saints to whom it was dedicated, Cosmas and Damian. When he was packed off to a Spanish prison, the peasants moved it to their own church. Since then the town has been devoted to the two saints. During the terrible drought of 1782, a statue of San Cosma was borne in procession through the streets of Selva with immediate results, a downpour falling out of a cloudless sky.

The last feudal lord of Selva, Count Giulio Antonio IV, Gentleman of the King's Bedchamber and Knight of San Gennaro, was hand-in-glove with the brigands who terrorised the little town. Eventually, in desperation, its long suffering inhabitants sent a deputation to King Ferdinand when he was staying at Tàranto with

Archbishop Capecelatro, a well-known foe to brigands, petitioning that their town should be administered by the Crown. The petition was granted in May 1797 and Selva renamed itself Alberobello.

In the centre of the Murgia dei Trulli, the round, gleaming white city of Locorotondo sits on a small hill. Unlike some of its neighbours, it is untouched by modern development, which has been diverted to a new town in the valley below. Locorotondo contains little of interest, apart from the church of Santa Maria della Greca, but there is a superb view of the Val d' Itria from the public gardens at the top of the hill. *Trulli* can be seen in every direction, from single houses to great clusters forming *masserie*, from aged *trulli* with tiny orchards and hens scratching round the doors to brand-new *trulli* with wrought-iron gates and crazy-paving. Dry-stone walls divide the fields and, on either side of the valley, herds of silvery grey cattle and black *Murgesi* horses graze on the green hills.

Until quite recently, hundreds of big, pure black horses were imported to the Murgia from Calabria, Northern Italy, Albania and Montenegro. All they had in common was their colour and their amount of bone. However, during the 1920s they were glorified with the impressive new name of *Murgesi*. Such horses must not be confused with the Conversano horse, a far more glamorous beast. The Val d'Itria used also to be renowned for its donkeys, which when crossed with *Murgesi* horses produced exceptionally tough mules.

While the old woodmen of the Murgia dei Trulli and Selva have vanished, together with their dense forests, their odd little houses continue to be built. Some are bought as weekend cottages by businessmen from Bari, who no doubt fancy that they are returning to their roots.

35

The *Difesa di Malta*

Lambs at the sound of a church bell,
lions at the blast of a trumpet.
R. dall Pozzo, "Historia della Sacra Religione Militare di San Giovanni"

THE COAST NEAREST the Murgia dei Trulli was known as the
Difesa di Malta (Challenge of Malta), because it was so well
guarded by the Knights of Malta. These were the Knights Hospital-
lers, the warrior monks who had defended Crusader Jerusalem, still
waging an unceasing war on the Infidel. In Italy they were popularly
known as 'Hierosolomitan' or 'Jerusalem' Knights. Even after the
decline of the Ottoman Empire ended the threat of invasion, Apulia
suffered from raids by North African and Albanian pirates, and the
brethren's policing of the Adriatic and Ionian Seas was of vital importance, often saving the crews of Apulian merchantmen and fishing
boats from enslavement. Locals saw the corn, wine and oil that went
out to Malta by felucca as a very good investment indeed. By the
mid-eighteenth century raids on the Apulian coast had ceased, but
they began again after Napoleon evicted the Knights from Malta in
1798, continuing well into the 1830s. Apulia must have sighed for the
galleys of Malta.

Apulian brethren also took part in wars on the mainland. During
the 1670s Fra' Giovanni Gadaleta from Trani fought as a captain of
horse in the Spanish service against the French when they tried to
relieve the rebellious citizens of Messina. Pacichelli heard about him
when he visited Trani, "A true Hierosolomitan ... who died soon after
in the flower of his youth and his courage", comments the *Abate*.

T.III.p. 54 An early 18th century
Knight of Malta

The Apulian Knights included the odd black sheep, however, such as "a tall, wild-looking man with red hair", Fra' Vincenzo della Marra, who belonged to a family from Sannicandro Garganico. Notorious for brawling and duelling, he "would have sold his Order for a crust of bread", but his bravery was admired; when taken prisoner by the Turks during a battle at sea, his brethren ransomed him immediately. In 1633 – with some friends – he dragged an enemy from his coach in the streets of Naples, and smashed his skull with an iron-tipped stave. Outlawed, Fra' Vincenzo fled to Malta and then became a colonel in the Papal army, only to be dismissed for insulting a cardinal. After joining the Venetian service, he was killed fighting the Turks in Greece.

Until confiscated by Murat in the early nineteenth century, the Order of Malta's estates in Apulia stretched from Venosa to Trani, from the Gargano down to Lecce and Òtranto, in a network of commanderies under the Prior of Barletta. Ever mindful of status, Pacichelli lists members of the nobility in each city he visits, who have "taken the Hierosolomytan habit". A successful Knight was rewarded with a commandery, retiring to administer it, sending the revenues to Malta, but keeping enough to support himself in the style of a nobleman. Rich old bachelors, the commanders entertained lavishly, occupying a prominent place in Apulian society.

The travellers' normal itinerary, from Bari to Brìndisi, went along the coast of the *Difesa di Malta,* passing through Mola, Polignano, Monopoli and Egnatia. Bishop Berkeley describes the country along this coast as extremely well planted and fruitful, but almost entirely lacking in houses, due to "fear of the Turks, which obligeth families to live in towns." He rode through great forests of olive trees interspersed with pears and almonds. At Mola, where the low, rocky coast was covered with figs, he found "no place in the town to dress or eat our victuals in; a merchant of the town gave us the use of an apartment to eat our meat in, as likewise a present of cherries." The town owes its existence to a fortress built here by Charles of Anjou in 1278, as linchpin in a line of coastal towers down to Brìndisi, that were intended to be a protection against piracy. At that time the Knights were still in the Holy Land and not yet active in these waters.

Monopoli was an important port under the Byzantines. There are Byzantine grotto churches in the city and in the fields outside, hidden among olive groves. However, the cathedral, the best piece of late Baroque in Apulia, did not exist in Berkeley's time, being begun only in 1742 on the site of a Romanesque predecessor. The *Difesa di Malta* was discreetly in evidence, the Knights' tiny medieval hospice standing next to their small thirteenth century church. Both survive, identifiable by the eight-pointed cross on the church. In 1358 the Knights had established an important commandery in the former Benedictine abbey of Santo Stefano di Monopoli, three miles down the coast, but moved it to Fasano during the seventeenth century.

All the travellers agree that the countryside around Monopoli was delightful. Today, fields of fruit trees and olives are still interspersed with pretty villages and handsome villas set on the slopes of the Murgia. But on reaching Egnazia, Horace's Gnathia, Bishop Berkeley went inland, a footnote in his Journal explaining: "This left on our left for fear of the Turks." Clearly, raiders were still slipping through the Order's patrols.

Sitting on the edge of the escarpment above the coast road, Ostuni – the same place as Pliny's Stulnium – was visible to every traveller on his way to Brìndisi. The Normans wrested it from Byzantium only as late as 1070. It has some fine churches, in particular its Gothic cathedral begun in 1435, and is certainly one of the most attractive of the *Difesa di Malta's* whitewashed towns. The citizens owed a good deal to the Knights' activities, even if some of the travellers were ungrateful.

On his way to Ostuni, Swinburne stopped for refreshment at what must have been part of the charming Masseria Difesa di Malta nearby, built amid the olive groves by the Knights during the 1770s:

> We arrived at a small single house, consisting of a kitchen, loft and stable, lately erected for the convenience of travellers, by the agents of the Order of Malta, to which the land belongs. The kitchen was too hot for me to breathe in, and the other two apartments as full of fleas as Shakespeare's inn at Rochester, so that my only refuge was the narrow shade of the house, which was contracted every minute more and more, as the sun advanced towards the meridian. Behind the house then I sat down, to dine upon the fare we had brought in our wallets. Unluckily I had not thought of wine or water, neither of which were now to be had tolerably drinkable; so that I was obliged to content myself with the water of a cistern full of tadpoles, and qualify it with a quantity of wine, that resembled treacle much more than the juice of the grape. While I held my pitcher to my lips, I formed a dam with my knife, to prevent the little frogs from slipping down my throat. Till that day I had had but an imperfect idea of thirst.

No doubt the water here was like that from all too many cisterns in waterless Apulia and the wine vile, but at least the Order was providing humble travellers with free food in the kitchen, free bedding in the loft and free stabling for their mules. This "small single house" was one of many maintained by the Knights in the *Difesa di Malta*.

Some idea of the Knights' wealth and standing can be gained at Fasano and Putignano. At Fasano, the palace of the Bailiff (now the *Municipio*) dates from the sixteenth century, but, with the adjoining church, was rebuilt in the eighteenth by a Knight of the Falcone family; his coat-of-arms, a bird of prey, can be seen on both buildings together with the eight-pointed cross. The cross of Malta is on other buildings too, while the city's main street is still Via del Balì. The Bailiff's role in the life of Fasano resembled the Count's at Conversano or the Duke's at Martina Franca; he was its feudal lord, the Order holding it in fee from the Crown. He spent the summer months at a villa in Selva di Fasano, on the edge of the escarpment looking out to sea, where he escaped from the heat and mosquitoes.

Nowadays Putignano, to the west, is a busy commercial centre, but the old city survives behind its white walls, amazingly intact. Here too, in what has been renamed Piazza Plebiscito, there is a Baroque Palazzo del Balì. This stands next to the ancient *chiesa madre* of San Pietro, rebuilt by the Knights in the seventeenth century with an imposing *campanile*, a double-decker high altar and an exuberant painted ceiling. The Knights prayed here and at the little Rococo church of the Purgatorio nearby, which has Maltese crosses over the portico. Putignano, with its white-washed houses and wrought-iron balconies, is the *Difesa di Malta* at its most elegant.

The Order of Malta's *palazzi* in Apulia have become offices or flats. Yet there are still one or two Apulian Knights, whose towers or *masserie* are decorated with the eight-pointed cross.

36

The Duel at Ostuni

The fencer is by fencing overcome...
Tasso, "Gerusalemme Liberata"

IN 1665, OSTUNI in the *Difesa di Malta* was the scene of a duel that, after the *Disfida* of Barletta, is the most famous personal combat in Apulian history. It was fought by two great noblemen, both of whose families had given many Knights to the 'Hierosolomitan Order' – Cosmo, Count of Conversano and Petracone V, Duke of Martina Franca.

Son of the terrible Giangirolamo II, Count Cosmo was thirty-eight years old. Just as his unloved father had been given a nickname, 'Il Guercio' (the Squinter), he himself was known as 'O Sfidante' (the Challenger). A lethal swordsman, the count was a veteran duellist who had already killed an alarming number of opponents. He had also taken a leading part in the bloodthirsty repression of the Neapolitan riots of 1661. Savagely morose, he was as dangerous as he was quarrelsome.

Count Cosmo nursed an especially bitter hatred for his Apulian neighbour, the elderly Michele Imperiali, Prince of Francavilla. This stemmed from a long-running family vendetta, that had begun when Cosmo was a child – erupting into a full-scale battle in a Neapolitan street in 1630 – between the Acquaviva of Conversano and the Caracciolo of Martina Franca, supported by their kinsmen, the Imperiali of Francavilla Fontana. Friends and servants joined in the fighting. By the time the police arrived several combatants had been killed while twelve were badly wounded. Everyone still on his feet was arrested, only Fra' Titta Caracciolo, a Knight of Malta, managing to escape.

Prince Michele had taken a leading part in the "battle". Meeting the Prince by chance one day in 1664 at the viceregal court at the royal palace in Naples, the count immediately challenged him to a duel and thrashed him with the flat of his sword. The Viceroy at once placed both men under arrest, hoping that their tempers would cool. But when they were released, Prince Michele, who was too aged and decrepit to fight, asked his nephew Petracone Caracciolo, Duke of Martina Franca, to do so in his place. The unfortunate Duke could not refuse. Since he was only seventeen, the duel was postponed until he came of age in twelve months time.

Understandably, young Duke Petracone grew very apprehensive. Keppel Craven tells us how he found out just what he would have to face:

> A gentleman, who had been sometime, as was the custom in those days, a retainer in his family, left it abruptly one night, and sought the Count of Conversano's castle, into which he gained admission by a recital of the injurious treatment and fictitious wrongs, heaped upon him by the tyrannical and arbitrary temper of the Prince of Francavilla. A complaint of this nature was always the passport to the Count's favour and good graces, and he not only admitted this gentleman to the full enjoyment of his princely hospitality, but having found he was an experienced and dextrous swordsman, passed most of his time in practising with him that art.

A few days before the duel, the gentleman, who was a spy – one source says he had been both men's fencing master – left Conversano and went to Martina Franca, where he reported to Duke Petracone:

> the only chance of success which he could look to, was by keeping on the defensive during the early part of the combat; he was instructed that his antagonist, though avowedly the most able manager of the sword in the kingdom, was extremely violent, and that if he could parry the first thrusts made on the first attack, however formidable from superior skill and strength of wrist and arm, he might perhaps afterwards obtain success over an adversary, whose person, somewhat inclined to corpulency, would speedily become exhausted.

Ostuni, one of the "White Cities"

When Petracone reached the age of eighteen in 1665, a meeting was arranged at Ostuni, on 19 July. Before he rode to meet his doom, the Duke made his will and confessed his sins, saying goodbye to his mother, who went into her chapel to pray. 'O Sfidante' ate an unusually good breakfast and then, taking leave of his wife muttered carelessly, "*Vado a far' un capretto*" – "I'm off to kill a kid."

The combatants had arranged to fight their duel as publicly as possible, on the forecourt of the great Franciscan friary just outside the walls, one of the city's most imposing buildings and only recently completed. Warned by the friars, however, the Bishop of Ostuni, in cope and mitre and bearing the Host, was waiting to stop them. Followed by an eager crowd, the two duellists looked for an alternative arena, settling on a little paved yard in front of the Capuchin church. Petracone's second was his sixteen year old brother, Innico, Cosmo's his eldest son, Girolamo – the same age as Petracone. Their weapons were rapiers with blades three foot long, balanced by daggers in their left hands.

When the combat started, according to a chronicler from Noci, Count Cosmo attacked Petracone so ferociously and skilfully that it seemed scarcely possible the young Duke could survive. Yet, somehow he warded off the Count's thrusts, letting him tire himself out. Then, to the crowd's astonishment, Petracone succeeded in wounding Cosmo. He asked if honour had been satisfied, but the enraged Count's only answer was to rush at the Duke. Receiving a second thrust, Cosmo fell to the ground, streaming with blood, whereupon Petracone and Innico mounted their horses and hastily rode away.

A friar helped Count Cosmo rise to his feet. Clutching his right breast from which blood was still pouring, he staggered into the friary, demanding a confessor. He died a few hours later.

Everyone had expected the duel to end very differently. A band of assassins, brigands hired by the Prince of Francavilla, waited in vain for Count Cosmo on the road home to Conversano.

37

Brigands

...a land
Where laws are trampled on and lawless men
Walk in the sun...
Samuel Rogers, *Italian Journal*

A PULIA SUFFERED FROM BRIGANDS until almost a century ago, as it had always done, even under Charles of Anjou. They multiplied during the unhappy reign of his great-granddaughter Giovanna I. In the fifteenth century Antonio Becadelli claimed, in his life of Alfonso the Magnanimous, how that unusually effective king had rid the realm of brigands, "something never known before." They soon came back, however, large armies of them fighting pitched battles with the Spanish viceroys' troops. The scourge was tamed by later viceroys and largely, if not entirely, eradicated under the Borboni, but revived in the early nineteenth century during the French occupation.

The caves in Apulia's ravines made good hideouts, and the olive groves that stretched for mile upon mile provided an escape from pursuing cavalry. A hollow tree trunk quickly hid someone on foot while, after putting fifty yards of trees behind him, even a horseman vanished. The woodland, formerly a feature of the Murgia dei Trulli, suited robbers particularly well, and the area around Alberobello, Noci and Martina Franca was infested with them. For centuries the valley of Ponte di Bovino, a long, narrow pass through which ran the only road from Naples into Apulia, was notorious for hold-ups. Crouched on a hill that dominated the pass, the town of Bovino was the birth-place of several famous brigands. They often ambushed the royal mail coach, although it was always heavily escorted; on one occasion a *comitiva* (band) found that the coach was carrying the robes of a newly appointed judge, so they amused themselves by dressing their leader in the robes and "trying" a captive traveller – who was sentenced to death and "executed".

Many of the brigands came from the Abruzzi, leaving its barren mountains for richer pickings; men such as Marco Sciarra in the sixteenth century, who led a *comitiva* a thousand strong, well armed and paid regularly, marching in three companies behind the banners of three lieutenants. For seven years they terrorised the Papal States and the *Regno,* including Apulia. Sometimes they stormed entire cities, such as Gioia del Colle, looting the houses of rich citizens. Marco always took care to hand out money and food to the poor. He genuinely believed in redistributing wealth, calling himself "a minister sent by God against usurers and drones." As the historian Rosario Villari explains, brigands like Marco were "shaped by a sense of justice and also by the standards and customs of a peasant world to which wild and primitive ferocity was far from alien."

He fought several pitched battles with government troops. Often he showed considerable chivalry, ordering his musketeers not to shoot at the enemy commander. When a traveller whose party he had ambushed strode up and announced "I am Torquato Tasso", he knelt down to kiss his hand, beseeching the great poet to remount and go on his way. For, Marco saw himself as more than a mere captain of *banditi;* in his own eyes, he was a patriot fighting Spanish invaders. Tasso understood this, commenting: "He waged a war like that of Spartacus."

In 1592, after defeating 4,000 troops sent against him by the Viceroy, Marco invaded the Capitanata. Here he captured Lucera, whose unlucky bishop, Don Scipione Bozzuto, was shot by a marksman when he peered down from the church tower where he had taken refuge. During the same year, however, Adriano Acquaviva, Count of Conversano, drove Marco out of both Apulia and his lair in the Abruzzi. Hired by Venice to fight Dalmatian pirates, Marco and his men refused to fight in Crete, so the Venetians slaughtered them. He escaped, trying to reach the *Regno,* but was murdered by one of his lieutenants for the money on his head and a free pardon.

In 1594, the traveller Fynes Moryson had been told of the hunted, wolfish existence led by such men all over Southern Italy. He was aware that many brigands had killed comrades for the sake of head-money and a pardon: "they are so jelous one of another, and so affrighted with the horror of their owne Consciences, as they both eat and sleep armed, and uppon the least noyse or shaking of a leafe, have their hands upon their Armes, ready to defend themselves."

Other brigand *comitive* (groups) were active in Apulia at the turn of the sixteenth century, especially in the Terra d'Òtranto, if not so well organised as Marco's. The peasants often helped them, regarding the Spanish soldiers as robbers and murderers – with good reason. The Benedictine monks of a priory near Troia not only gave shelter to brigands but helped to dispose of their plunder.

The most dangerous *comitive,* usually about thirty strong, were those around Cisternino and Martina Franca: those in the Lecce area led by the Lubelli brothers, and those near Ceglie Messapico under Cataldo and Nunzio, whose other hunting ground was the Monopoli district. For many years Antonio Rovito of Ugento was popularly known as "King of the Brigands" in his neighbourhood, while in 1608, Stefano Calò was wanted in Ostuni for more than twenty murders. Two years later the authorities congratulated themselves on having rid Apulia of *banditi,* which was clearly wishful thinking.

Sometimes the *comitive* were led by local noblemen, like Giovan Vincenzo Dominiroberto, Baron of Palascianello, who once escaped from prison in the basket in which his food had been delivered. In 1631 the baron was finally run to ground in a church at Serracapriola, dragged out from sanctuary and beheaded, despite the local bishop's protests; presumably his head was sent off to obtain the head-money, while his four quarters were hung from roadside trees.

In the 1630s magnates began recruiting small armies of *banditi,* to enforce their dominion over the peasants and cow the commons in the towns. "Never before had Southern Italian brigandage ... been so closely linked with the barons' activities and interests", comments Villari. The wool merchants grew frightened of doing business in the *dogana* at Foggia where the magnates' new henchmen bullied them into paying robbers' prices. Feudal privilege enabled barons to give their brigands virtual impunity, although many were hunted down by revengeful peasants during the revolt of 1647.

Later in the century the authorities almost eradicated brigandage, but it revived during the 1760s. The *comitiva* of Nicola Spinosa, or '*Scanna Cornacchia*' ('Carrion Crow') as he was popularly known, a murderer and escaped convict from Castellana, became a useful

Castello Marchione, the hunting lodge of the Counts of Conversano, where they held secret meetings with brigand chieftains

political tool for Count Giulio Antonio IV of Conversano, who protected its members in return for favourable results in the elections to his city's commune. He regularly received the 'Carrion Crow' after dark at his hunting-lodge of Marchione outside Conversano, turning a very blind eye to murder, robbery, rape and extortion.

Giulio Antonio was also Count of Castellana, where *'Scanna Cornacchia'* was no less active. In 1782 its people petitioned King Ferdinand, imploring him to save them from the 'Carrion Crow', and explaining that the *comitiva* was under their feudal lord's protection. In response, the count was ordered to hand the *comitiva* over to justice within a month; otherwise, His Majesty would put in train "certain steps of an economic nature." Giulio Antonio thereupon bribed Gregorio Matarrese, whom he knew was in their confidence, to murder them and gave him guns. The *comitiva* was planning to rob the King's Messenger near Tàranto so Matarrese laid a lethal ambush. Most of its members were killed or captured, but the 'Carrion Crow' escaped into the woods. He went to ground with his mistress, Domenica Pugliese – *'La Falcona di Putignano'* in a *masseria* near Putignano, where the couple were at last tracked down by a company of Swiss soldiers. Realising he had no hope of escape, the 'Carrion Crow' ordered his mistress to kill him, the 'Falcon' shooting him in the neck. Stuck on a lance, his head was paraded through Castellana.

"Many abandon their wretched way of life and turn to robbery", Galanti wrote of the *Regno's* peasants in the 1790s, yet when de Salis visited the Terra d'Òtranto at this time he noticed that guards were not needed – although their presence was a help in dealing with extortionate innkeepers. By then the authorities seldom executed brigands since they were useful as convict labour.

However, in 1806, Joseph Bonaparte became king, succeeded by Marshal Murat two years later, and brigandage broke out all over Southern Italy. *'Il Pennacchio'* ('the Plumed One') stormed through the Gargano, claiming he was under orders from the exiled King Ferdinand, killing French supporters and plundering their property. In 1808, Major Courier reported that the area around Foggia was a land of thieves: "They hold up travellers and have their way with the girls. They rob, rape and murder."

During Joseph's reign they terrorised the Bovino valley, along which ran the main road from Naples. Charles Macfarlane writes, "rarely could a company of travellers pass without being stopped; a Government officer, a Government mail, or the revenue from the province, never without a little army for an escort. And all these troops were at times unable to afford protection, but were themselves beaten off, or slaughtered by the brigands." They even dreamt of capturing Joseph and taking him prisoner to King Ferdinand in Sicily. However, Murat eventually brought the situation under control.

The most notorious *comitiva* was led by Gaetano Vardarelli and his brothers. After deserting from Murat's army in 1809, Gaetano harried northern Apulia with 300 horsemen, one of his bases being the Bovino valley. He and his band encouraged the country people not to pay taxes, burning conscription lists. Since salt was a government monopoly, they broke into state warehouses and handed out the salt. They lived off the land, raiding *masserie*; if resisted, they set fire to the buildings and the crops, driving off the livestock. When the hunt finally grew too hot, many of the *comitiva* fled to Sicily, including Gaetano, who became a sergeant in King Ferdinand's guards. But Apulia had not heard the last of Don Gaetano Vardarelli.

Part IX

Tàranto and Brìndisi

38

Classical Tàranto

Taranto is in many ways the most remarkable city left to us in all
Magna Graecia ... The ancient city spread itself out over the mainland
eastward, its acropolis alone occupying the peninsula, which is now
an island.

Edward Hutton, "Naples and Southern Italy"

THE TWO GREAT PORTS of southern Apulia are Tàranto and
Brìndisi, on the Ionian Sea and the Adriatic. Since the third
century BC they have been linked across the Heel of Italy by the Via
Appia. Famous in Antiquity, they fascinated the travellers, who had
read about them in Polybius or Livy. To understand how they saw
these venerable cities and what they hoped to find there, you have to
look at the history of Taras and Brentesion.

According to legend, Tàranto – in Greek, Taras – was founded
by a divinity of that name, son of Poseidon, the god of the Mediterranean, and of the nymph Saturia, who was a daughter of Minos of
Crete. She had set out for Italy from Crete with Iapyx (ancestor of
the Messapians), but en route she had been raped by Poseidon. Taras
arrived in Apulia on a dolphin, having ridden over the sea from Cape
Matapan. He was worshipped as a demi-god by the Tarentines, who
put him on their coins, and even today he appears on the city arms,
riding on his dolphin.

The Cretan elements in the story, however fantastic, are probably
significant. Minoan ships could well have visited the Gulf of Tàranto.
Strabo says that the Cretans were here before the Spartans while
Herodotus thinks that the Messapians came from Crete. (Although

Herodotus admits that he is not infallible – "my job is to write down what has been said, but I don't have to believe it.") In reality, the Messapians came from the other side of the Adriatic; their pottery, unique in Italy, is relatively common in the Balkans. Yet there were undoubtedly Greek links from a very early date, with a small Mycenean trading colony on a site at Scoglio del Tonno – near today's railway station – which flourished from about 1400–1200 BC. Even after the collapse of Mycenae, when most of the West lost contact, the Messapians kept in touch with Greece.

During the eighth century BC, a band of young Spartans left home because their countrymen refused to treat them as equals. They were bastards, born to women whose husbands had been away at war for nineteen years. The legend is that, led by Phalanthus – another dolphin rider – the youths sailed northwest into the Ionian Sea and founded Taras. What is certain is that Spartans established a colony here at about this time, administered by a 'nomarch'. Trading with the Messapians, they were no doubt attracted by the marvellous harbour and beautiful coastline. "The landscape, vegetation and intensity of light all recalled Greece", Francois Lenormant points out: "The first colonists from Hellas must have thought they were still in their own country... Here you enter a new land ... which really does deserve the name 'Greater Greece'."

Predictably, there was unending war between colonists and natives. Yet there must also have been cultural exchange since the Messapians adopted the newcomers' alphabet. This was realised in 2003 when archaeologists unearthed a 'map' on a shard of black-glazed terracotta, which is the size of a large postage stamp and dates from about 500 BC. The oldest example of western cartography, it shows thirteen towns including Òtranto, Soleto, Ugento, Leuca (Santa Maria di Leuca) and Taras. Save for Taras their names are in Messapian, but written in ancient Greek script.

Until the fifth century Taras was governed by kings. Like all Greek colonies its citizens frequently faced extermination by the natives; as late as 474 BC they suffered a terrible defeat. However, they won a decisive victory in 460 at Carbina, when, as Hutton puts it, "the Messapian women were outraged upon the altars of their gods with such refinements of lust that one must suppose an extraordinary corruption of manners among the Tarantines." Carbina is modern Carovigno.

During the fourth century BC, its most prosperous period, Taras had a population of 300,000 and covered much the same area as modern Tàranto. Its first citadel was an acropolis, on a rock on what was then an island, but is now the peninsula occupied by the Old Town, guarding the entrance to the Mare Piccolo. The chamber tombs were the most magnificent in Magna Graecia. Later, elegant suburbs with wide streets, theatres and baths were laid out on the site of today's New Town.

Tarantine pottery was more florid than any in mainland Greece, while Tanagra figurines originated here, being afterwards copied at Tanagra in Boeotia. The city's craftsmen made enchanting gold jewellery – wreaths, bracelets, earrings – some of which have been recovered from graves at Mottola and Ginosa, where the richer Tarantines had summer villas. (There are superb examples in the museum.) The coins were among the most elegant in the entire ancient world; the silver staters show Taras or Phalanthus riding on a dolphin, while the reverse usually has either a horse, Tarantines being renowned for their horsemanship, or a murex shell.

All this wealth came from orchards, fisheries, sheep and the famous Tarantine purple dye. Each spiny-shelled murex (or rock-whelk) exudes a few drops from which a dye can be extracted, varying between dark purple and pale rose; since no other fast dye for these colours was then available, it was much prized, Tarantine purple costing only less than Tyrian. The merchants of Taras had depots all along the Adriatic coast besides close links with the Greek traders further east.

Janet Ross was told the legend of the dye's discovery; one day the hero Hercules's dog had found a murex on the beach and, crunching it between its teeth, it had stained his jaws purple for life. She also heard the theory that the citizens of Taras had been the first Europeans to keep domestic cats. Previously, like other Greeks, they seem to have used tame 'weasels' – probably pine martens – for keeping down rats and mice. Some Tarantine coins of the fifth and fourth centuries have a youth on the reverse holding a bird, with a cat climbing up his leg to catch it, while one or two vases show cats hunting birds. Presumably they were imported from Egypt or Persia.

The later Tarantines grew so effete and unwarlike that in retrospect Horace gave their city the damning name *molle Tarentum* (soft Tàranto). Perhaps their decline was due to drinking a little too much of their good wine, which the poet compared favourably with his famous Falernian. Despite walls ten miles in circumference, they lived in daily fear of the Messapians and Lucanians, depending for protection on mercenaries who were not always victorious. The Romans became steadily more threatening, and in 280 BC Taras sought help from King Pyrrhus of Epirus.

Pyrrhus, who in Hannibal's opinion was the finest general of his lifetime, possessed a great toe rumoured to have divine powers. When he landed at Taras, because of a storm he had only a handful of cavalry, 2,000 infantry and two elephants. Learning that the Tarantines expected him to do all the fighting, he at once conscripted the male population, banning drinking parties and banquets. He managed to beat the Romans twice, but his losses were so heavy that he evacuated his troops to Sicily. The second of these battles, Asculum, was the original 'Pyrrhic' victory; "One more victory over the Romans like that and we're done for", he told a soldier. When the Romans marched on Taras, he rushed back to relieve it but was defeated, and in 272 BC the city finally fell to the Romans.

Taras became Tarentum, a Roman garrison occupying the citadel. However, in 212 when some Tarantine hostages tried to escape from Rome and, after being caught, were flung to their deaths from the Tarpeian rock, there was widespread revulsion against Roman rule among the citizens. Two young cousins of the victims, Philomenus and Nicon, wrote to Hannibal, offering to hand over the city to him. His army was camped nearby and he had ingratiated himself by releasing all the Tarantine prisoners taken at Cannae – if he could capture the port of Taras, he would be able to get badly needed reinforcements and supplies from Carthage.

The Romans were accustomed to letting Philomenus in after dark because of his passion for hunting, and because he always gave them some of his game. One night, while the garrison were having a party, he came back with an enormous wild boar; when the sentry bent down to admire it, he stabbed him with his boar-spear and then opened the gate for the waiting Carthaginians. Nicon had already opened another gate for Hannibal with the main storming party, and together they quickly overran the city. However, the Romans held out in the citadel, protected by the sea on three sides, and guarded on the landward by a deep moat and a strong wall. It bottled up the Tarantine fleet, so Hannibal had the ships dragged across the isthmus on huge wagons. Then they blockaded the citadel, but it still refused to surrender.

Three years later, when the Carthaginians were busy elsewhere, a Roman army besieged Taras. A traitor opened the gates, and after half-heartedly throwing a few javelins at them, the panic-stricken Tarantines ran into their houses. The Romans enslaved 30,000 men, women and children, besides sending home an immense quantity of gold, silver and statuary. "I see the Romans have their own Hannibal" was Hannibal's comment. "We've lost the city in the way we took it."

This was the end of Taras as a great city-state, Brundisium swiftly replacing it as Southern Italy's principal port. Yet Roman rule cannot have been all that harsh, since after two centuries Strabo reported how Tarentum still kept its Greek language and way of life. It charmed both Horace and Virgil, who, like most cultivated Romans, revered everything Greek. Horace swore that if the Fates did not allow him to live out his last days at Tivoli, then he would do so near Tarentum. He praised the wine, the *merum tarentinum,* claiming that it was far better than the bland vintages from the vineyards around Rome, while Virgil wrote lyrically of the Tarantine countryside.

About 95 AD, Marcus Cocceius Nerva, a kindly, dignified senator, was exiled here by the paranoiac Diocletian. Too gentle to fear as a murderer, the savage and tyrannical emperor may have been afraid of him as a potential replacement. When Diocletian was assassinated in 96, Nerva was summoned to the throne although in his sixties. He only lived for another two years but his reign was one of the most benevolent in Roman history. No doubt, he rewarded the pleasant place of his banishment.

Centuries later, the River Galaesus, so often mentioned by the two poets, attracted classically minded travellers to the city. But they could not credit that any of the wretched, swampy little streams flowing into the Mare Piccolo could possibly be the beautiful river of Horace and Virgil that had once "soaked the golden fields."

39

Two Men from Taras

I die far from the land of Italy and from Tàranto, my home,
and for me that is a harder fate than death.

Leonidas, "Epigrams"

V ERY FEW GREEK TARANTINES are remembered as recognis-
able historical personalities, as people in their own right. There
are two exceptions, however. These are a brilliant scholar-statesman,
Archytas, and a minor poet, Leonidas.

It was under Archytas, who was born about 400 BC, that Taras
became the head of a formidable confederation of the Greek city-states
of Magna Graecia. He was arguably the greatest Apulian in history,
not excepting the Emperor Frederick II. Not a lot is known about him,
and what we do know coming mainly from a few pages in an ancient
Greek collection of lives of the philosophers. Chosen seven times by
the Tarantines to be their leader, Archytas's head remained unturned
despite winning many victories over the Messapians and the Lucanians,
and never once losing a battle. Because of his gifts as a statesman, as well
as a military commander, the Tarantines reached the summit of their
prosperity and the Tarantine fleet ruled the waves in the Ionian and
Adriatic seas. Thanks to his alliance with Dionysius, tyrant of Sicily,
several cities of Magna Graecia that had been conquered by Dionysius's
father recovered their freedom. Dionysius felt such respect for him that
in his honour he sent a gigantic bronze candelabrum to light the Tarantine senate-house, with a burner for every day in the year.

Archytas wrote on astronomy, music, geography and politics, but
only a few fragments of his books survive. A pioneer of mathematical

mechanics, he developed new methods of weight-lifting with pulleys, constructed a wooden dove that flew, and solved the problem of duplicating the cube by building a scale model. His discoveries were so important that they influenced Plato and Euclid, possibly even Aristotle.

After the death of his mentor, Socrates, Plato took refuge with Archytas and his Pythagorean circle at Taras. When Plato went on to Syracuse and infuriated Dionysius, Archytas saved his life by writing an eloquent letter of intercession and then sending a galley to take him away quickly. A man who looked after his slaves as well as he did his family, he was probably a model for the philosopher king in Plato's "Republic".

He was drowned in a shipwreck off the coast of the Gargano. Three centuries later, Horace wrote a wistful ode to his memory, "Te maris et terrae", in which he lamented how the superb genius, who had known how to measure the earth and the ocean, even all the grains of sand, was now himself "a little mound of earth near the Matine coast."

The Tarantine poet Leonidas, who appears to have escaped from the city when it fell to the Romans in 272 BC, was neither a genius nor a very important poet. He seems to have been poor and obscure even before the fall of his beloved native city, knowing little of Tarantine luxury, a friend of peasants, fishermen and artisans, and writing how he found love in hovels. Yet, for all his terseness, or perhaps because of it, his poems have a gentle charm which inspired at least one really great poet, André Chenier.

He used a humble verse form, the epigram, which never consisted of more than a few lines. He wrote some lines in praise of Pyrrhus's victory at the River Sinni in 274, when the king was trying to save Taras from the Romans, that give us the only clue to when he lived. He is most likeable, however, in his country mode, as in the four lines of Greek which form "The Farmer's Rest" (translated by E.F. Lucas):

> Spare to this humble hillock, this stone that stands so lowly,
> Where poor Alcimenes slumbers, one word in passing, friend,
> Though beneath briar and bramble it now lies hidden wholly
> These same old foes that, living, I fought with to the end.

Leonidas's descriptions of nature can still move. In one epigram, "The Goatherd's Thank-offering", he describes a very old lion, "time-worn in every limb", who is so grateful at finding shelter from a snowstorm in a goatherd's fold that he does not harm any of its terrified goats. In another, "The Cricket's Grave", he writes of "the wild thistle-climber ... the corn-stalk scaler".

In yet another epigram (translated by Kenneth Rexroth), his husband from Magna Graecia sounds just like a certain sort of Apulian farmer who even today is not yet quite extinct:

> Here is Klito's little shack.
> Here is his little corn patch.
> Here is his tiny vineyard.
> Here is his little wood-lot.
> Here Klito spent eighty years.

After escaping from Taras, Leonidas roamed the shores of the Aegean, especially those of the island of Kos off Asia Minor, lamenting that he was going to die in exile after so many wanderings. Yet, like Archytas, he had shown the world that not all Tarantines were heartless voluptuaries. Sadly the countryside the poet loved, all around Tàranto, is now covered with plastic tunnels for early vegetables.

40

The Princes of Tàranto

The most powerful Prince of Tàranto, Gianantonio del Balzo Orsini ...
could ride on his own land from Salerno to Tàranto.

Benedetto Croce, "Storia del Regno di Napoli"

GUIDEBOOKS GIVE THE IMPRESSION that nothing happened at Tàranto from the Classical era until modern times. Yet it was in turn a bastion of Byzantine Italy, a Saracen pirates' nest, a Byzantine city again and then the capital of a great feudal principality. Few Anglo-Saxon historians have written about the fifteenth century *Mezzogiorno* when the Prince of Tàranto decided who should wear the crown at Naples, Gianantonio del Balzo Orsini being a southern Italian version of Warwick the Kingmaker. His name, with that of his father Raimondello, crops up all over Apulia.

During the Barbarian invasions and the Byzantine reconquest, Taranto suffered severely. It was occupied by the Saracens from 842–80 under Sahib al-Ustul, Abu Ga'far, and finally Uthman, who used it as a base for raiding instead of making it into an emirate like Sawdan's Bari. Regained by the Byzantines, it was sacked by the Saracens, then rebuilt by Nicephorus Phocas and re-colonised from Greece. One should always remember that all the Greek survivals encountered in Apulia are not so much the last traces of Magna Graecia as relics of the Byzantine Empire. If he was an educated man, the Strategos of Taranto may perhaps have seen himself as heir to the Nomarchs of ancient Taras, but he must have known very well that what he ruled was a Latin and Lombard port – only in the eleventh century did sufficient colonists arrive from Byzantium to make it once more a truly Greek city.

It fell to the Normans in 1063. Bohemond of Hauteville became its first prince in 1085 and, although he left it to go on Crusade, this was the start of its history as the most important feudal fief in Apulia. Significantly, before becoming king Manfred was Prince of Tàranto.

Charles II created his younger son, Philip, Prince of Tàranto and Despot of 'Romania' – the Latin name for Byzantine Greece. If Philip made little impact on Greece, when he died in 1331 he left his titles there to his eldest son Robert, who through his mother was Latin Emperor of Constantinople. Philip's second son Louis inherited Tàranto. At Louis's death in 1362, Tàranto passed to another Philip, to whom Robert bequeathed the titular Empire. Philip died childless in 1374. Behind these Imperial pretensions lay Apulia's eternal tie with the Levant.

In 1346, Louis of Tàranto married his beautiful, doomed cousin, the twenty-year-old Giovanna I. Her first husband, Andreas of Hungary, had been strangled and castrated, so his father invaded the *Regno* at the head of a Hungarian army, under a banner that bore a murdered king and the word *vendetta*. For a time the young couple were forced to go into exile. After Louis's death, Giovanna married two more husbands, until in 1382 she was deposed by her cousin, Charles of Durazzo, who had her smothered with a bolster.

Among the new King Charles's opponents was a Raimondello del Balzo Orsini, who from his boyhood had "loved to tempt fate" as an adventurous knight errant, and whose life was a long series of battles and chivalrous duels. A great Roman family, the Orsini and their Colonna rivals dominated Rome during the century when the Popes lived at Avignon. They also acquired lands in Southern Italy, Raimondello being a younger son of Niccolò Orsini, Count of Nola near Naples. Born about 1350, he was bequeathed the county of Soleto by his grandmother's brother, Raimondo del Balzo. Niccolò, however, insisted that his eldest son should inherit the county. Raimondello went off to the Crusades, but on his return he took Soleto by force, putting 'del Balzo' before his name. In 1384 he married Maria d'Enghien, Countess of Lecce in her own right and a famous beauty.

During the war that followed Giovanna's death, he led a company of seventy knights who had sworn to avenge the murdered queen, supporting her heir, Louis of Anjou, against Charles of Durazzo. Among Charles's commanders was the English *condottiere* (mercenary warlord) Sir John Hawkwood, and there was some fierce fighting; after being badly wounded in the thigh Raimondello always wore one leg of his hose white and the other red. Charles became King of Hungary as well as Naples in 1386, but was murdered. When the Angevin party collapsed, Raimondello went over to Charles's son Ladislao, his reward being the principality of Tàranto.

A megalomaniac, Ladislao planned to become King of Hungary and all Italy, occupying Rome on two occasions. As lustful as he was ambitious, he employed pimps to kidnap pretty girls, whom he kept in a secret harem at Naples. He was also violent-tempered and murderous.

At the end of 1405, when Ladislao had finally been evicted from Rome and the Angevin cause was reviving under a new pretender, Raimondello led another revolt, but died at Tàranto in February 1406 while the King was marching to besiege him. Knowing that an Angevin expedition was on its way, his widow concealed his death, evacuating useless mouths and revictualling the city by sea. The siege dragged on for so long that Ladislao nearly gave up. Eventually he offered to marry Maria, although she was twenty years older. Since there was no sign of the Angevins, she accepted, the ceremony taking place in the castle chapel at Tàranto in April 1407. The Angevin galleys arrived just too late and had to sail back empty-handed to Provence.

Ladislao died in 1414, killed by a mistress after his enemies had told her to anoint her private parts with poison, pretending that it was an aphrodisiac. His sister and successor Giovanna II imprisoned Maria, but she soon escaped with her children. Among them was Gianantonio del Balzo Orsini, born in 1385; the new Prince of Tàranto.

A childless widow of forty-five, Giovanna was only interested in handsome lovers, leaving affairs of state to her favourites. Civil war broke out from time to time, since Alfonso V, King of Aragon and Sicily, and Louis II, Duke of Anjou were busily competing for the succession. The regime tried to buy Gianantonio's loyalty, making him Prince of Altamura as well as Tàranto in 1431, but two years later he fell out with the queen. Led by Louis of Anjou, a group of courtiers besieged him at Tàranto in 1434, hoping to seize his estates. Fortunately Louis suddenly died of a fever.

Queen Giovanna herself died in 1434, leaving her throne to Réné of Anjou, Louis's younger brother. During the same year, fighting for Alfonso, Gianantonio was captured by Réné's Genoese allies in a sea-battle off the isle of Ponza. When released, he went home to raise the Apulian barons against Réné in a long war that involved all the other states of Italy. Alfonso only survived because of the Prince of Tàranto and his Apulians.

Alfonso finally won in 1442, a parliament recognising him as the first King of the Two Sicilies; but Gianantonio refused to ride in his 'Roman triumph' into Naples, saying that the place assigned to him was too low for the man who had made it possible. Even so, he was appointed Grand Constable and given the Duchy of Bari. In 1444, the King married his son Ferrante to Gianantonio's favourite niece, Isabella Chiaramonte, and although he rarely left his lands he attended the wedding. It was his last appearance at court.

Alfonso dared not antagonise Prince Gianantonio, however. He was too powerful, lord of seven cities with archbishops, of thirty cities with bishops and of more than 300 castles. Not only did he control the entire heel of Italy, but large areas of Basilicata and the Neapolitan Campagna.

Gianantonio respected the brave, chivalrous and learned King Alfonso, but resented the greedy Catalans who now ran the *Regno.* Nor did he care for the King's false, cruel son, Ferrante. When Alfonso died in 1458, from malaria caught while hunting in Apulia, Gianantonio welcomed the Angevin pretender the Duke of Calabria, who came and defeated Ferrante at the River Sarno.

Luckily for Ferrante, his beautiful, high-spirited queen, Isabella Chiaramonte, raised money to equip another army for him, tramping the streets of Naples with a begging box. Disguised as a Franciscan friar, and accompanied only by her chaplain, she went to Tàranto and pleaded with her uncle, who, after the battle at the Sarno, had occupied the royal cities of Andria, Trani and Giovinazzo. She found a sympathetic listener, for by now Gianantonio had begun to dislike the arrogant Duke of Calabria. He sat on the fence, giving the duke deliberately bad advice, and refusing to lend him money or troops. When the king routed Calabria at Troia in 1462, Gianantonio openly joined Ferrante, dooming the Angevin cause.

He died in his castle at Altamura in November 1463, rumour claiming that King Ferrante had bribed the old prince's servants to strangle him in his bed. Gianantonio was childless and, ignoring his will and his widow's protests, the king seized everything he left. Besides vast estates and huge flocks, there were a million ducats in cash and warehouses filled with merchandise. Ferrante became the richest ruler in Christendom.

You can gain an idea of what Raimondello and Gianantonio del

Balzo Orsini looked like from their effigies in the church of Santa Caterina at Galatina where both are buried. Kneeling in prayer, Raimondello wears the courtly clothes he wore during his life, red and white; another effigy below shows him in a Franciscan habit. Dressed as a friar, Gianantonio lies under a canopy in an octagonal chapel; below are painted the words, "From perfect and gentle deeds a noble spirit never recoils", an ironic epitaph for so cynical a career. Beneath the friar's hood his face, with its huge, hooked nose, appears surprisingly gentle.

Yet the castle of Tàranto, properly known as the Castel Sant' Angelo, is the best monument to the del Balzo Orsini, even if Ferrante made great changes. The chapel can still be seen, where in 1407 Raimondello's widow, the beleaguered Countess Maria, married the priapic King Ladislao.

41

The Travellers' Tàranto

...we glide into the sunshine of Hellenic days when the wise Archytas,
sage and lawgiver, friend of Plato, ruled this ancient city of Tarentum.
Norman Douglas, "Old Calabria"

"TODAY IT IS MUCH REDUCED from its former expanse", Pacichelli wrote of Tàranto after his visit here in 1687. He was impressed by St Cataldo's life-sized silver statue in the cathedral, noting that it contained the saint's skull, together with his tongue, "uncorrupted after a thousand years." He also tells us that at Pontifical Masses in the cathedral the Epistle and Gospel were sung in Greek as well as in Latin, which suggests that at that date the Tarantines still remained partly Greek-speaking.

A century after Pacichelli, Swinburne commented: "The streets are remarkably dirty and narrow, especially the Marina, which runs along the Mare Piccolo, and is, without dispute, the most disgustful habitation of human beings in Europe, except, perhaps, the Jewish Ghetto in Rome." But Swinburne enjoyed the sea-food, when he was a guest at a convent:

> The prior received me with great politeness, and at supper
> treated me with the most varied service of shell-fish I ever sat
> down to. There were no less than fifteen sorts, all extremely fat
> and savoury, especially a small species of muscle (sic), the shell
> of which is covered with a velvet shag, and both inside and
> outside is tinged with the richest violet colour. I tasted of all,
> and plentifully of several sorts, without experiencing the least
> difficulty in the digestion.

The "muscle" sounds like a murex. Among the other shell-fish he ate would have been the sea-date, or dactylus, that according to Pliny shines in the dark. "In the mouth, even, while they are being eaten, they give forth their light, and the same too when in the hands." Oysters, for which Tàranto has always been famous, would not have been included, the oyster season here lasting only from 5 November to Easter Sunday.

When Count de Salis returned from the Salento, his interest in agriculture resulted in an invitation to stay at the house of Giuseppe Capecelatro, Archbishop of Tàranto from 1778 to 1836. Sir William Hamilton was a fellow guest at the delightful Villa Santa Lucia on the shores of the Mare Piccolo, its gardens filled with pagan statuary and acacia, myrtle and every kind of rose; an inscription over the main gate read, *"Si Adam hic peccasset, Deus ignovisset"* (If Adam had sinned here, God would have forgiven him). A worldly prelate, who criticised clerical celibacy, Jesuits and the enclosure of nuns, he told his seminarians to forget theology and teach modern farming. He was on friendly terms with King Gustavus III of Sweden and Grand Duke Pietro Leopoldo of Tuscany, corresponding with Catherine the Great, to whom he sent a collection of Tarentine shells. Another friend was Goethe. The Prussian scholar Herder wrote to his wife, "I have made the acquaintance of the Archbishop of Tàranto, the most discerning, high-spirited, learned, intelligent and likeable ecclesiastic I have ever met."

In 1801 the Neapolitan government agreed to let the French garrison occupy certain ports, including Tàranto. In 1803, it looked as if the English would invade the Two Sicilies, so a French artillery general was sent to organise its defences. He was Choderlos de Laclos, author of "*Les Liaisons Dangéreuses*", 63 years old and in poor health, but forced by poverty to resume his military career. Exhausted by the journey, he was struck down by dysentery as soon as he arrived. From his sick bed Choderlos wrote, *"Tarente est une assez vilaine ville dans un assez vilain pays"* (Taranto is a nasty city in a nasty country), commenting that the inhabitants ate nothing but fish. Two months after, he died and was buried under the tower on the off-shore island of San Pietro in the Gulf of Tàranto, his tomb being broken open and his bones scattered in 1815.

In the Old Town, in Via Paisiello, a plaque on a modest seventeenth century house commemorates the birth here in 1741 of Giovanni Paisiello, "reformer of music, who discovered in his heart a fount of harmony and channelled it into songs of love and grief, honoured by Kings and Emperors." He composed many successful operas, such as "*L'Idole Cinese*", and spent eight years in St Petersburg at Catherine the Great's court where he produced his masterpiece, "Il Barbiere di Seviglia". In 1803 he went to Paris to work for Napoleon, having caught his attention with a march for General Hoche's funeral, but after only a year went back to Naples to serve Joseph Bonaparte and Murat, dying in 1815. Already his music had gone out of fashion, yet Beethoven admired the "Molinara". His "Inno Reale", a noble and melodious tune, remained the national anthem of the Two Sicilies until the end – at church parades it was played at the elevation of the Host, soldiers singing it on bended knee.

When Ferdinand Gregorovius came here, Paisiello's house reminded him of Mozart's birthplace at Salzburg. Despite writing that "cultural life is dead in Tàranto", he had been impressed by a scholarly booklet on the ancient city by a certain Francesco Sferra. He tracked down the sage with difficulty, eventually directed by a priest to Via Paisiello. Here, in what he calls a "Temple of Aesculapius" (a pharmacy), he found a sickly looking young man with a dirty towel round his head making pills. The chemist's apprentice admitted that he was Sferra and immediately tried to sell Gregorovius another learned work.

Lenormant observed in 1880 that, because of the Tarantines' fish diet, they suffered from rickets and even elephantiasis. Augustus Hare found a "miserable, filthy, scrofulous population, which has been confined in the narrow space occupied by the Acropolis of the Greek city since the eleventh century." Yet he could not forget the legend that Plato had landed at the ancient bridge, to be welcomed by the Tarantine philosophers. He was also intrigued by the muslin produced from a shell-fish, the *lana-penna,* from the rocks around Punta Penna, its long, silky, golden-brown filaments being dyed purple and woven into a filmy gauze. (The veils of the dancing girls in the murals at Herculaneum were made of this material.) "Taranto has been compared to a ship", observed Hare with his painter's eye, "the castle at its east end representing the stern, its great church the mast, the tower of Raimondo Orsini the bowsprit, and the bridge the cable."

Mrs. Ross believed the Tarantines "show their evident Greek descent by their shapely hands and ears and well-poised heads", although this was wishful thinking. She thought the Old Town's side alleys so narrow that they "seem built for shadows, not men", but in

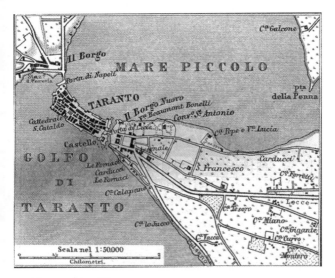

Baedeker 1890 Map of Taranto

the upper town "Some of the palaces are handsome in a baroque, rococo style, with balconies which bear witness to the Spanish rule, and are suggestive of serenades." She says the fishermen dread moon-rays: "They carefully protect the fish from them when caught, and if they find a dead one on board after a night's fishing, declare it is *allunato,* or moon-struck, and nothing will persuade them to eat it."

"Old Taranto glimmers in lordly fashion across the tranquil waters", observes Norman Douglas, "a sense of immemorial culture pervades this region of russet tilth, and olives, and golden corn." He considered the cathedral "a jovial nightmare in stone", but was fascinated by the fishermen's huts on the banks of the inland sea, built of branches and grass-ropes. "There is a smack of the stone ages, of primeval lake-dwellings, about these shelters." They must have been descendants of the fishermen's huts Leonidas knew. Even so, "Hellenic traits have disappeared from Taranto", Douglas comments: "It was completely Latinised under Augustus, and though Byzantines came ... they have long ago become merged into the Italian temperament."

Edward Hutton agreed that everything from ancient Greece had vanished:

Here in Taranto, the last city of Magna Graecia, let us confess the appalling change this whole country must have suffered from earthquake and neglect since classic times", he wrote after his visit. "Everywhere it is a prey to malaria, because it has so long lacked a population which may pursue the art of agriculture in peace; everywhere, save for its noble outlines, its mountains and its sea, it is a bitter disappointment to those few fantastics who hold a memory of the ancient world dearer than any mechanic triumph of today. Magna Graecia is not here but in our hearts ...

Visitors of a new and unpleasing sort came in November 1940 when Tàranto was attacked by British biplanes. Their bombs sank the warship "Conte de Cavour", together with two other battle-ships and a cruiser, crippling the Italian Royal Navy. The damage was greater than that inflicted by the Grand Fleet at Jutland on the Germans in 1916, and far more decisive, changing the course of the war. But little damage was done to Tàranto itself.

Even today, Tàranto's fishermen rarely face the perils of the open sea, fish of every description flooding into the Mare Piccolo. Their old method of farming mussels is documented as far back as the twelfth century, but probably dates from long before the founding of Taras. Row upon row of pales are stuck in the shallow water, with ropes slung between. From these ropes are suspended others in rings, to which the baby shellfish cling in colonies, reaching maturity within a few months.

The ropes have, however, been replaced by plastic netting. In the past, garlands of mussels were brought to the market, where a housewife could choose the ones she wanted, but nowadays, with the advent of plastic, it is easier to sell them strips of netting. From the housewife's point of view, this is cheating since she has to pay for many too small to eat; from the mussels' it is infanticide and possibly, in the long term, genocide.

42

Brìndisi

That Brentesion of the Greeks where Virgil died, that Brundisium
of the medieval chronicles where Frederick II married the beautiful
Yolande of Jerusalem.
Paul Bourget, "Sensations d'Italie"

IF BRÌNDISI CANNOT CLAIM so glittering a past as Tàranto, it
has had moments of glory. One of the few sheltered harbours on
the Italian Adriatic, Brentesion, as the Greeks called it, has been an
important port since at least the sixth century BC. The Messapians,
who founded it, traded with their kinsmen in the Balkans. Later
a dependency of Taras, it was conquered by Rome and became a
Roman colony, remaining loyal despite Hannibal's seeming invinci-
bility. As a reward, it was made a *municipium*. Its name comes from
the Messapian word for a deer's head, *brunda*, so-called because of
the shape of the harbour, and its coat-of-arms is still a stag's head.

Julius Caesar fought Pompey here in 49 BC, blockading his rival's
fleet in the port. He filled the narrow harbour entrance with huge
rafts, building a causeway over them, but Pompey escaped. (Piles
sunk into the sea bed during the operation led to the gradual silting
up of the harbour.)

Julius's nephew Octavius took the title 'Caesar', when he and
Mark Antony divided the Roman world between them at the Treaty
of Brundisium. However, in 32 BC, Octavius Caesar, the future
Emperor Augustus, assembled his fleet here for the campaign which
would destroy Mark Antony and Cleopatra. Shakespeare makes
Mark Antony say:

Is't not strange, Canidius,
That from Tarentum and Brundisium,
He could so quickly cut the Ionian Sea ...?

Virgil died here aged fifty-one, in 19 BC. After spending ten years writing the "Aeneid", on his deathbed he gave instructions that his work should be destroyed as unworthy, but the Emperor Augustus countermanded them. Augustus Hare was another admirer, suggesting that throughout Apulia:

the traveller will be perpetually reminded of the Latin poets,
especially of Virgil's "Georgics", which may well be taken as
his companion. Fields are still covered with lupin – the "tristis
Lupinus", and the peasants still in cloudy weather, tell the hour
by the position of the flower, which, like the sunflower, turns,
as Pliny describes, with the sun. The wood of the plough is still
elm ... and the oxen still drag back the inverted plough ... and the
wild fig-tree still splits the rocks with its evil strength.

Despite the damage done by Julius Caesar, Brìndisi remained a principal port for both Roman warships and merchantmen. A scene on Trajan's column at Rome shows him leaving from Brundisium to conquer the Dacians. He erected two lesser columns in the port to mark the end of the Via Traiana and the Via Appia. (One was moved to Lecce in the seventeenth century.) Every July, Brundisium was full of ships being loaded with Apulian wool.

Sacked and razed to the ground by the Saracens, Brundisium was rebuilt by the Byzantine Lupos Protospata, who had his name carved on the great pillar marking the end of the Appian Way. The city surrendered to the Normans in 1071, and ten years later was used against its former masters, when Robert Guiscard tried to make himself Emperor of Byzantium, assembling a fleet here. In the twelfth century Anna Comnena spoke of Brundisium as "the sea-port with the finest harbour in the whole of Iapygia." It was still capable of taking ships that could carry a thousand pilgrims.

Countless crusaders sailed from this secure harbour, then the main port for the Holy Land. Many Apulians were among them, not just potentates like Bohemond, who had made himself Prince of Tàranto, but humble people who formed a large proportion of the settlers in the new Kingdom of Jerusalem. Knights Templar, Knights Hospitaller and Teutonic Knights were constantly travelling to and fro between Brìndisi and Acre.

In 1225 Emperor Frederick II married the heiress to the throne of Jerusalem, the fourteen year old Queen Yolande. After a wedding by proxy at Acre, she sailed to Brìndisi for a second ceremony in the cathedral. The Emperor ignored her on her wedding night, seducing her cousin with whom he fell passionately in love. Immured in his harem, Yolande lasted long enough to give him an heir, Conrad, dying in childbirth. Frederick wrote the poem "Oi lasso non pensai" for her cousin whom he calls "The Flower of Syria".

Two years later, the nobles of Germany and Italy rode down to Brìndisi, summoned by the Emperor to join him on a Crusade. Soon there were too many in the camps outside the city, bad weather, poor hygiene and lack of food causing an epidemic which decimated them. Both the Emperor and his second-in-command, the Margrave of Thuringia, caught it, although their head-quarters were on the island of Sant' Andrea in the outer harbour. Frederick set sail, but the margrave was dying so he put in at Òtranto. The Emperor abandoned the Crusade to recuperate, and was promptly excommunicated by Pope Gregory IX.

Frederick finally left for the Holy Land in 1228, from Barletta. After recovering Jerusalem, he was informed that hostile Papal troops had entered Apulia. He returned to Brìndisi as fast as he could, driving out the invaders, and sacking towns such as Troia which had welcomed them.

During the late Middle Ages Brìndisi entered a long decline. In the fourteenth century it was sacked by Hungarians while a hundred years later Gianantonio del Balzo Orsini jammed the harbour entrance by sinking boats in it. The city's misery was compounded by an earthquake in 1458. For three centuries the port remained blocked, from fear of the Turks.

Swinburne was amused by a privilege granted by Frederick that still existed at the time of his visit – the cathedral canons could have "handmaids" free of tax, so long as they were old and ugly and no threat to celibacy. When he came, the city was ruinous and half empty, the only decent building being Frederick's castle next to the port, by now a malarial swamp. However, work had started in 1775 on a canal to reopen the outer harbour, and galley slaves were refacing the quays with stone from a medieval palace. He was more impressed by the hunting: "a few miles from the town, there is a good deal of woodland, where sportsmen find very good diversion. Gentlemen hunt hare, fox and sometimes wild boar, with hounds or lurchers, and sometimes with both. In autumn, fowlers use nets, springs or birdlime; in winter, guns. All the country is free to whoever buys the King's licence, except some few enclosures where the Barons endeavour to preserve the game."

Keppel Craven had a bizarre experience here. Visiting the seventeenth century church of Santa Maria degli Angeli, to his surprise he was invited into the convent. The nuns were convinced he was the Crown Prince of Bavaria, travelling incognito. Seated on a red and gold chair surmounted by a crown, he was plied with coffee, cakes and *rosolio* (rose petal liqueur), while the convent's most precious relics were shown to him. "Among the relics which were named to me, I remember some fragments of the veil and shift of the Virgin Mary, a thumb of St Athanasius, a tooth of the prophet Jeremiah, and some of the coals which were used to roast St Lorenzo." The nuns filled his pockets with presents, oranges and lemons, "among which I afterwards discovered, to my great consternation, a pair of cotton stockings, and two of woollen gloves."

Like Swinburne, Craven admired the castle at Brìndisi, considering it to be one of the most beautiful he had ever seen. By then it had become "a prison for malefactors: I heard one hundred and eighty of these wretches clanging their irons in time to the most discordant melodies that ever struck the human ear, the melancholy monotony of which was only broken by vehement appeals to the charity of the stranger."

After the opening of the Suez Canal in 1870, the port became a staging-post on the new, fast route to India, bringing many British. Even so, Janet Ross did not like it very much in the 1880s, although she had enjoyed Tàranto. She could not find a cab at the station: "We were evidently not going to India; the mail steamer left two days ago. What could we want a cab for? Besides, it was raining; the harness would be spoiled, and the driver would get fever." The city could "vaunt an unenviable superiority over most places in the shape of dirt and bad smells", sniffs a ruffled Mrs. Ross, "It needed all the classical reminiscences we could conjure up to make our two hours' pilgrimage bearable."

During the Second World War Brìndisi had a brief moment of importance when for a few months it became the Italian capital. King Victor Emmanuel III and his government took refuge here in September 1943, before moving to Salerno the following February. After the War the port was kept busy by ferry services to Corfu and to mainland Greece, besides exporting farm produce from the Salento, which ensured a certain atmosphere of bustle. Some years ago, however, the port departed to a new location outside, a move that has been described as taking away the city's heart and soul.

Yet the port's departure was not such a bad thing for the nostalgically minded tourist, for nothing can ever deprive Brìndisi of its ancient memories of splendour. Regardless of decline, the Emperor Trajan's solitary column still broods at the top of a flight of majestic steps, looking out over the Adriatic Sea and you do not need too much imagination to marvel at what it must have seen.

Part X

Lecce and the Baroque

43

Lecce

> To walk once more through the streets of Lecce, gazing up at the great
> golden bouquets of stone flowers which adorn its palaces and churches.
>
> Sir Osbert Sitwell, "Winter of Content"

FORMERLY THE *REGNO'S* SECOND MAINLAND CITY, outranking
even Bari, Lecce is the capital of the Terra d'Òtranto. Although
farmed meticulously since ancient times, the area around the city
has never known sheep-ranching or wheat-growing on the massive
scale seen in the Tavoliere, and a large percentage of smallholdings
has meant less discontent among the country people than elsewhere
in Apulia. Founded by Messapians, from the start Lecce owed its
importance to being in the centre of the Salentine peninsula, equi-
distant from Òtranto, Brìndisi and Gallipoli.

The Romans knew it as Lupiae. There is a legend that Christianity was introduced here by St Paul's landlord at Corinth, where the
Apostle had lodged with Justus, "whose house is hard by the Synagogue." Justus came to Lupiae, says the legend, staying with a local
patrician called Publius Orontius, whom he converted and who was
later made bishop by St Paul – both Justus and Oronzo being subsequently martyred under Nero. Clearly Roman Lecce grew extremely
prosperous, as can be seen from the magnificent amphitheatre in
Piazza Oronzo, built by Emperor Hadrian.

Destroyed by the Goths and then rebuilt, Lecce suffered the usual
horrors at the hands of the Saracens, but stayed under Byzantine rule
until captured by the Normans in 1053. Tancred, Count of Lecce
became the last Norman King of Sicily in 1189, entertaining Richard

Coeur-de-Lion on his way from England to the Holy Land. Under the Angevins the county of Lecce was inherited by the Enghien family, descended from the Dukes of Athens.

When Count Pirro died in 1384, he was succeeded by his seventeen year old sister, the beautiful Maria d'Enghien, who became Countess of Lecce in her own right. According to Janet Ross, even in the 1880s *La nostra Maria* was still remembered affectionately as the best ruler in the city's entire history. As we have recounted, her first husband was Raimondello del Balzo Orsini, her second King Ladislao of Naples. After Ladislao's death in 1413, she went home to Lecce where she spent the rest of her life, dying at nearly ninety. Maria was famous for her kind laws; the old and the helpless being exempt from taxes, while strangers who settled in the city need not pay any for three years.

The ruler who has left the most visible mark on Lecce, however, is the Emperor Charles V. He had the huge castle rebuilt in 1539–49, to guard against the Turks, employing a Salentine architect, Gian Giacomo Dell' Acaja, who erected diamond-shaped bastions and palatial apartments on top of the old Norman fortress. Charles also gave the city unusually massive walls, with four great gates. The walls were demolished well over a hundred years ago, but the majestic Porta Napoli (or Arco di Trionfo) survives, still bearing the Imperial coat-of-arms.

Although the eclipse of Òtranto ensured Lecce's eventual predominance over the Salento, during the sixteenth century the city had to endure a long lasting economic slump that bankrupted even Salentine magnates, while a population boom forced up food prices. In 1647 the anti-Spanish, anti-feudal revolt spread from Naples, and the combined forces of the viceroy and the nobles had difficulty in putting it down, shedding plenty of blood. Then came the 1656 plague when a quarter of the population died. However, towards the end of the century Lecce started to prosper again, with a surplus of corn, wine, oil, almonds and fruit; tobacco began to be grown, producing excellent snuff, while a famous race of mules was bred. And, as the region's principal city, Lecce attracted legal and administrative business, besides becoming the centre of the Salentine nobility's social life. In consequence, there was a steady demand for new *palazzi* and churches.

The Baroque architecture they used here until late in the eighteenth century was religious in origin, an exuberant glorification of

Catholicism. "Leccese Baroque" is a highly distinctive form, however, warmly admired by some, but fiercely condemned by others. The local stone, a pale honey colour, is very easily carved and purists object to what they regard as wildly extravagant ornamentation.

Anthony Blunt (in "Baroque and Rococo"), however, queries the very existence of the Baroque in Lecce:

> The phrase Barocco Leccese appears in every Italian text-book on architecture, and the concept is to be found in most English works that mention the architecture of the seventeenth and eighteenth centuries in South Italy, but it can be argued that there is not a single building in Lecce or the surrounding district – the Salento – which can properly be described as Baroque... Both the façades and the altarpieces of the churches show a richness and gaiety of decoration which have perhaps no parallel, save in Sicily. The decorative motifs employed are, however, mainly derived from a sixteenth century vocabulary which had long been out of date in Rome or even Naples... Leccese architects must have relied primarily on decorative engravings or pattern books and it seems that they continued to use those published in the late sixteenth or seventeenth centuries long after they had been abandoned elsewhere.

He also points out that not even the design of the churches was remotely Baroque, Romanesque rose windows continuing to be employed even in new buildings.

The most typically *Leccese Baroque* buildings are the group around the Piazza del Duomo. Bernard Berenson thought the cathedral the most beautiful in Italy, but few people can agree with him. It was designed and built between 1659 and 1670 by a local architect, Giuseppe Zimbalo, popularly known as 'Lo Zingarello', The Little Gypsy. The *campanile* is 270 feet high. ("In the good old times when corsairs ruled the sea, the high *campanili* all over this country were used as watch towers", Mrs Ross tells us. "In the one at Lecce was a bell, which a sentinel struck in a peculiar way, to give the alarm if he saw suspicious vessels on either sea.") Another good example of Zimbalo's work is the former convent of the Celestines, now known as the Governor's Palace, which Edward Hutton sums up rather well – "the amazing baroque façade, with its appalling general design."

There are countless Baroque *palazzi* in Lecce, often surprisingly small but no less embellished than the churches. The pompous coat-of-arms at their corners or over the doorways enthral students of Italian heraldry.

Pacichelli liked the style, commenting how suitable the local stone was for "Venetian windows, cornices and other gallant ornament." The *duomo* was "new and likewise superb." He admired the long, wide street, the gardens with orange trees, and the low cost of food. Less cheerfully, he records how the plague of 1679 had reduced the population to 9,000 souls, although among them were "Patrician families living in great splendour and divers Barons, some of whom have feudal rights, and many doctors and magistrates." But in 1734 the sober Bishop Berkeley thought the "gusto too rich and luxuriant, occasioned without doubt by the facility of their working their stone." He found the people "civil and polite, and so far as we had dealings, honest and reliable." The Abbé de Saint-Non commissioned an etching of the cloister in the Dominican convent, which he found restful after the façade's wearying extravagance. Of Lecce as a whole he says, "This modern town would be one of the most beautiful in existence had it been built with a little taste; for the beauty of the stone and the materials employed give an appearance of grandeur, but the method is detestable; all the edifices are covered with the worst and most useless sculpture."

Both Swinburne and Riedesel were impressed by the citizens' skills in dancing and making music. The former comments, "Music is here cultivated with a degree of enthusiasm. Many of the nobility are good performers, and proud of exhibiting their skill on solemn festivals. The Leccian music has a very plaintive character, peculiar to itself."

"I enquired throughout Italy at what place boys were chiefly qualified for singing by castration", Dr Burney relates delicately. He was told:

> the young *castrati* come from Lecce in Puglia; but before the operation is performed, they are brought to a Conservatorio to be tried as to the probability of voice, and then are taken home by their parents for this barbarous purpose. It is said, however, to be death by the laws to all those who perform the operation and excommunication to everyone concerned in it, unless it is so done, as is presented, upon account of some disorders, which may be supposed to require it, and with the consent of the boy.

Burney particularly admired Leccese folk songs he had heard sung at Naples.

In 1797 Lecce received a visit from the King and Queen of the Two Sicilies, Ferdinand and Maria Carolina, who stayed in the Bishop's Palace. If the Leccesi liked the amiable, long nosed king, they must have found the tiny, haughty queen – Marie Antoinette's sister – somewhat forbidding. Six years later, the king would be distressed by the news that slave-raiders had abducted 164 people from the province of Lecce.

In 1805 Major Courier of the newly installed French garrison at Lecce reported to his colonel that Captain Tela had been murdered by Don Giuseppe Rao on whom he had been billeted. Seeing his wife going into the captain's room, Don Giuseppe stabbed her and the captain to death with a stiletto. There had been no affair – she was delivering his laundry – while her husband took little interest in her. But, according to Courier, Don Giuseppe lived in dread of being called a *becco cornuto*, a cuckold. "In this part of Italy it is the most sensitive point of honour", says Courier. "Here *"Becco cornuto"* is the most terrible of all insults, worse than thief, murderer, swindler, blasphemer or parricide." He adds that the towns-people were saying they would never catch the murderer, however hard they might look.

Lecce had a resident British governor from 1817 to 1820, General Sir Richard Church, given the job of putting down the brigands who terrorised Apulia. He liked "the bright little capital with its white houses, and the little streams running through the streets", and soon got rid of the brigands. The general gave a ball every other week, alternating with one given by the *intendente* (revenue officer).

Keppel Craven spent a week here in 1818, enjoying "the friendly hospitality of General Church", but found the streets oddly deserted. The city "would commodiously admit a population of 30,000 souls, whereas the present amounts to no more than 14,000." As for the architecture: "extravagant and almost incredible bad taste is exemplified in every building of consequence." Even so, the snuff was excellent, and the people "renowned for their courteous, polished manners."

On a snowy January morning in 1859, Ferdinand II, his queen and his eldest son Francis entered Lecce on their way to meet Francis's bride at Bari; their carriage preceded by four mounted carabinieri bearing torches and followed by six with drawn sabres. In the afternoon the king went to the *duomo* for a sermon by the bishop, a *Te Deum* being sung. In the evening he attended a performance by a popular comedian at the Teatro Paisiello, after which there was a banquet and fireworks. (The theatre, built in 1768, is still standing). But Ferdinand was ill, dying from a mysterious disease that had begun after an assassin's attempt to bayonet him two years before. He had to remain at Lecce, in the Governor's Palace, for nearly a fortnight. Characteristically, he summoned up enough energy to order the demolition of the medieval walls. This was the last visit to the city by a Borbone sovereign, although during his brief reign Francis II gave orders to extend the Naples railway to Lecce by way of Brindisi.

Charles Yriarte went to a reception at the prefecture in 1876, finding:

> Elegant, amiable, cultivated people, well informed on every subject, everybody speaking French fluently – which is unusual on the coast farther down than Ravenna – learned archaeologists, distinguished naturalists, administrators, rich landowners from the area around Naples on holiday, glittering officers and, finally, smart women in the latest Paris fashions without the overdressing that is so common among Southern Italians, who gave me plenty of serious, scholarly conversation, with all the amiable courtesy and friendly outspokenness which is typical of Italy.

"I was told several times, 'Oh Lecce is so gay, the very name calls up a smile; and the Leccese are so civil and pleasant.' All of which we found quite true" observes Janet Ross. But while her hotel, the *Risorgimento* (still there) was comfortable and clean, the host was put out by her ordering boiled eggs, bread and butter, and coffee with milk at nine every morning: "The idea was so novel, and the mixture so extraordinary, that we always had to wait half an hour. 'Why did we not have a cup of black coffee in bed like other people, and then breakfast properly at mid-day?' " She did not like the architecture – "very ugly", "a very orgy of baroque rococo, quite overpowering in the excess of ornamentation."

"Every night during our stay at Lecce we saw rockets, Bengal fire, &c." she records. After one of these displays,

I insisted on going into a booth with a large doll hanging outside, to see marionettes as done for the people, not for the gentlefolk. We paid a halfpenny each and clambered up a rickety ladder into the "*posti distinti*", where our appearance created quite a sensation.

The play was Samson and Delilah: "When Delila came on, with that queer, spasmodic, irresponsible walk belonging to a marionette, and sheared Samson of his mass of hair with an enormous pair of scissors, the audience applauded vigorously, 'Well done', 'She's the hairdresser for me'."

The highlight of Mrs Ross's visit was meeting a hero of the *Risorgimento*, the Duke Sigismondo Castromediano. He lived at his castle of Cavallino some miles outside Lecce and came in to show her the city museum. "A very tall half-blind, courteous old man, leaning on the arm of his secretary and surrounded by various professors, some of whom had put on tail-coats and white gloves in honour of the visit of a learned lady." He told her of his life as a political prisoner under the Borboni, "among convicts of the lowest description, imbued with every vice, the refuse of humanity." His health had been broken and he was very poor, reduced to living in one room of his castle. Something of a showman, he had left instructions that his fetters and convict's red jacket should be placed on his coffin at his funeral. He recalled how touched Mr Gladstone had been to hear about his sufferings, especially "the killing out of sheer spite by the gaolers, of a pet nightingale which the poor prisoners had tamed." The Duke told Janet that "nothing gave him such pleasure as to see an English-woman" and asked permission to embrace her, after which he kissed her on both cheeks.

The Baroque was still unfashionable during the 1890s when Paul Bourget visited the city. "Here the bad taste is too intense, fancy carried to such extremes with such genius, that the term loses its meaning."

However, in 1902 an architect called Martin Briggs "discovered" Lecce. Eight years later, he published a book, "In the Heel of Italy: a Study of an Unknown City", calling Lecce "a veritable seventeenth century museum", and claiming that here "Baroque architecture may perhaps be seen at its best." Brigg's book persuaded the Sitwells to visit Lecce in 1922, the city elders insisting on paying their bill since they were obviously so distinguished. Sir Osbert Sitwell admired the

Detail of the facade of
S. Croce, Lecce

city even more extravagantly than Martin Briggs: "Lecce, peer of any
Italian city in loveliness", was his verdict.

Its citizens are still passionately proud of Lecce. They tell strangers
how until only recently the *palazzi* were occupied by *duchi*, *marchesi,
conti, baroni*, and how they speak better Italian than the Florentines.
They talk of Bari as a hideous, heathen place, inhabited by decadent
Levantines who have vile manners.

44

Don Cirò, the Bandit Priest

...a robber by profession – an unholy wizard in the imagination of other
men – a devil in reality.

Charles Macfarlane, "The Lives and Exploits of Bandits and Robbers"

O NE WET, WINDY NIGHT in December 1814, a wayfarer
hammered on the gate of the castle of Martano in the Terra
d'Òtranto. Because of the torrential rain the old steward let him
in, only to be shot down at once. Fifty horsemen galloped into
the courtyard, then ran through the castle, murdering every single
servant, including the chaplain and the housekeeper. The 'wayfarer',
whose name was Don Cirò Annichiarico, burst into the bedroom of
the Princess of Martano – twenty years old, famous for her beauty,
a great heiress and still unmarried – demanding her strongbox and
her jewel-chest. After finding in them 36,000 gold ducats with diamonds, rubies and pearls, he stabbed the princess and her maid to
death, shouting, "Philosophers say that dead bitches don't bite!"

Then Don Cirò and his followers banqueted in the castle hall,
drinking the health of *La bella principessa* with her fine wines, before
riding off into the night and the rain. The only person they left alive
was the princess's eight year old cousin, who had hidden under a
heavily draped table. But for this little boy, no one would ever have
known who was responsible for the massacre at Martano.

Brigands took full advantage of the confusion after Murat's
fall in 1815. The harvest that year was the worst on record, causing
famine and then starvation, followed by outbreaks of plague and
scarlet fever; in the Terra d'Òtranto 17,000 people would die from

cerebro-spinal meningitis in 1817. Law and order collapsed, brigands raiding ware-houses and ambushing grain-convoys, besides robbing and kidnapping. After unsuccessfully campaigning for five months against them in the Capitanata, Colonel del Caretto warned, "They are endangering the realm's food supplies since, as we all know, Apulia is its granary." The campaign that at last broke the brigands was directed from Lecce, by an Irishman.

The Neapolitan commander-in-chief, General Count Nugent (an Irishman formerly in the Austrian service) called in his old friend, Colonel Richard Church. Born in 1784 at Cork, during the Napoleonic Wars, Church had served in Egypt, Calabria and Capri, and in the Ionian Islands, where he commanded a regiment with the unlikely name of "The Duke of York's Greek Light Infantry". Military governor of the Terra di Bari and the Terra d'Òtranto with the rank of General, he established his head-quarters at Lecce in 1817, and brought the situation under control in less than two months, after a ruthless campaign of what would now be called counter-insurgency, with shrewd intelligence work and cynical bargaining.

Hunting down Cirò Annichiarico was among his greatest successes. In retrospect one can see that Don Cirò never had much chance of escaping General Church. Yet at the time it did not seem at all like that to the Leccesi, who feared the terrible Annichiarico more than any other living man.

Cirò Annichiarico, the son of a prosperous farmer and nephew of a canon, was born in Grottaglie in 1773. At twenty he entered the Tàranto seminary, studying under Archbishop Capecelatro and acquiring the prelate's revolutionary politics. But in 1803, by then a priest and choir-master, he committed a murder. Some reports say he killed a rival for the favours of a local beauty, or even the girl herself. The most likely version, however, is that Cirò cut the throat of a certain Gisuseppe Mottolese because he refused to marry his sister after seducing her. Sentenced to fifteen years in the galleys, he spent four in an underground dungeon at Naples, before escaping with another prisoner, who introduced him to a secret society known as the *Decisi* (the Resolute).

At that date the *Fratelli Decisi* were a group of young men recruited by Pietro Gargano, a cavalry trooper who had deserted from Murat's army. Political outlaws and hardened criminals, they terrorised the Terra d'Òtranto, while at the same time enjoying a certain amount of popular support. In order to join this organisation, whose real name was "The Society of Jupiter the Thunderer", the applicant had to commit at least two murders and then undergo tests of courage before his final acceptance. Senior members possessed the power of passing death sentences on somebody they disliked. Writing to a victim selected for extortion, they would add four dots in blood to their signature to show they were serious. The society had some of the trappings of freemasonry, such as signs of recognition, passwords and far from empty threats of dire consequences if secrets were betrayed. But although professing liberal opinions and recruited "to make War against the Tyrants of the Human Race", the society – certainly after Cirò became its leader – appears to have been primarily a means of lining its members' pockets or settling vendettas by murder.

There is a vivid description of Don Cirò Annicchiarico in General Church's reminiscences. Although coarse-featured and scar-faced, with an upturned nose and red, pig-like eyes, the unfrocked priest had become a dandy:

> His usual dress was of velveteen, highly laced, with many rows
> of buttons, and belts in every direction. He also always wore
> several silver chains, to one of which was attached the silver
> death's-head, the badge of the secret society, the Decisi ... On
> his breast he wore rows of relics, crosses, images of saints, and
> amulets against the Evil-Eye. His head-dress was a high-peaked
> drab-coloured hat, adorned with gold band, buckle, and tall
> black feather, and his fingers were covered with rings of great
> value.

Armed to the teeth with carbine, pistols and daggers, he carried poison hidden in a red pocket book.

Even if Cirò denied killing Giuseppe Mottolese, he admitted to many other murders during his career as a brigand, lasting for nearly ten years. Often disguised as Punchinellos (Neopolitan puppets), he and his band terrorised the Terra d'Òtranto. When a girl refused to sleep with him, he went to a dance at her parents' home in Carnival time, wearing his clown's costume, and gave her a last chance. She still refused, so he drugged the party's wine, left the house and then burnt it to the ground with the entire family inside.

Sometimes he said Mass for his men in an underground chapel before galloping out under his black standard to rob and kill. Macfarlane comments, "banditti ... will send a knife into your bosom while a crucifix and a reliquary repose on their own." He also tells us, "Not one of his band could fire his rifle with so sure an aim, or mount his horse like the priest Don Cirò". Living in caves or the forest toughened him and, always well mounted, he would ride forty miles a night along lonely paths to *gravine* where he could hide. His amazing escapes convinced the peasants that "the Abate Annichiarico" must be a necromancer protected by demons and they always gave him warning of approaching troops.

Cirò shared the *Decisi*'s dream of a *Carbonari* republic, persuading them to ally with another secret society, the *Patrioti Europei*, and try to build an army. Late one night during spring 1817 two of Church's officers were riding to Barletta when they saw a light flickering in the distance. The guides claimed it was a will-o'-the-wisp, but as the horses approached, the officers hid in the undergrowth beside the road. The horsemen halted a few yards away, and they heard them say that Cirò and Gaetano Vardarelli, another brigand leader, were at Castel del Monte to discuss joining forces. Since both were *Carbonari* supporters and might well have led their united bands in a full scale rising, the government hastily signed a treaty with Vardarelli to prevent a link-up. Cirò immediately offered to clear the Terra d'Òtranto of brigands in return for a similar agreement, but was refused.

Church gave a dinner at Lecce where he publicly promised, "I swear never to rest till I have destroyed Cirò Annichiarico and all his blood-hounds." He met with constant obstruction, local troops arguing that Cirò was a popular hero. The general had to rely on his Swiss officers and Greek irregulars. Often Cirò left a *Masseria* or a wood just before their arrival, alerted by peasants. When the soldiers raided a safe-house, the *Masseria del Duca* near Martina Franca, where he and his brigands had been enjoying a hearty meal, they simply slipped away through the olive groves.

At last, Church learnt that Don Cirò was attending a wedding at San Marzano di San Giuseppe, some miles off the Manduria-Tàranto road. "A mountain village, straggling up and down among crags and walls, the houses jumbled among patches of olives", is how Church remembered it, "At the top of all a castle, and below the village a belt of woods." The Marchese Bonnelli's castle (still there) had been lent for the wedding by a terrified steward. "The bride, a strapping *brigandessa*, did not depend on her splendid costume, bright eyes, and straight black brows entirely for her conquests", says the general,

"The wine flowed freely, the people gathered round and swore fidelity to Cirò and the Decisi with brimming glasses and ringing cheers."

However, the troops had followed close on Don Cirò's heels. After fighting for several hours, the guests surrendered. Including the bride and bridegroom, caught hiding in a cellar, the survivors were taken prisoner to Francavilla Fontana with 130 horses and 2,000 muskets. Among those executed was the bridegroom, who confessed to having committed twenty-three murders. Cirò, however, had escaped on his fast English mare.

Even so, the brigand-priest knew he was doomed. He had already tried vainly to make his peace with the government, and then to take a ship from Brìndisi but he could not find the 2000 ducats demanded by the skipper. He realised too that his friends, the *Decisi*, were betraying his hiding places. Ten days later he was trapped in the *Masseria Scaserba*, only ten miles from General Church, who was at Francavilla Fontana. For forty-eight hours, he held out with three companions in the *Masseria's* tower, against 130 regular troops and numerous militia, killing or wounding over a dozen of them. Finally, the usual Apulian lack of water forced him to surrender.

Asked by the military tribunal at Francavilla Fontana how many people he had murdered, he replied "*E chi lo sa? Saranno tra sessanta e settanta.*" ("Who knows? Maybe between sixty and seventy.") When a fellow-priest offered him the last rites, the Abate Annichiarico declined the offer with a grin: "*Lasciate queste chiacchiere! Siamo dell' istessa professione – non ci burliamo fra noi.*" ("Let's not bother about that nonsense! We belong to the same profession – we don't want to laugh at each other.")

On 8 February 1818 he was marched through crowded streets to his death in the main piazza at Francavilla Fontana, which was guarded by troops with cannon. Again refusing the last rites, he was blindfolded and made to kneel down with his back to the firing-squad. After a first volley, he was still breathing, muttering to himself. Later a soldier explained what happened next. "Seeing that he was enchanted, we loaded his own musket with a silver bullet, and this destroyed the spell". His head was cut off, and displayed with the words, "Here is the head of the chief of assassins, Cirò Annichiarico of Grottaglie." Then it was taken away, to be hung in an iron cage above the main gate of Grottaglie, his birthplace.

Shortly after, Church arrested Don Cirò's betrayers, the council of the *Decisi*, when they met at Grottaglie to plan the general's murder.

Presepio by Stefano di Putignano, Chiesa del Carmine at Grottaglie (detail)

The troops found them sitting beneath a black banner, not a band of brigands filthy from living rough in the *gravine*, but ten of Grottaglie's leading citizens, grown rich on extortion and blackmail. They were shot and then beheaded in the same *piazza* as Cirò.

45

Baroque in the Salento

The Baroque does not know what it wants...
Eugenio d'Ors, "Du Baroque"

THERE IS A MISTAKEN BELIEF that the Baroque in Apulia is confined to Lecce. There are fine examples of Baroque at Apulian cities further north, like the Palazzo del Monte di Pietà at Barletta or the *duomo* of Monopoli. But it is certainly true that there is far more in the Salento than anywhere else in Apulia. Many of the smaller Salentine cities have churches with wildly extravagant façades and *campanili, palazzi* with frenziedly elaborate balconies and doorways. Although the style, as at Lecce, sometimes seems to be ornament for the sake of ornament, these are often delightful buildings.

After being destroyed by an earthquake in 1743, the city of Nardò spent over forty years rebuilding itself in imitation of Lecce. Even by Leccese standards the church and convent of San Domenico in the *piazza* of that name are ornate. The façade of the church, attributed to Tarantino, which survived the earthquake of 1743 was built in two phases; the lower part covered with caryatids typical of the earlier period and the upper very much more restrained. There are attractive little palaces in and around the triangular Piazza Antonio Salandra, like the white Palazzo della Pretura, which has an elegant loggia on the first floor over an open arcade. The *guglia* of the Immacolata in this *piazza* erected in 1769, is one of only three in Apulia – the others being at Ostuni and Bitonto. (A *guglia* is a Neapolitan folly of Austrian origin, a fantastically decorated, free-standing column.) The streets in the city centre are full of ironwork balconies with swags and caryatids.

Piazza Salandra,
Nardò with
the Guglia
dell'Immacolata

The largest city in the Salento after Lecce, Nardò has had a peculiarly tragic history. During the breakdown of Spanish and feudal authority in 1647, many of its citizens rose in revolt against their tyrannical feudal lord, the Count of Conversano, Giangirolamo II Acquaviva d'Aragona, who was also Duke of Nardò. The count-duke crushed the rebels with a systematic, murderous savagery that has never been forgotten. Even today, the blood-stained Giangirolamo is still one of the great ogres in local folklore, '*Il Guercio di Puglia*' – 'The Squinter of Apulia'.

There have been other tragedies at Nardò, and in more recent times, some of them almost within a very bitter living memory. Because the city was the centre of a highly profitable wheat-growing enclave, during the late nineteenth and early twentieth centuries its people suffered all the horrors of labour gangs. In April 1920 they disarmed the *carabinieri*, seized their weapons and hoisted the red flag over the *Municipio*. The authorities had to use artillery and armoured cars to regain control.

Copertino was home to that supremely Baroque figure, Giuseppe da Copertino, the 'Flying Saint' of whom Norman Douglas makes fun in "Old Calabria". In his ecstasies Fra Giuseppe flew into the air, usually up to the chapel ceiling though, if outside, to the treetops; occasionally he took a passenger, such as his confessor whom he held by the hair. More than seventy flights were logged, the most famous being in 1645, in the presence of a Spanish viceroy. As soon as the great man entered the church, the friar shot up to kiss the feet of a statue above the altar, then flew back over the congregation. The viceroy's wife fainted. He repeated the performance for Pope Urban VIII, flying on the day before his death in 1663.

The ancient castle of Copertino is the largest inland fortress in the Salento other than Lecce. Given to the family of the Albanian hero Skanderbeg, in 1540 they employed a local architect, Evangelista Menga, to add diamond-shaped bastions, sumptuous apartments, gardens on the ramparts and a slanted terrace to channel rainwater into the only bathroom. When Pacichelli visited Copertino during the 1670s, it had passed to the Genoese Pinelli, Dukes of Acerenza, who were clearly excellent hosts, the *Abate* remarking on "very comfortable and well arranged accommodation."

There is some dramatic Apulian Baroque at Ruffano, a city unvisited by any early traveller, on an unexpected hill rising sharply out of the Salentine plain. The hill is crowned by two palaces and a church. Built in 1626 by Prince Rinaldo Brancaccio, according to an inscription in the courtyard, Palazzo Brancaccio is linked by a great bridge to Palazzo Licci, smaller and of about the same date. The early eighteenth century *chiesa madre* in the tiny city's main square is another typical piece of Leccese Baroque with an exuberant high altar. A first glimpse of Ruffano is unforgettable.

Most of the Salento's Baroque churches were inspired by Lecce; a good example is that at Galàtone, near Nardò, where the Sanctuary of the Crocefisso della Pietà has a façade of 1710. Several towns here are a mixture of Romanesque and Baroque, but Galatina is Gothic as well. During the 1390s its Italian-speaking citizens collected 12,000 ducats to ransom their lord, Raimondello del Balzo Orsini, who had been captured by the Turks. In gratitude he built a Latin rite church for them since the *chiesa madre*, San Pietro, used only the Greek rite. This new church, Santa Caterina, has fine frescoes that were painted during the 1430s. They seem Western enough, with their kings and knights, until you realise that most of the subjects and nearly all of the saints are those venerated by Eastern Christians, such as the

Virgin's Dormition or the Emperor Theodosius. Even Raimondello's patron saint turns out to be that Byzantine favourite, Antonio Abate.

Janet Ross was so overwhelmed by the frescoes, "a perfect glory of colour", that a local antiquarian had dark suspicions about her motives for visiting the church. He "dropped behind my artist friend and inquired whether I was a spy of the English government; such things had been heard of, and England was so rich that she could afford to buy the whole church of Santa Caterina and carry it bodily away. It certainly was a curious thing to see a woman travelling about and reading inscriptions on old tombs; he thought it praiseworthy, but very odd."

She was intrigued by much else about the city, including the fast disappearing local language, Greek with many Italian words. "Galatina so enchanted us that when we went to lunch at the small inn we asked whether we could sleep there for the night", she recalls, "It was with difficulty that we could make the people understand but at last they showed us a long room with five beds in it close together. Two were already engaged, and they offered us the other three. So reluctantly we had to go back to Lecce late in the evening."

During the early seventeenth century, egged on by Jesuits the bishops of Apulia banned Mass in the Greek rite. To suppress it at Galatina, the former parish church of the Greeks, SS Pietro e Paolo, was rebuilt between 1633 and 1663 in the style of Zimbalo. A vigorous example of Counter Reformation triumphalism, its façade is one of the best pieces of Baroque in Apulia.

46

A Band of Brigands – the Vardarelli

*Well armed and accoutred, and excellently mounted, their troop was
also trained to the most rigid discipline; and Don Gaetano, the elder of
the brothers Vardarelli, as well as commander of the band, displayed an
activity and skill worthy of a nobler profession.*

Keppel Craven, "A Tour through the Southern Provinces of Italy"

ANOTHER OF GENERAL CHURCH'S problems was Gaetano
Vardarelli. He had deserted from the Borbone army in 1815,
reassembling a *comitiva* of fifty, and within a year, says Macfarlane,
the Vardarelli were "in high feather". They lived off the country, plundering *masserie*, extorting money and the grain that was so valuable
because of the famine. A raid on Alberobello was beaten off, largely
by a farmer's wife, ironically known as 'La Brigantessa' on account
of her skill with a musket. Although they seldom murdered travellers, they often kidnapped them or made them change horses with
their own tired mounts. The Vardarelli's sister rode with the band,
dressed as a man, but she was so badly wounded during a skirmish
with troops that Don Gaetano killed the girl to save her from falling
into the hands of the soldiers.

A peasant himself, during the famine he tried to help the starving
country people. He wrote to the mayor of Foggia, demanding that
massari leave nearly harvested fields to be gleaned as formerly, instead
of grazing animals on them. Otherwise, he threatened he would burn
everything that belonged to the landowners.

Throughout the French occupation, brigands had regularly lain in
ambush in the vital Bovino pass, eluding all attempts to hunt them

down. When they had not been heard of for months, they would suddenly strike, attacking the royal mail coach especially when it had bullion on board, or holding travellers to ransom. The Vardarelli appear to have joined the bands which preyed on the pass.

"I passed by the Ponte di Bovino early in the year 1816, when the mere mention of its name caused fear and trembling", recalled Macfarlane:

> The pass is in general steep, and in some points very narrow; a deep ravine, through which froths and roars a mountain stream in the winter season, is on one side of the road – hills covered with trees or underwood lie on the other. In its whole length, which may be about fifteen miles, there are no habitations, save some curious caves cut in the face of the rock, a post-house, and a most villainous-looking taverna ... And then, as regards security, who would follow the experienced robber through the mountain-wood, or down the ravine, or be able to trace him to the hiding-places in the rocks that abound there? Across the mountains he has a wide range of savage country, without roads – without a path; on the other side of the chasm the localities are equally favourable; here he can, if hard pressed ... throw himself into the impenetrable forests of Mount Garganus, or into the not less remote and safe recesses of Monte Vulture.

Macfarlane tells us that a journey by coach from Apulia to Naples, the capital, was "to the peaceful inhabitants (always, be it said, rather timid travellers) an undertaking of solemn importance and peril; before embarking on which, not only were tapers burning under every saint of the calendar, and every Madonna that could show a portrait, but wills were made, and such tearful adieus, that one might have thought the Val de Bovino the real valley of death".

As for escorts, "four miserable-looking gendarmes *á pied,* with their carbines slung over their shoulders, got up in front of our still more miserable-looking vettura for our protection", Macfarlane recalled. Travellers who were ambushed were forced to lie on the ground to shouts of *Faccia in terra* (Face to the ground), brigands holding guns to their heads while others rifled their pockets. "Of one thing I was quite sure – that the soldiers, in case the robbers conde-scended to assault us, would be the first to run away, or perform the *Faccia in terra* movement."

General Church met Gaetano as soon as he arrived in Apulia. Spending the night in a *masseria* just outside Cerignola, with only his ADC and his batman and, learning that the Vardarelli *comitiva* – by now over a hundred strong – was nearby, he boldly sent an order for them to present themselves:

"Am I not King of Apulia?", boasted Don Gaetano, when he came. "Have I not beaten three of your sovereign's generals? The troops in Apulia are on my side, the civil inhabitants do what I tell them. I can take as many travellers' purses as I please. All the aristocracy, the entire middle classes, fear me. You know very well, Your Excellency, that (King) Ferdinand can do nothing against me".

Church rather liked the brigand chief and his band, recalling years later, "They harassed the provinces, fought the troops, robbed right and left, but seldom if ever committed murder in cold blood."

A treaty signed by King Ferdinand in July 1817 enrolled the Vardarelli *comitiva* as highly paid auxiliary troops in the royal army, with the job of clearing the brigands out of the Bovino valley. Don Gaetano performed his new duties admirably, but he had made too many enemies. In September 1817 he was ordered to leave the Capitanata for the Molise. He obeyed very reluctantly, only leaving in February the following year. At Ururi, just inside the Molise, during a morning inspection of his men, he and his brothers were shot from the balcony of a nearby *palazzo*. Their killer was Don Nicola Grimani, a landowner whose sister Gaetano had raped – he bathed his face and hands in Vardarelli blood, shouting "I am avenged."

About forty of the *comitiva* escaped. In April 1818 they rode into Foggia, reporting to the district commander, General Amato, who ordered them to go to Lucera. They objected so strongly that, after a long argument, shots were exchanged and one of the band fell dead. Some galloped off, firing as they went, while the remainder barricaded themselves in a cellar. Four who surrendered were sent in to tell them they would be smoked out, and were promptly murdered. Sporadic shooting came from the cellar, killing a soldier. Bales of straw were lit and pushed through its entrance, which was then blocked by huge stones. After two hours soldiers went in, to find seventeen men dead or dying; several had stabbed each other. Once the citizens realised the danger was over, the dead brigands became objects of pity, the general being blamed for the tragedy.

Keppel Craven had arrived in Foggia at the moment when the firing started. He was taken into the ground floor of his inn, with his guide, servants and horses, and not allowed to emerge for several hours. That evening, he was shown the corpses at the prison:

> They had been stript of every article save the reliquaries or consecrated images, which the lower classes in Italy invariably wear around their neck, and which now rested on the ghastly wounds that disfigured their bodies, some of which were also blackened by smoke.

There were other Apulian *comitive* besides those of Gaetano Vardarelli. When Craven went on to Cerignola he was informed that a band had kidnapped the *sindaco*. (As ransom, its members were demanding 1,200 ducats, 100 yards of pantaloon velveteen and silver buckles.) A raid described to Janet Ross seventy years later by the old inn-keeper at Manfredonia, Don Michele Rosari di Tosquez, a 'baron' from Troia who had lost everything at the hands of brigands, may have been by a Bovino *comitiva*. "'My ancestors were Spaniards and I was born at Troia; but when I was a small child the brigands came, burnt the *masseria,* hung my father from the pigeon tower, and killed my two elder brothers. My mother died of fright. Curse them,' he exclaimed, bringing his fist heavily down on the table, 'that ruined us.'"

While General Church was able to put down brigandage and secret societies in the Terra d'Òtranto, he failed to crush the *Carbonari* revolutionaries, who were demanding a constitution. In 1820 they marched on Naples. General Nugent fled and King Ferdinand reluctantly granted a constitution. Church was briefly imprisoned in the Castel del' Ovo and, on being released, continued to serve the king until 1825. Two years later he was persuaded by Theodore Colocotrones, a former bandit and member of the Duke of York's Greek Light Infantry, to fight in the Greek War of Independence. Sadly his career in Greece was undistinguished – at Pireus and the Siege of the Acropolis he never left the safety of his yacht.

In 1824, when staying with the Prince of Ischitella at Peschici in the Gargano, Macfarlane met a survivor from the Vardarelli *comitiva* called 'Passo di Lupo', who described the reality of brigand life.

Most of the loot was taken by the *guappi* (bullies) while Passo di Lupo could not go into a town to spend his small share; often he could not even buy pasta or wine. Stolen sheep were roasted whole in their wool, sometimes eaten raw. Since they were without doctors or medical supplies, wounds were left to fester, so that many of them were covered in sores. For years after ceasing to be a brigand, Passo di Lupo "could never enjoy a sound sleep in his bed, but ... was constantly starting up convulsively, and shrieking out his former companion's names."

When Macfarlane last visited the bridge at Ponte di Bovino in 1824, "General del Caretto has decorated it with the heads and mangled quarters of some half dozen of more modern, but less conspicuous brigands." He adds that even when there were not organised *comitive*, the locals lay in wait in the pass: "In some places the hill and the wood, or concealing thicket, is so close to the road on the one hand, and the ravine on the other, that it is really enticing. A shot from the one, and the man's business is done – and there yawns a dark capacious grave, to receive his body when deprived of what it is worth."

Ramage came across brigands four years later, but he was unmolested since they were only interested in rich landowners who could pay a big ransom. Nevertheless, when in 1836 Saverio Mercadante from Altamura wrote the opera "I Briganti", its theme still remained unpleasantly familiar to Apulians.

47

Tarantismo

St Vitus's dance and that other one which cured,
they say, the bite of the Tarentine spider.
Norman Douglas, "Old Calabria"

DESPITE TELEVISION and consumer society, a very old Apulia
lingers on secretly, with amazing tenacity. *Tarantismo* is a dramatic example of pagan survival in this ultra-conservative land. An
ancient form of therapeutic magic, no doubt familiar to the shamans
during the Stone Age, it is popularly supposed to be a cure for the
bite of the venomous tarantula. In reality, tarantism is a form of exorcism, a means of healing mental disturbance.

Because one of its churches is dedicated to St Paul, Galatina is
said to be free from snakes and poisonous spiders, although surrounded by mile upon mile of vineyards. Throughout Southern Italy
the Apostle Paul is invoked against venomous creatures, since he was
unharmed by the viper that bit his hand when he was washed ashore
at Malta. This is why the church of S.Paolo at Galatina is a place of
thanksgiving for those cured by tarantism.

Some writers believe *tarantismo* is a relic of the Bacchic rites but
most think it is caused by a bite from a tarantula. In the early eighteenth century Maximilien Misson was fascinated by the affliction:

> The true tarantula resembles a spider and lives in the fields. There
> are many, it is said, in the Abruzzi and in Calabria, and they
> are also found in some parts of Tuscany. When bitten by this
> accursed insect one takes a hundred postures at once – dancing,

St Paul expelling snakes
from the Salento

vomiting, trembling, laughing, turning pale, swooning – and
one suffers very greatly. Finally, without help, death follows in
a few days. Sweatings and antidotes relieve the sufferer, but the
best and only remedy is music.

Bishop Berkeley records:

The P. Vicario [Superior of the Theatines at Barletta] tells us of
the tarantula, he cured several with the tongue of the serpente
impetrito, found in Malta, and steeped in wine and drunk
after the ninth or last dance, there being 3 dances a day for
three days; on the death of the tarantula the malady ceases; it is
communicated by eating fruit bit by a tarantula. He thinks it is
not a fiction, having cured among others a Capuchin, whom he
could not think would feign for the sake of dancing.

There was some confusion about the precise definition of a tarantula. Sandys, in his "Relation of a Iourney begun in An. Dom, 1610",
says it is:

a serpent peculiar to this country; and taking that name from the city of Tarentum. Some hold them to be of the kind of spiders, others of effts; but they are greater than the one, and lesse than the other, and (if it were a Tarantula which I have seen) not greatly resembling either. For the head of this was small, the legs slender and knottie, and the body light, the taile spiny, and the colour dun, intermixed with spots of sullied white. They lurke in sinks and privies, and abroad in the slimy filth betweene furrows; for which cause the country people do reap in bootes.

Sandys appears to have seen a scorpion.

Misson (who did not visit Apulia) wrote in 1722 to a certain Domenico Sangenito of Lucera, asking for information. He was told: "They vary in colour and I have seen ashy ones and those of a dark tawny hue, like a flea, and with markings which look like little stars. We have them in the mountains as well as in furthest Apulia, but however their bite does no harm." Sangenito was apparently referring to a spider. Yet it is likely that the spider exists only in the sufferer's imagination and is an illusion caused by hysteria.

"In the seventeenth century the belief in the tarantula bites began to subside, and nothing now remains of *tarantismo*", Hare declared in 1882. But two reliable witnesses told us that during the 1980s they had been to Galatina and seen women, and on one occasion a man, dancing to relieve the malady. The *tarantolata,* or supposed sufferer from the bite, believes the cure can only work if she is surrounded by the right colours and the right tune is played. Red, green, yellow or black are most likely to suit a spider and the music must match its mood, happy or sad. The musicians, who play the violin or guitar *battente* accompanied by cymbals and an accordian, need a large repertoire to find the right tune, as well as the stamina to go on playing for hours on end. The dancing generally takes place in a room, occasionally in the street. A sheet with a portrait of St Paul is spread on the floor and the *tarantolata* starts to move in imitation of a spider, while the musicians try various tunes for her. When they find the right one she begins to dance, not alone, but with anyone among her friends who is wearing the spider's colour. She dances for a few minutes, then takes another partner. At first she dances lethargically, but after a few hours becomes increasingly elated, ending in a state of ecstasy.

Perhaps half a dozen *tarantolate* go secretly each year to the church of S.Paolo, to imitate a spider, crawling and running, flinging themselves on the altar. Their torn stockings are left hanging up as votive offerings. The decline in *tarantismo* seems to be due to fewer people working in the fields, rather than disbelief in the spider's bite. (One should not confuse the colourful dancing displays for tourists with the real thing.)

No one has ever been able to give a really convincing explanation. The travellers disagree on the details, if not on the importance of colour and music. Some describe the woman as dancing in front of mirrors, others with a drawn sword in her hand. Keppel Craven says she dresses in white and is decked in "ribands, vine leaves and trinkets of all kinds." He considers the whole thing an excuse for a party:

> While she rests at times, the guests invited relieve her by dancing by turns after the fashion of the country; and when overcome by restless lassitude and faintness she determines to give over for the day, she takes a pail or jar of water, and pours its contents entirely over her person, from the head downwards. This is a signal for her friends to undress and convey her to bed; after which the rest of the company endeavour to further her recovery by devouring a substantial repast which is always prepared on the occasion.

Janet Ross heard a story which should be a warning for anyone inclined to be sceptical. There was a master mason living near Taranto, who:

> got new-fangled ideas into his head and mocked at the idea of a spider's bite being venomous, threatening to beat any of his female belongings who dared to try the dancing cure in case they were bitten by a "Tarantola". As ill-luck or San Cataldo would have it, he was himself bitten, and after suffering great pain and being in a high fever for several days, at last sent for the musicians, after carefully locking the door and closing the windows of his house. But the frenzy was too strong, and to the malicious delight of all who believed in "Tarantismo", he tore open the door and was soon seen jumping about in the middle of the street, shrieking, "*Hanno ragion' le femine! Hanno ragion' le femine!*" (The women are right! The women are right!)

Part XI

Greek Apulia

48

The Byzantine Terra d'Òtranto

...that abode of Greeks, that unreassuring land.
Virgil, "Aeneid"

THE TERRA D'ÒTRANTO was the last part of Apulia to be conquered by the Normans and still has something unmistakably
Greek about it. After losing Ravenna in the eighth century, Byzantine
Italy, re-organised as the Theme of Lombardy, was ruled from here
by a *strategos* (or general) until 975 when the *catapanate* was established at Bari. The strategos worked closely with the archbishop, who
sometimes represented him. In the tenth century Archbishop Vlattus
of Òtranto led an embassy to the Zirid sultan at Mahdia in Tunis to
buy the freedom of Apulian slaves – inspired by his sister being in the
sultan's harem – but when he returned privately to redeem more of
them he was put to death.

The navy of Nicephorus Phocas (963–69) routed the Arabs.
"I alone command the seas", claimed the Emperor, who began the
Greek colonisation of southern Italy, settlers flooding in under Basil
Boiannes during the next century. Discreet contact with Constantinople lingered on until the Turkish conquest of Greece, while Mass
was said in the Greek rite up to the Counter Reformation. Even
today, although the language has almost ceased to be spoken, certain
Greek customs survive south of a line from Ostuni to Tàranto . The
most obvious example is harvesting olives in the Greek way. The trees
are barely pruned so they grow very high and the ripe fruit is left to
drop into nets spread on the ground below instead of being picked
by hand as in the Terra di Bari.

The underground churches contain some of the Byzantine frescoes that are among Apulia's greatest treasures. During the eighth century Byzantium forbade celibacy and the veneration of icons. When monks were ordered to marry or lose their eyes, 30,000 fled to Italy, founding small monasteries in caves, especially in Calabria and the Terra d'Òtranto. Sicilian monks, refugees from Islam, joined them in the ninth century. They decorated the churches they carved into the rock with frescoes of Christ, the Virgin and the Saints. The tradition continued for centuries.

The grotto church of San Biagio near San Vito dei Normanni owes its preservation to an enlightened landowner putting a door over the entrance. This was the church of a group of hermits and, judging from its size – over forty feet long – served a large community. Signed by the artist Daniel with the date 1197, the frescoes are unmistakably Byzantine, and Charles Diehl thought that, together with the magnificent Archangel Michael at San Giovanni nearby, they were the most important in the Terra d'Òtranto. He blamed the destruction of many other frescoes on the navvies who built the railways. Using the cave churches as shelters where they could light fires, they seem to have taken a fiendish enjoyment in disembowelling the painted saints or gouging their eyes out. San Biagio had a lucky escape.

Converted to the Latin rite during the seventeenth century, few surface (as opposed to underground) churches in Apulia retain any traces of their Byzantine past. The exquisite little church of San Pietro at Òtranto is an exception, with drums and cupolas, and some of the Greek cycle of frescoes – the Last Supper and the Harrowing of Hell. The fifth century church at Casarano has been enlarged and its walls redecorated with Western frescoes, but the brilliantly coloured Byzantine mosaics are still in the dome and chancel, the dome dotted with stars. There is also the Romanesque abbey of Santa Maria di Cerrate, south of Brìndisi, which although built by Normans belonged to the Eastern rite, as you can see from its frescoes and from an altar inscribed in Greek.

On the other hand, there are Greek grotto churches throughout the stony hinterland of the Salentine peninsula, secret, haunted places that are often very hard to find, sometimes underground, sometimes dug into a bank or the side of a cliff. They stretch in a diagonal band twenty-five miles wide from Roca Vecchia in the north to Poggiardo and Ugento in the south. Some are locked, the key kept by a seemingly mythical custodian, while others have frescoes that are visible

The Byzantine church of San Pietro at Otranto

only by the light of a powerful torch. Often it is difficult to recognise them as churches or chapels, especially when they are used as cattle-byres or tool-sheds. Among the most important are those at Vaste, Giurdignano and Supersano. The earliest frescoes, from the tenth century, are in the church of Sante Marina e Cristina at Carpignano Salento, while the most beautiful are in a small museum in the public gardens at Poggiardo – having been taken from the nearby grotto chapel of Santa Maria under the town centre, discovered when a lorry fell into it in 1929.

You can best see the slow transition from Byzantine to Western above ground, however, at Soleto, near Galatina, where the tiny chapel of Santo Stefano is filled with frescoes, mostly from the mid-fourteenth century. The Last Judgement was obviously done by a Greek, but others could have been painted by some obscure follower of Giotto. The Byzantine saints are westernised – St Nicholas, St George, and St Onophrius with his loin-cloth and long white beard.

In contrast, the *campanile* of the *chiesa madre* at Soleto, built in about 1400 for Raimondello del Balzo Orsini, is totally Latin. Although Raimondello had been all-powerful here, Janet Ross was told that his *campanile* was the tomb of "some great king, whose name is not known, he died so long ago." She thought Soleto "so eastern-looking with its one-storied, flat-roofed, white houses, that I expected the people to speak Arabic."

Early Greek settlers from Tàranto called Gallipoli on the Ionian coast the 'beautiful city' and it still has enormous charm. It fell to the Normans in 1071 but was not totally subjugated for another sixty years, the Greek rite being used in its churches until the sixteenth century. It rose against Charles of Anjou in 1268, 34 rebellious barons being besieged in its castle for six months and hanged as soon as they surrendered. It beat off the Turks in 1481 but was occupied by the Venetians four years later, although briefly. The Spaniards gave the castle four great round bastions; mounting heavy cannon, these guarded the harbour and the landward side of the island on which the city is built. The last siege was in 1809, when the castle stood up to a bombardment by the British Navy.

"Here are fish and exquisite meat of every sort," we are told by Abate Pacichelli, who says that English and Dutch ships put in to Gallipoli every day to buy olive oil. According to de Salis, in the eighteenth century the streets were narrow and dirty, and harbour facilities virtually non-existent, although the port was a centre for exporting oil from all over Apulia, stored in rock cisterns. Keppel Craven thought it "the most opulent and gayest town upon the coast. The inhabitants do not succeed six thousand in number; but they are easy in their circumstances, lively and merry, and in general well informed." However, "Consumptions and spitting of blood are rather frequent here, occasioned by the great subtlety of the air, which is ventilated from every quarter." He liked the pleasant suburbs on the mainland, now under ugly modern buildings, their gardens reminding him of "those so often seen round English ornamented cottages", with "plants that will scarcely live out of a hothouse in our climate."

Craven also noticed good paintings in Gallipoli's churches. The cathedral still has a fine collection of pictures by a local artist, Giovanni Andrea Coppola (1597–1659), whose work was admired by Riedesel. Coppola's house can be seen in Via Nicetti, a yellow corner building with an ornate doorway, which Riedesel visited to see more of his paintings.

Gallipoli is joined to the mainland by a bridge built in 1603, fifty years after cutting the isthmus to make the city impregnable. It is possible to drive round the old walls, but better to walk since it is no more than a mile and the view marvellous. You can see the island of Sant' Andrea and, on a clear day, the Calabrian mountains across the Gulf of Tàranto.

In the triangle formed by Gallipoli, Òtranto and Lecce, *Griko* is spoken at a few places. Greek visitors have difficulty in understanding this Italiot Greek, which is really a separate language of its own, with many Italian words. It has no literature although poems and songs are sometimes published, printed in the Latin alphabet. As late as the 1970s, 20,000 people spoke it at Calimera and the surrounding villages. It is odd to hear young women talking Griko in the early twenty-first century.

In addition to the descendants of the Greek colonists of the tenth and eleventh centuries and of the refugees from northern Apulia in Norman times, Greek speaking Albanians settled on the vast estates in the south granted by King Ferrante in 1460 to their leader, George Castriota Skanderbeg. A street in Gallipoli is still named after his soldiers, Via Stradiotti – the famous 'stradiots' or Albanian light cavalry.

49

The Castle of Otranto

...send for the chaplain, and have the chapel exorcised,
for, for certain, it is enchanted.
Horace Walpole, "The Castle of Otranto"

ONE REASON WHY early travellers came to the Salentine peninsula was to see Òtranto, because they had read Horace Walpole's "Castle of Otranto". Published in 1764, the first "Gothick" novel,
full of ghosts and horror, for many years it was enormously popular,
translated into fourteen languages. But its author had never been to
Apulia, let alone to Òtranto.

In his preface, Walpole says, "The following work was found in
the library of an ancient Catholic family in the north of England. It
was printed at Naples, in the black letter, in the year 1529." The title
page claims it is "A story translated by William Marshall, Gent. From
the Original Italian of Onuphrio Muralto, Canon of the Church of
St Nicholas at Otranto." Yet while there was a church of St Nicholas
here, it was staffed by monks, not by canons, and Onofrio Muralto
never existed. Finding the name "Otranto" in an atlas in his library,
Walpole decided that if the second syllable were stressed, wrongly, it
would sound nice as a title. His "castle" was modelled on Strawberry
Hill, his house at Twickenham.

"The Castle of Otranto, a name calculated to awaken feelings of
pleasing recollections in an English mind, is far from realising the
expectations created," grumbled Keppel Craven. Even so, the castle's
real history was hair-raising enough on more than one occasion.

The Normans occupied Òtranto in 1071, Isaac Contostephanos,

Grand Duke of the Fleet, unsuccessfully trying to retake it for Byzantium a few years later. It was an important port throughout the Crusades for all those preferring to stay on land as much as possible when they travelled to Palestine. The Byzantine citadel was replaced with a castle by Frederick II, who waited there with Queen Yolande while his fleet was at Brìndisi during the abortive Crusade of 1227. King Ferrante rebuilt the castle, much as it looks today, after his son had recovered it from the Turks. A dry moat filled with wild chrysanthemums lies behind the massive walls.

Consecrated in 1188, the cathedral has a splendid Norman crypt with forty-two columns, each with a different capital; Classical, Byzantine, Egyptian and even Persian. A capital with four birds that Riedesel thought were harpies probably symbolised Mahomet's ascent into heaven.

The cathedral's Norman floor is the most important mosaic in Apulia, its theme the struggle between good and evil. A Tree of Life starts at the door, filling the whole nave. In its branches are animals representing virtues and vices, with figures from the Old Testament. King Arthur is here too, clean-shaven like a Norman and riding on a goat, the earliest pictures of him since the floor dates from 1163–66. So is Alexander the Great, in a chariot drawn by two griffins. The middle part of the floor has the signs of the Zodiac with each month's activities. The farmers of Òtranto kept sheep, goats and pigs, worked in vineyards and cornfields, ploughed with oxen – and apparently spent March picking their feet with an iron scraper normally used for cleaning hoes.

The ruins of the church of San Nicola de Càsole are on a hill south of the city. Bohemond, Prince of Tàranto and Lord of the coast between Bari and Òtranto, rebuilt the monastery here, destroyed in 1032 by Saracens. Its monks followed the rule of St Basil, growing corn and vegetables, fishing in the bay below, or working in the famous library. Scholars came from all over Italy to study Greek. Although their rule and their liturgy were Byzantine, they accepted the Pope's authority, which gave them unusual influence after the schism between East and West. When Pope Gregory IX contemplated compulsory rebaptism of those baptised in the Greek rite, Abbot Nettorio dissuaded a tribunal of cardinals, while a later abbot went to the Council of Florence, trying to reconcile Catholics and Orthodox. However, the community was wiped out in 1480.

In July that year the Turkish Grand Vizier arrived before Òtranto with a hundred ships. Both castle and city fell after a fortnight, 12,000 out of a population of 22,000 perishing during the sack. Among them were 800 men and women who refused to renounce Christianity, so impressing their executioner that he was converted and died with them. But Sultan Mehmet II died before he could invade Italy, and at the news of his death the Turkish garrison surrendered. They had converted the cathedral into a mosque, white-washing the walls and using the *campanile* as a minaret. When it was reconsecrated the martyrs' bones were enshrined in a chapel. Hundreds remain in cupboards behind the altar, one near the entrance holding mummified feet and hands, shrivelled intestines, and skulls with eyelashes and scraps of hair.

The martyrs had died on the Hill of Minerva, once dedicated to Apulia's favourite goddess, their corpses rotting next to a pyramid of their skulls for a year until King Ferrante ordered their burial. A church on the summit has a tablet inscribed with their names and the name of the converted executioner, Berlabey. Every 14 August Òtranto commemorates their death.

The stone cannon-balls lining the city streets are reminders of the Turkish occupation. Janet Ross heard from the station master how memories of the massacre lingered, mothers warning disobedient children that the Turks would come back and "get them". The city never recovered; by 1600 its population had dropped to 3,000 and by 1818 to 1,600. Every watch-tower along the coast had once had its own small settlement, but all were abandoned. The reason, however, was not so much "fear of the Turk" as malaria.

On a clear day, you can see Albania's snowy mountains from the Hill of Minerva. Eighteenth century travellers say that snow was brought to Òtranto by Albanians and landed on the beach. Plague and cholera being common in the Balkans, payment was left on the sand to avoid physical contact. The snow was stored in cisterns in the tufa and used to cool medicines.

Visitors admired the country around the city for its gardens and citrus groves, but they have gone beneath modern housing or have been replaced by rough grazing for sheep and goats. Inland, there are forests of unusually tall olive trees, vineyards and plots of corn or tobacco. Many olive trees are so gnarled that it is easy to suspect they were alive in the days of the Caesars – undoubtedly some of them witnessed the sack of Òtranto.

South of Òtranto, towards the Capo di Leuca or Finibus Terrae, the land is fertile and hilly. It has always been thickly populated despite the destruction of whole villages by Saracens and Turks, putting de Salis in mind of a garden, instead of the bare rock he had expected to find at the "End of the Earth." The tip of the Salentine peninsula, a dazzling white finger of low cliff, is topped by a church built over a temple to Minerva. The Sanctuary of Santa Maria di Leuca houses a Byzantine icon of the Virgin; a pilgrimage here has been considered a passport to Heaven since pagan times – those who do not come in their lifetime must do so after death. Capo di Leuca was thought by Ramage and Hare to be the harbour described by Virgil in the "Aeneid" when the Trojans sailed past the Terra d'Òtranto on their way to found Rome. They did not land because it was "an abode of Greeks."

50

Manduria

Manduria is a nice, clean town, very oriental looking with its flat-roofed
houses, and the inhabitants seem well-to-do, old-fashioned people.

Janet Ross, "The Land of Manfred"

BETWEEN TÀRANTO AND GALLIPOLI, Manduria is one of the
Terra d'Òtranto's most interesting cities. In its great days, in
Classical times, the inhabitants were not Greeks but Messapians,
who have left impressive remains. After being sacked by the Saracens,
the city lay deserted for centuries until re-founded in the thirteenth
century as "Casalnuova", only reverting to its ancient name in 1799.

Whether Manduria or Casalnuova, it was on every educated traveller's itinerary, as the site of Pliny's uncanny well. "In the Salentine,
near the city of Manduria, there is a well full to the brim, whose water
is never reduced by any quantity withdrawn nor ever increased by
any added," says Pliny. Still in existence, this never runs dry, not even
during the most blistering Apulian summer. Inside a grotto within
the walls of the ancient Messapian city, the well seems to be just as it
was when Bishop Berkeley, Swinburne, Keppel Craven, Ramage and
Janet Ross saw it.

Swinburne was amused by the citizens' reputation as dog-eaters:

> Casalnuova contains about four thousand inhabitants, noted
> for nothing but their taste for dog's flesh, in which they have no
> competitors that I know of, except their neighbours at Lecce
> and the newly discovered voluptuaries of Otaheite (Tahiti). We
> did not see one animal of the canine species in the streets; and

woe be to the poor cur that follows its master into this cannibal
settlement. I could not prevail upon my conductor to own
whether they had any flocks of puppies, as of sheep; or took any
pains, by castration or particular food, to fatten or sweeten the
dainty, before they brought it to the shambles.

He adds that dogs were kidnapped by tanners, their skins making
fine "false Morocco" leather, their meat food for under-nourished
workmen.

The massive remnants of the Messapians' double walls, five miles
in circumference, are often over fifteen feet thick and sometimes
nearly twenty high. They were built during the fifth century BC as a
defence against the Tarantines. Almost as striking are the dozens of
rectangular graves carved out of the rock, and the elaborate chamber
tombs that contain frescoes and have rafters painted on their ceilings.
A couplet in the Aeneid (Book VI) gives us some idea of the after-life
that they hoped to live in such tombs:

They lie below, on golden beds displayed;
And genial feasts with regal pomp are made ...

The Messapians spoke an extinct Indo-European tongue, probably akin to modern Albanian, which was written in a script derived
from Greek. The language ceased to be spoken shortly after the birth
of Christ, but its intonation lingers in the stressed first syllable of
place-names such as Tàranto, Òtranto and Brìndisi.

"There is a fine *palazzo,* which belonged to the Princes of Francavilla", Mrs. Ross noted, when she could spare the time from inspecting
the Messapian remains. Begun in 1719 by Prince Michele II, with its
long balcony of iron scroll-work and its row of tall windows, this has
a distinctly Spanish appearance. It was still unfinished when Swinburne visited "Caselnuovo" nearly sixty years later. He commented,

The suite of apartments is grand, but the situation
uncomfortable without garden or prospect. Nearby lie the
remnants of a ghetto from which the Jews were expelled at the
end of the seventeenth century; some of the houses, one dated
1602, have curious windows whose heavy tracery is designed to
conceal the occupants from being seen by passers-by in the street
below.

Janet Ross visited Manduria while staying at Leucaspide near Tàranto as the guest of her friend Sir James Lacaita. A notary born in Manduria, he had become legal adviser to the British legation at Naples. After giving information about political prisoners to Mr Gladstone, who then described the Borbone regime as "the negation of God," Lacaita fled to England. Here he failed to become Librarian of the London Library, but was employed as secretary by Lord Lansdowne, acquiring many influential friends, including the Prime Minister, Lord John Russell; he was knighted in 1858 for organising Gladstone's mission to the Ionian Islands. In 1860, in desperation, the Neapolitan government asked him to become its ambassador in London and persuade the British to stop Garibaldi invading the mainland from Sicily. As he afterwards admitted, it took him three days to decide, but he refused, helping to destroy the old *Regno*.

No Apulian profited more from the *Risorgimento*. A director of Italian Lands Ltd., a London based firm formed in 1864 to handle the sale of all Neapolitan crown and church lands for the new regime, he quickly amassed a large fortune, and in 1868 bought Leucaspide with other former monastic property. Certainly the best known Pugliese in Victorian England (not excepting the Duke of Castromediano), he entertained English visitors lavishly. A small man with simian features, lowering eyebrows and bushy side-whiskers, despite his charm and scholarship, he had a slightly unsavoury air, even if it was not apparent to Mrs. Ross.

She was escorted from Massafra station to Leucaspide by a guard "with a big pistol stuck in his belt and a gun slung over his shoulder." The drive was lined by agaves, tall as small trees. Behind the house her host had planted a ravine with bushes in imitation of an English shrubbery, rosemary and cistus covering its sides. There was a view of olive groves sweeping down to the Gulf of Tàranto with, far off, the rugged Calabrian mountains. "We were never tired of looking down from the *loggia* or arcade, which ran all along the south-west front of the *"impostura"* ("imposter"), as Sir James laughingly called Leucaspide, so imposing in its dazzling whiteness from a little distance, and giving itself the airs of a large *palazzo*", Mrs. Ross recalled. "From the garden below came the scent of lemon and orange trees, laden with fruit."

In 1988, exactly a century after her visit, we went to Leucaspide. Lacaita's son had left it to his agent, a descendant of whom lived in a small house behind the villa, empty for twenty years. A nervous German shepherd dog patrolled its vast, flat roof. Yet white roses

Leucaspide where Janet Ross stayed with Sir James Lacaita

clambered up the *loggia*, which seemed as if sleeping, waiting for the labour gangs to dance for the guests. We might even have fancied that the ghost of Janet Ross was sitting on the terrace in her Turkish trousers, smoking one of her infamous cheroots. But on the far side of the ravine and to the south of the farm buildings, loomed the sprawl of the Italsider steel-works, coming nearer and nearer. We have not been back.

Apulians are a superstitious race, a trait sometimes exploited for political ends. During the revolutionary troubles of 1799, the Mandurian royalists, using a belief that on 2 November the dead come out of their tombs and walk the streets, staged a procession of "ghosts" chanting "Be calm, be faithful to Ferdinand!" Apparently the ruse worked.

Many travellers describe seeing votive offerings at churches, like the round stones hung outside the sanctuary of the Archangel at Monte Sant' Angelo. Some years ago, at the rupestrian chapel of San Pietro Mandurino, we saw the skin of a fox stuck on a tree just outside the door. A Mandurian said it was a thanks-offering to St Peter for saving a hen from the jaws of death. But Janet Ross heard that the skin of an animal always hung on the great walnut tree of Benevento, a meeting place for witches. Inside the church there were intricate circles of pebbles in front of the altar. When we asked a friend in Gioia about what we had seen, he laughed: "I don't take that stuff seriously." But then he changed colour, adding "It's very dangerous, like using cards to get control of someone's soul."

Shortly after, we read in Norman Lewis's "Naples '44" that he had come across fox-magic at Sagranella, up in the hills behind Benevento. "This village seems hardly to have moved out of the Bronze Age," he writes. "I am told it has a fox-cult, and every year a fox is captured and burned to death, and its tail is hung, like a banner, from a pole at the village's entrance." Benevento was neither Greek nor Messapian territory but Samnite. Even so, we feel sure that the Messapians would have had no difficulty in explaining the significance of our Mandurian fox hanging in a tree.

Part XII

Three Little Courts

51

Conversano

Supported by a vast following, that included many kinsmen together with large bands of unruly retainers, magnates like the Count of Conversano ... were able to bloody their hands with crimes against their vassals.

Rosario Villari, "La rivolta antispagnola a Napoli"

FEUDALISM SURVIVED IN APULIA until the French invasion of 1806, even if "vassals" no longer went out to battle. Sometimes the feudal lords were tyrants, oppressing their vassals and levying their dues mercilessly, like the notorious Count Giangirolamo II of Conversano. There is a lurid legend that he claimed the *jus primae noctis* (Law of the First Night) and had every peasant girl from his estates on her wedding night, or else gave her to one of his cronies.

In the midst of cherry orchards, Conversano is up on the Murgia dei Trulli, between Bari and Martina Franca, with beautiful views out to sea. Crouched almost menacingly above what are now the public gardens, despite an elegant Baroque gateway and apartments, the counts' massive castle keeps its Angevin towers and ramparts, a polygonal bastion from Aragonese days bearing the coat of arms of the Acquaviva. The Acquaviva were one of the 'Seven Families of the Kingdom of Naples', the others being Aquino, Ruffo, Sanseverino, Del Balzo, Celano and Piccolomini, to whom the county came through the marriage of Giulio Antonio Acquaviva to Caterina del Balzo Orsini in 1456; its territory then included Bitetto, Gioia del Colle and Noci, with several other towns. Count Giulio Antonio I was killed by the Turks in 1481, during the campaign to retake

Òtranto, his horse galloping back to his tent with his decapitated body. His head had been stuck on a Turkish pike, but eventually the corpse was reassembled and brought home to Conversano. His family were consoled with the right to use the royal arms and name of Aragon.

His son, Count Andrea Matteo Acquaviva d'Aragona, a leader of the pro-French party, advised the French to seize Bari, and in consequence spent two years in a dungeon at Naples after the Spanish victory in 1503. Learned in both letters and the military arts, he installed a printing press at Conversano, and printed a book of Plutarch's "Moralia", which he had himself translated from Greek into Latin. He also completed the nearby church of Madonna dell' Isola, which had been begun by his father, commissioning a monument of painted stone by an Apulian sculptor, Nuzzo Barba of Galatina; beneath it lie the recumbent effigies of Giulio Antonio I and his countess, their son kneeling next to them in full armour.

By the seventeenth century, like all great noblemen in Apulia, the Counts of Conversano were facing ruin, they were victims of an unending recession, owing vast sums to money-lenders at Naples. The ruthless exploitation of feudal dues meant the difference between survival and bankruptcy.

Because of a cast in one eye, 'a singular mark of the Fiend', Count Giangirolamo II was nicknamed '*Il Guercio di Puglia*' ('the Apulian Squinter'). Born in 1600, at seventeen he led 300 horsemen from Conversano to help repel a Turkish attack on Andria. As soon as he became Count in 1626, hiring an army of brigands he extorted his dues mercilessly – tolls, levies on grain, oil and wine, compulsory use of his mills and ovens, of his wine and olive presses. Every non-noble landowner in the county of Conversano and the duchy of Nardò (inherited from his mother) suffered, whether peasants or *borghesi*. The mayor of Nardò tried to stop him, so in 1639 he arranged for the mayor to be strangled, and then, to conceal his involvement, had the murderer throttled in the church where the murder took place. Later, he was accused of twenty other murders. He was greatly respected by fellow magnates.

In 1640, encouraged by a heavily indebted Viceroy, the richest banker in Naples, Bartolomeo d'Aquino, who was "of a dirty and mean appearance in keeping with his birth", tried to marry Il Guercio's sister, Anna, offering to pay 40,000 ducats. Having just been accused of the mayor's murder and in sanctuary in the friary of San

Lorenzo at Naples, Giangirolamo could not intervene. But he summoned his friends, who rode to the palace where the girl was staying, beat off the Viceroy's guard, and escorted her at sword-point to a convent in Benevento outside the Viceroy's reach. He then gave his sister a more acceptable husband and a dowry of 9,000 ducats.

Although he escaped prosecution over the mayor, he was arrested in 1643 for involvement in a pro-French plot and sent to Madrid. When the news reached Nardò, its delighted citizens wanted a *Te Deum* sung, but a priest, Don Ottavio Sambiase, told them an exorcism was more fitting, making everyone repeat, "O Lord, may you hurl the Count of Conversano down to Hell!". However, at Madrid both Philip IV and Il Guercio were charmed by each other, the king sending Giangirolamo home in 1645 as Captain-General of Nardò with even stronger powers over his vassals.

He was zealous in crushing the 1647 rebellion, which was as much against feudal magnates as against Spain, his equally ferocious wife, Isabella Filomarino, selling her jewels to pay for troops. Raising eighty cavalry and 300 foot-soldiers, within a few months he had pacified Apulia, where every town except Manfredonia and Lucera had joined the rebellion. There had been peasant revolts everywhere; as Rosario Villari writes in "La rivolta antispagnola a Napoli", it was "basically a peasant war, the biggest and most dramatic in Western Europe during the seventeenth century." Giangirolamo commanded only a few troops and a handful of nobles with their retainers, but fought a very effective campaign, even if his son Don Giulio was shot dead at his side. In 1648 he won a decisive victory at Foggia, whose citizens opened their gates in abject surrender, and another at Lecce. Generally he pardoned the townsmen, merely fining them.

During the previous summer Giangirolamo's city of Nardò had declared that it no longer owed allegiance to him as feudal lord, only to the King of Spain. But there was no resistance when he entered with his soldiers in 1648 and its citizens renewed their allegiance. Scarcely had he left the city, however, when they rebelled again, besieging the garrison of a hundred men he had left in the castle, who were joined by citizens supporting him. The count-duke returned swiftly, investing the city's twenty-four towers with 400 troops, directing operations from his *masseria* of Lo Stanzio. After the rebels had fought for two days and nights, inflicting heavy casualties, the castle garrison routed them in a surprise attack. Giangirolamo then promised a general pardon, whereupon they laid down their arms.

Tancred and Clorinda from Tasso's Gerusalemme Liberata, by Finoglio, at Conversano

As soon as Giangirolamo's men entered the city a reign of terror began, 'traitors' being tortured and hanged. The septuagenarian Baron Sambiase was hung up to die by dangling from one foot, the mayor, who had fled to Gallipoli, was pursued and killed, while four canons were shot and beheaded; their heads, wearing birettas, were nailed over their choir-stalls in the cathedral; it was rumoured that their bodies were flayed and the skins used to cover chairs in the *gran salone* (grand gallery) at Conversano. The houses of many other rebels were razed to the ground. Il Guercio's governor continued the hangings for several months. Count Giangirolamo was arrested for a second time in 1651 and once more taken to Spain. He never saw Conversano or Nardò again, dying in 1655 when about to sail home. It was probably a stroke, but popular legend claims that the Spaniards had him torn to pieces by wild horses.

This bloodstained ogre was one of the greatest patrons of art in Apulian history. The church of SS. Cosma e Damiano, which he built at Conversano between 1636 and 1650, is a Baroque jewel-box. The most important artist he employed was Paolo Domenico Finoglio, born about 1590, who had made his reputation at Naples, helping Ribera and Artemisia Gentileschi decorate the Certosa of San

Martino. He arrived at Conversano in 1635 with less than ten years to live, and, leaving the frescoes in SS. Cosma e Damiano to Fracanzano and Carlo Rosa, concentrated on painting the altar-pieces, together with a moving "Martyrdom of San Gennaro" in the cloister.

Finoglio's finest paintings have returned to Conversano after a long absence, restored to their glory, and may be seen again at the castle. These are ten scenes from Il Guercio's favourite epic, Tasso's "Gerusalemme Liberata", a fantastic reconstruction in verse of the first Crusade; a world of jewelled grottoes, magic islands and enchanted forests, full of golden serpents and goblins with dragon-wings, inhabited by heroes (such as the Norman Godefroy de Bouillon), guardian angels, fiendish witches and ladies in armour, especially a dying Saracen sorceress of wonderful beauty who begs for baptism. The sub-plots are stories of love for unattainable heroines by knights errant driven out of their wits by spells. Holding a torch, the artist himself appears in "The Torture of Olindo and Sofronia", with melancholy eyes, a huge fleshy nose and a cleft chin.

One of Finoglio's finest sacred paintings, "St Benedict and St Sabinus", is in the nearby abbey church of San Benedetto. The Counts of Conversano certainly left their mark on this abbey, their preferred burial place. An ancient foundation, whose church dates in part from the eleventh century, it later became a convent of Cistercian nuns under a mitred abbess. The counts' daughters supplied most of the haughty abbesses, who were a byword for truly staggering arrogance when they dealt with bishops, neighbouring magnates or anyone else, until the abbey was dissolved in 1809.

Il Guercio had three sons, all men of the sword. Cosmo, ('O Sfidante'), was slain in the duel at Ostuni, Giulio fell in battle, while Giantommaso took vows as a Knight of Malta. But Cosmo's son prospered. "The ancient castle or palace is most majestic, newly refurbished as a splendid dwelling by Count Acquaviva, lord of the city and of the surrounding region", wrote the Abate Pacichelli, who came to Conversano during the 1680s. He tells us reverently that the count's courtiers are "all titled people", admires his fine furniture with its gilt and embroidery, and is dazzled by "an almost unbelievable abundance of silver plate, mingled with vases of porcelain and rock crystal." (This was the Count Giulio who threatened to cut off the Duke of Noja's nose and ears.)

The Counts of Conversano were famous for their magnificent horses. After the invention of firearms heavy mounts for carrying men in full armour had to be replaced by swift, athletic animals that were capable of taking evasive action when necessary. From the fifteenth century the Counts imported Andalusian and Arab stallions to cover local mares, and by the eighteenth their offspring were being offered to half the courts of Europe; Lippizaners trace some of their blood-lines to Conversano stallions. Cirò Annichiarico, the brigand priest, who had ridden some of the finest horses in Apulia, thought that Conversanos were faster than Andalusians.

The Acquaviva d'Aragona's final years were embittered by sordid wrangles over feudal dues. Even the brigands whom they had been employing as their enforcers were unable to help them after the crown's draconian new measures against *banditi*. In 1801 Giulio Antonio IV, thirty-eighth Count of Conversano, left the city in disgust to live at Naples. Five years later, King Joseph Bonaparte abolished feudalism and the Acquaviva sold the castle soon after. They retained many of their Apulian estates, however, together with their lordly hunting-lodge of Marchione.

Built about 1740 by Count Giulio Antonio III, between Conversano and Putignano, Marchione is unique in Apulia because the Apulian magnates normally stayed at a *masseria* when they went hunting. In design it is a beautiful little castle whose four squat towers are crowned by terraces, and whose elegant *piano nobile* (noble floor) has an arcaded loggia that is reached by ascending a majestic double staircase. Despite standing among almond and cherry orchards today, as a hunting-lodge it once stood in an oak forest and two sole surviving oak-trees are lovingly preserved in the grounds. The game hunted was wild boar.

The last Acquaviva d'Aragona left Marchione to her son, the late Prince of Boiano (and Count of Conversano) who restored it. The house contains what must be the only surviving portrait of Il Guercio. Count Giangirolamo is shown as a stocky man with a Vandyck beard, a smiling face and a huge rapier – and no trace of a squint.

52

Martina Franca

some barons are like sovereigns in their lands
Paolo Maria Doria, *Vite Civile*

FORTY KILOMETRES TO THE SOUTH EAST, Martina Franca is an even prettier little city than Conversano. On a hill at the highest level of the Murgia del Trulli it dominates the fertile Val d'Itria and, although nowadays its white walls are masked by high-rise flats, the centre remains unspoilt, with narrow white-washed streets and small Baroque *palazzi* that have wrought-iron balconies. A local historian, Michele Pizzigallo, describes it proudly as "belonging to yesterday, like a flower always in bud."

Founded in the tenth century by refugees from the Saracens, Martina expanded in the fourteenth, being granted many privileges and adding "Franca" to its name. Raimondello del Balzo Orsini built a castle in 1388 while a hundred years later its lord was Francesco Coppolo, Count of Sarno, whom King Ferrante made his finance minister and then destroyed. In 1507 Martina Franca became a duchy and was given to Petraccone III Caracciolo del Leone, Count of Buccino in Basilicata. The family descended from 'Sergianni' Caracciolo, Grand Seneschal of Naples and lover of Queen Giovanna II, who amassed a vast fortune before being murdered. The Caracciolo del Leone took their name from the lion on their coat-of-arms, to be seen all over Martina Franca.

The Masaniello of Martina Franca, who led the 1647 revolt here, was a blacksmith, Vivantonio Montanaro, called 'Capo-di-Ferro', ('Iron Head'). Duke Francesco I routed him by importing 300 mercenaries. But generally strife was less bloody, mainly wrangles over the ducal feudal dues that were levied by professional tax-gatherers. They caused chronic resentment, which was why most dukes preferred to spend much of their time at Buccino, until the accession of Petracone V in 1655.

Duke Petracone was always loyal to the *Regno's* Spanish King and when only thirteen served in Spain against the Portuguese. On his return two years later he married Aurelia Imperiali of Francavilla. After killing the Count of Conversano, he and his brother Innico were imprisoned, but so many nobles interceded that they were soon released. When he came out of prison in 1668, Petracone began building a palace.

The old Orsini castle was pulled down, replaced by a *palazzo*, so beautifully proportioned that it has been attributed to Bernini. The main façade has a balcony with iron scroll-work running the length of the building beneath a long line of windows, and a tall gateway flanked by two great columns leading into a large courtyard. Pacichelli thought it "a work of perfection ... very like the Casa Pamphilij in Piazza Navona at Rome", noting that each façade has sixteen windows, and that there is a gallery, a theatre and a roof-garden. He reminds us that "The Lord Duke is also Marquis of Mottola ... Lord of Bovino ... and Baron of many other lands in Calabria and Lord of Locorotondo nearby, which produces horses and mules and supremely good milk, and is best for cheese."

A portrait of Petracone V shows a self-satisfied face with a big nose verging on the bulbous, a low forehead and a pointed beard. According to Pizzigallo, he was "narrow and obstinate with his family, haughty and offhand with local gentry, open and generous with the people." He lived in great splendour. When his son Francesco, Count of Buccino, married Eleanora Gaetani in 1700, Martina was illuminated for nights on end and horsemen carrying torches serenaded the *palazzo,* which was lit by splendid fireworks.

The duke had a favourite, Gaetano Faraone, an avaricious tailor, who became both informer and adviser. He ran everything in Martina Franca, but acquired some dangerous enemies, among them the Count and Countess of Buccino. When Petracone died in January, 1704, Faraone was immediately put in a dungeon and accused of dominating the late duke by witchcraft, with the aid of Nardantonia Casparro and Grascia di Mascio, "women commonly reputed to be expert at spells and magic." Nardantonia's daughter testified how one night the tailor had come to her mother's house with dough from which five crosses were made. "The said Faraone crushed each in turn, stamping his feet as he did so crying 'Devil, Devil, Devil, Beelzebub, give me entire ownership of the will and desires of Don Francesco, Count of Buccino, as I have over the Duke his father!'" He then placed the crosses in a bag, saying that he would drop them in a well. Five pieces of dough were found in a cistern at his house, wrapped in paper on which was written "Gaetano Faraone".

When interrogated in February Faraone was very ill because "he had struck his breast with a stone while calling on God to pardon his sins." He was placed in a "horrible dungeon" where he was found dead in May, the official cause of death being "gangrene of the bladder." Forty years later, some citizens of Francavilla Fontana accused Francesco II of murdering him. He was so alarmed that he contemplated giving the duchy to his son and going into a monastery, but eventually escaped with a fine of 20,000 ducats.

Francesco II made feudal dues even more burdensome, with a new poll-tax. Martina Franca was divided into two parties; the duke's followers and the moderates, the *Ducalisti;* and the radical *borghesi,* called *Universalisti.* However, as feudal lord the duke controlled elections to the commune and the appointment of most officials, including the mayor, and during the eighteenth century his vassals grew still more frustrated. Petracone VI, a straight-forward soldier who succeeded in 1752, did his best to make life easier, consulting both *Ducalisti* and *Universalisti,* but after seven years, exasperated by constant litigation, he handed the duchy over to his son.

Francesco III, who became duke in 1772, was much liked, his love of the country and interest in agriculture endearing him to the peasants. He and his wife, Stefania Pignatelli, modelled their little court on the royal court at Naples, plays being regularly produced in the palace theatre. In 1773 they commissioned Domenico Carella to paint the rooms of the *piano nobile;* the Mythology Room, the Bible Room and the Arcadia Room. As Rococo decoration they are superb, especially the Arcadia Room. On the ceiling are painted the Four Seasons. On the walls you can see the duke and his court. Francesco, in striped breeches and waistcoat, carries a tricorne hat while Duchess Stefania has a towering mass of powdered hair. They are surrounded by their courtiers, the local nobility, in a fête champêtre with fiddlers, a flautist and a huntsman with a hunting horn, and a background of country people. A beaming *Carella* watches from his easel in a corner. There are dogs everywhere, since the painter adored them.

Despite feudal dues, mules and horses brought prosperity to Martina Franca, as can be seen from its Rococo palaces. The best are Palazzi Panelli, Stabile, Martucci and Conte Barnaba, all graceful (yet surprisingly restrained for the period) and all built by the same unknown architect. The civic buildings are equally elegant, the Torre dell' Orologio (1734) and the Palazzo della Corte (1763) in what is now Piazza Roma. Both saw many angry confrontations between *Ducalisti* and *Universalisti*.

Count de Salis, who, with Archbishop Capacelatro, visited the duke at his *masseria* at San Basilio on their way from Bari to Tàranto in 1789, recalled Francesco III's friendly, unaffected manners. Dinner at the *masseria*, the Casa del Duca, was "a plain, almost rustic repast". During the meal, the archbishop sang the duke's praises to de Salis for preferring country life to the pleasures of the court at Naples.

Next morning Duke Francesco took de Salis to see his flock of 3,000 sheep and the dairy farm where cheese was made from their milk. All were purebred *pecore gentili,* descendants of the white Apulian sheep admired by the Romans, although by this date the hardier black sheep with a higher milk-yield was becoming more popular. On the way to the sheepfold the party met a band of shepherds, who walked before their flock carrying a banner, and playing a horn, an oboe, bagpipes and a curious local drum. They were also shown the duke's horses, mules and donkeys, at a stud near the *masseria*.

When Francesco III died in 1794, feudalism died with him, even if legally it lingered on for a few more years. His son, Petracone VII, died prematurely in 1796 and the next duke, Placido I, was only eleven. After the *Universalisti* welcomed the Neapolitan Republic, the city was sacked by Cardinal Ruffo's *Sanfedisti* and swelled by 7,000 recruits from the Murgia dei Trulli, whose wilder elements ripped up floors in a search for hidden money, plate or jewels. Silks and linen, china and furniture, wine, cheese and salami, were flung out of the windows to gangs waiting below. Some women had rings pulled off their fingers or earrings torn out of their ears.

Predictably, *Universalisti* supported the Napoleonic regime. So did Duke Placido, whom Murat made Esquire to the King, a high court appointment. He died at Martina Franca in April 1815, a month after Murat's fall.

In 1816 the restored Borbone monarchy issued a decree confirming the abolition of feudalism, although Placido's sickly little son, Petracone VIII, retained the palace with much of his wealth. When he died in 1827 the male line of the Caracciolo del Leone became extinct, the title passing to his sister Argentina. Through her it went to the Dukes of Sangro.

Sold in 1914, the palace became the Municipio, but in recent years a programme of systematic restoration has given back the state rooms something of their charm. For over a decade a music festival celebrated throughout Europe has been held annually in the courtyard.

53

Francavilla Fontana

...immense, majestic and well built...
Giovanni Battista Pacichelli, "Il Regno di Napoli in Prospettiva"

ANOTHER GREAT FEUDAL FIEF in central Apulia was Francavilla Fontana. Unlike the Acquaviva and the Caracciolo, its lords, the Imperiali, were Northerners by origin, Genoese bankers. They also spent far more time at Naples. It is possible that their enormous wealth made for an easier relationship with the locals than at Conversano or Martina Franca, since they did not have to depend so much on feudal dues for their income.

The foundation of Francavilla Fontana was, once again, the story of finding a wonder-working icon. In 1310, Philip of Anjou, Prince of Tàranto, was hunting when he saw a stag kneeling by a fountain in a valley and shot at it; to his amazement, the arrow turned round in flight and came back to him. He had the valley searched, a small grotto being discovered which contained a portrait of the Madonna and Child, "painted in the Greek manner". The Prince built a church and, to encourage people to settle around it, granted land to all comers, free from taxes for ten years, giving the settlement the name of Francavilla or 'Free Town'. Many settlers were attracted by the miracles which were worked by the icon. The most famous was on 24 January 1520, when a severe frost and then snow threatened to destroy the crops; everyone prayed before the Madonna of the Fountain and, on rising from their knees, they found that every plant, every leaf and stem, was free from frost or snow. Given walls in 1364 and a castle in 1450, Francavilla Fontana eventually passed to the Borromeo. Cardinal Carlo Borromeo sold it in 1571, to feed the poor of Milan.

The purchaser was Davide Imperiali, who already possessed vast estates near Genoa and also in Spain, besides a huge banking fortune. In the same year, 1571, he equipped four galleys at his own expense and took them to fight the Turks at Lepanto. As a reward, King Philip II made him Marquess of Oria. Davide's son, Michele, acquired the lordships of Avetrana and Massafra in 1647, together with the title 'Prince of Francavilla'.

Pacichelli is curiously unenthusiastic about the Princes of Francavilla, although he admits that their fief is one of the largest in the realm. However, he admires the wealth of the surrounding countryside – its grain, wine, oil, almonds and "other delights", remarking also on the town's "commodious, white-washed houses". He visited it when Michele II was its Prince. This Michele, who reigned from 1676 until 1724, rebuilt the castle as a palace, one of the largest in Apulia. The basic plan remained unchanged, four square towers at each angle and crenellated battlements, but the interior was modernised, the famous Neapolitan architect Ferdinando Sanfelice designing the double staircase which leads to the great hall where the Imperiali displayed their collection of paintings. There were superb guest-rooms, and a small theatre. There was also Cardinal Renato Imperiali's library, one of the best in Europe, which was open to the public.

The *duomo* at Francavilla, housing the miraculous icon, is large and Baroque, rebuilt in 1743 after an earthquake. Henry Swinburne describes it as "new, gay and well lighted; but so stuccoed, festooned and flowery, that the whole decoration is mere chaos." He says the plans were drawn in Rome, but muddled up by a local architect. It has paintings by the prolific Domenico Carella, a native of the town. Among them is "Il Caduto del Fulmine" ("The Fall of the Thunderbolt"), commemorating the drama of Palm Sunday 1779. Six hundred of Francavilla's leading citizens met in the church to discuss public affairs, the debate growing so heated that the Archpriest had to beg them "to respect the house of God." A certain Angelo Cosimo Candita standing near the main door was particularly noisy. Suddenly a thunderbolt struck the church, killing Candita. His horrified friends commissioned the painting, which still hangs over the main doorway.

Andrea II (1724–38) was a benevolent ruler who gave the town a school and an orphanage. His son Michele III, fifth and last prince, spent most of his time in Naples where he rented the Cellamare Palace, entertaining seven or eight hundred guests a week; among them was Casanova, who commented that "this amiable and magnificent Prince ... preferred the love of Ganymede to Hebe." Even so, he made the steward of his Apulian estates build villages, schools and workshops, and turn scrub into farmland.

When Swinburne visited Francavilla Fontana, Prince Michele had told its citizens to make him welcome, with "honours sufficient to turn the head of a plain English gentleman." Don Domenico, formerly Clerk of the Chamber to the Princess, showed him the town, a mob accompanying them throughout. He thought the houses "showy", but admitted the main street would be "handsome even in a capital city." As for the palace, "The apartments are spacious; but, as the owner has been absent above fourteen years, everything wears the face of neglect and decadency." He gives a patronising account of what must have been the town's most prized diversion:

> I was left to take my afternoon nap, and in the evening entertained with the tragedy of Judith and Holofernes, acted by the young people of the town, in a theatre belonging to the castle. Their rude accent, forced gestures, and strange blunders in language, rendered their dismal drama a complete farce. When the heroine murdered the general, the whole house shook with thundering bursts of applause; the upper part of his body was hidden by the side scenes; the lower parts lay on a couch upon the stage, and in the agonies of death were thrown into such convulsions, kickings and writhings, as melted the hearts and ravished the souls of the attentive audience. Judith then came forward, and repeated a long monologue, with her sword in one hand, and a barber's block dripping with blood, in the other. Never was a tragedy-queen sent off the stage with louder or more sincere acclamations.

Although the Imperiali family was very far from being extinct in Apulia, when Michele III died in 1782 he had no heirs within the fourth degree of consanguinity. The entire fief of Francavilla Fontana therefore reverted to the Crown, together with his other great castles and estates at Manduria, Massafra, Oria and Messagne. Despite having spent so much time away at Naples, he was deeply mourned. When visiting Oria, de Salis heard that Prince Michele had been a man of "rare knowledge and qualities", who by his kindness had doubled the population of his estates, encouraging many peasants to leave their former lord and settle on his land. But even in 1789, only seven years after the Prince's death, under the Crown's management the Imperiali estates had begun to be less prosperous. Due to being run from Naples by bureaucrats who never set foot in Apulia, "the population had dropped by a third, the newly cultivated ground had deteriorated and the manufacturing industries were completely exhausted."

Francavilla Fontana was very badly bombed in 1944, losing many of the historic "showy" houses next to the *duomo*. Nevertheless, the main street admired by Swinburne two centuries ago remains much as it was during his visit; the palace has been restored, and the little theatre where he saw the tragedy of Judith and Holofernes is still there.

Among the other great houses that once belonged to the Imperiali Princes of Francavilla Fontana, the palace at Manduria also survives intact, although broken up into flats, a bank and a restaurant. The castles at Massafra and Messagne have been restored. Best preserved of all, however, is the beautifully maintained castle at Oria, which since 1933 has belonged to the Counts Martini Carissimo.

Part XIII

Risorgimento?

54

The Death of the *Regno*

To many it was as if the kingdom had disintegrated with Ferdinand II.

Sir Harold Acton, "The Last Bourbons of Naples"

KING FERDINAND OF THE TWO SICILIES died on 22 May, 1859, two months after his last visit to Bari. His death paved the way for the *Risorgimento*: the unification of Italy. Nowhere would he be more regretted than in Apulia where, like the Emperor Frederick and King Manfred, he had hunted in the forests. If he did not build castles, he keenly encouraged New Bari's development, besides giving Apulian titles to three of his sons, the Counts of Bari, Trani and Lucera.

Nicknamed 'Bomba' for supposedly threatening to shell rebels into submission, a lie spread by enemies, Ferdinand was hated by liberals. He kept the absolute monarchy he had inherited, imprisoning his opponents. Mr Gladstone described his government as "the negation of God", conveniently ignoring England's own prison-hulks and record in Ireland. Yet no Southern ruler has been more popular. A big, bluff, virile man, he was a type whom the *Mezzogiorno* (southern Italians) understood, the perennial *'capo'* or boss, constantly sticking cigars into deserving mouths. A Southerner to his fingertips, who spoke and thought in Neapolitan dialect, and whose staple diet was *pasta*, he always listened to petitions, granting generous pensions. If he was superstitious, making St Ignatius a field-marshal on full pay, so were his subjects.

Under his firm rule, the South prospered. Despite lower taxes than other Italian states, it had more money in circulation than any,

Ferdinand II, King of the Two Sicilies from 1830 to 1859. Unjustly known as 'Bomba' by his enemies, he was a man of the *Mezzogiorno* heart and soul.

with the biggest gold reserves; 443 million in gold lire in 1859 compared with Piedmont's 27 million. In the same year the Royal Navy of the Two Sicilies included ninety-five steam ships, far more than Britain's Royal navy, though admittedly most of them were tiny. His government built the first Italian railways, steamships, electric telegraph and lenticular lighthouse. Dockyards at Naples and Bari were the most modern in the peninsula. So were the new roads. "Anybody who avoided subversive politics enjoyed complete freedom and could do what he liked", Giacinto De Sivo wrote in 1868. "Countless foreigners prospered so much that they settled here", he adds bitterly: "Then Gladstone came and ruined us ... unbelievable calumnies were repeated in newspapers all over the world."

The men of the *Risorgimento* had once hoped Ferdinand would become King of Italy, but he refused, from respect for the rights of other Italian sovereigns, especially for those of the Pope. Had he lived longer and, however unwillingly, granted a constitution and Sicilian autonomy, the South might have been much happier. But he died at forty-nine from a mysterious disease – probably diabetes – which, characteristically, he ascribed to the Evil Eye.

In June 1859 the French defeated the Austrians, who ceded

Lombardy to Piedmont. Then the central Italian duchies turned against their Austrian-backed rulers and by March 1860 the Piedmontese were in possession of Tuscany, Parma and Modena, besides occupying part of the Papal States. Yet Piedmont had no intention of invading the *Mezzogiorno*.

In April, however, Garibaldi landed in Sicily where Palermo had risen in revolt. The late king had put down an earlier Sicilian rising and would certainly have known how to deal with this one, but his twenty-two year old son, Francis II, did not. He had already disbanded the Swiss regiments who had been his best troops. After Garibaldi overran Sicily in May, Francis granted a constitution, only hastening the regime's collapse.

Many Southerners lost confidence in their inexperienced young king. When Garibaldi landed on the mainland in August, a handful of liberals tried to start risings, supported by a few business men eager for new markets in the North and by peasants who hoped naively that the great estates would be shared out. Foggia declared for Garibaldi, but in Bari and other Apulian cities royalist mobs routed similar demonstrations.

In September King Francis abandoned Naples to Garibaldi, withdrawing to the fortress city of Gaeta to concentrate his troops. Piedmont, saddled with an astronomical national debt, realised that it could take over the rich Southern kingdom. In October, a Piedmontese army invaded the *Regno,* occupying Naples and besieging Gaeta, bribing generals and officials. Even the most loyal despaired and at the end of the month, in a carefully rigged plebiscite, Apulians voted with the rest of the South for 'unity'.

The *Risorgimento* must be judged by its fruits, and for Apulia they were very bitter indeed. Far from improving conditions, the destruction of the ancient *Regno* made them much worse, just as de Sivo claimed. Here is how a recent historian, Roger Absalom, describes the impact of 'unity':

> To most southerners the experience was indistinguishable from
> harshly rapacious colonisation by a foreign country, which
> introduced a totally new set of laws and regulations governing
> every aspect of civil society, in the name of free trade substituted
> shoddy and over-priced imports for the familiar products local
> handicrafts and industry had previously provided, imposed
> ruinous and unaccustomed levels of taxation, conscripted the

young men into its army and added insult to injury by the promulgation of contemptuous attitudes towards them.

Few dreams have ended in such disillusionment as the *Risorgimento* did for the *Mezzogiorno*. Too late, Southern Italy realised that, far from being liberated, it was the victim of another Northern conquest, by arrogant invaders who sneered that "Africa begins south of Rome." The Duke of Maddaloni (head of the great Carafa family) protested in the new Italian parliament, "This is invasion, not annexation, not union. We are being treated like an occupied country." That was what the death of the *Regno* meant for Apulia.

If brought up to date politically, the Borbone monarchy could have offered the *Mezzogiorno* a chance of becoming a self-governing, prosperous Southern Italy. Instead, the *Risorgimento* handed over the South to Northern asset-strippers, to be misgoverned from a far away capital. What had been a prosperous country soon became an economic slum in which the Apulians suffered as much as anybody. Some of them, however, were not going to give up without a fight.

55

The Brigands' War

We swear and promise to defend, with our blood
if need be, God, the Supreme Pontiff Pius, Francis II,
King of the Two Sicilies, and our column commander.

Sergeant Pasquale Romano

O N 13 FEBRUARY 1861, King Francis sailed into exile. Gaeta, his last stronghold, surrendered to the Piedmontese besiegers and the Borbone army was disbanded. It was the end of the seven hundred year old *Regno*.

The Piedmontese tried to win over the Borbone officers, giving over 2,000 of them commissions in the new Italian army or paying pensions to those who preferred to retire, but in March Constantino Nigra, a senior Piedmontese official at Naples, reported they were angry and resentful. As for the other ranks, "we have a horde of Borbone soldiers, disbanded without work or food, who will take to the mountains when spring comes." He adds that the clergy are hostile and the aristocracy "in mourning for the Borboni." Farini, governor of 'The Neapolitan Provinces', openly admitted that not even a hundred Southerners wanted a united Italy.

Even if the Southern leaders who now emerged were peasants and sometimes criminals, what the Piedmontese called 'The Brigands' War' was none the less a genuine civil war. For a decade 120,000 Piedmontese troops were needed to hold down Southern Italy. Between April 1861 and April 1863 nearly 2,500 "brigands" were killed in combat, over 1,000 shot after surrendering and another 5,500 taken prisoner. These figures are for the *Mezzogiorno* as a whole – no breakdown is available for Apulia alone – and does not include casualties among the handful of die-hards who went on fighting.

Some of the leaders were former Borbone NCOs, discharged without pensions unlike their officers. Their sole hope was Francis II's return and they were fighting for his restoration. Large numbers took an oath of loyalty to him, some men continuing to wear the Borbone army's blue tunic and red trousers, others using as a badge a silver piastre coin with the king's head. Afraid of losing their pensions, Borbone officers dared not join them openly, but instead organised committees at Trieste, Marseilles and Malta to smuggle guns. Money and more guns came from Rome, where King Francis had established a government in exile, since the Two Sicilies was still recognised by the Papacy and Austria. Papal officials turned a blind eye to gun-running over their frontier and frequently gave shelter to brigands who were pursued by Piedmontese troops.

Bases were set up in the hills or in the Apulian ravines, where self-appointed leaders recruited ex-soldiers returning penniless to their villages. Mounted and flying the Borbone flag, they ambushed enemy troops or, after cutting the telegraph wires, galloped into isolated cities to shoot the *sindaco* and his officials. They were aided by landowners and former Borbone officials, by priests and peasants. In the opinion of the Peasants, Hare noted, "brigands were always *poveretti* [poor things], to be pitied and sympathised with."

In April 1861 Carmine Donatello Crocco, a huge man with a black beard down to his waist, made a triumphant entry into Venosa at the head of a brigand army. On hearing the news, nearby Melfi, led by its most respected citizens, promptly hoisted the Borbone flag. Three days later, however, General Crocco hastily retreated at the approach of Piedmontese troops.

Throughout the summer the Capitanata was terrorised by bands like Crocco's, all flying the old royal flag. The governor of Foggia reported that *masserie* were being raided daily, their owners or managers abducted and held to ransom.

When in July Luigi Palumbo seized Vieste with 400 men, welcomed by shouts of *"Viva Francesco II!"* the new Italy's supporters were rounded up and shot, their *masserie* sacked, their corn and wine shared out among the peasants. Warned that an enemy force was on its way, Palumbo rode off to occupy Vico del Gargano, where he had a *Te Deum* sung to celebrate the restoration of Borbone authority.

Carmine Donatello Crocco the brigand leader and a self-styled 'general' during the terrible Brigands' War of 1861–65

When the Piedmontese arrived, he and his men took refuge in the Foresta Umbra.

All over Apulia brigands were entering large towns with impunity, buying food and medical supplies. They had spies everywhere, including a group of ex-officers at Bari, together with agents and depots. Persuaded that the entire South was going to rise for him, in early autumn 1861 King Francis sent a veteran Carlist general, José Borjès, to Calabria to take command. Unfortunately, as a Spaniard, Borjès found it impossible to assert his authority over the Calabrians and moved to Apulia, where for a time he joined Crocco in the western Murgia. Towards the end of 1861, however, after two months spent hiding in woods and caves, he despaired and with his small Spanish staff and a few brigands made for the Papal States. "On their being surrounded just before reaching the frontier, they surrendered without a fight, in the confident belief that their lives would be spared", writes Ulloa, prime minister of the Borbone government in exile: "Otherwise they would have fought to the death. But they were at once disarmed, and sent before a firing squad."

By then, in Apulia and indeed all over the South, it had started to look as if the Piedmontese troops were winning the war. A bitter winter set in. Disheartened by the cold and damp of their miserable lairs in the ravines, many Apulian brigands gave up what had become a merciless conflict.

Among those who lost hope in the 'Brigands' War' was General

Crocco, who fled to Rome, abandoning his mistress, Maria Giovanna of Ruvo. His career was extraordinary yet far from untypical.
Although he had deserted from King Ferdinand's army in 1851, after
killing a fellow soldier, at the *Risorgimento* he had become the brigands' leader in western Apulia and Basilicata. In 1872 he would make
the mistake of returning to Basilicata, to be caught and sentenced to
life imprisonment.

At the close of 1861, the journalist Count Maffei, an enthusiastic
supporter of the new Italy, was genuinely convinced that the brigands
were beaten, "reduced to a few wretched wanderers, hunted like wild
beasts." He was wrong. The war had only just begun and, despite its
initial successes, the Piedmontese army would suffer more casualties
then it had during all the battles of the entire *Risorgimento*, many of
them killed in Apulia.

56

"A War of Extermination"

Piedmontese troops occupy all Southern Italy, only because of savage
and merciless enforcement of martial law ... Those who will not submit
are slaughtered .. in a war of extermination, in which 'pity is a crime'.
When an insurgent is captured by the Piedmontese he is shot.

P Cala Ulloa, "Lettres Napolitaines"

NORTHERN OCCUPATION, heavy new taxes and rising inflation
had enraged the Southerners. Conscription into the Italian
– formerly Piedmontese – army fuelled their resentment, partly
because all the NCOs were Piedmontese who spoke an incompre-
hensible dialect, and many unwilling conscripts preferred to join the
brigands instead. Sometimes there were other reasons for joining.
New farm-managers, imported to run confiscated royal or church
estates, often raped the labourers' pretty daughters, threatening the
parents with eviction if they complained, so a brother or male cousin
would knife the rapist, and then go off to be a brigand.

As has been seen, the wooded Murgia dei Trulli around Alberobello was perfect bandit country. Among the brigands' friends here
were the Gigante, a prominent Alberobello family. (Their Masseria
Gigante, now an hotel, is just outside the town.) Both the priest Don
Francesco Gigante and his brother Luigi, who was in the National
Guard, were in touch with the famous Sergeant Romano. During
the night of 26 July, 1862 Romano led twenty-six picked men into
Alberobello, crept up on the Guard House and took it at bayonet
point; the plan, instigated by Luigi Gigante according to a captured
brigand, was to kill six pillars of the new government at Alberobello,

including the mayor. But the local National Guard commander happened to look out of his window, saw the brigands and alerted the town by firing his revolver. Romano and his men ran off, taking thirty rifles. When charged, the Gigante brothers bribed the police who came from Altamura to investigate, and the magistrate at Bari, who secretly loathed the new regime, found that there was no case for them to answer.

Pasquale Romano was the best known *capobanda* (leader) in this part of Apulia. An educated man and a devout Catholic, he wrote of his hatred for "the treacherous, invading usurpers who are trying to hunt us down." He survived in the woods of the Murgia dei Trulli longer than most brigands because of his many friends among the peasants, who fed him and warned of the enemy's approach. Sheltering by day in the little stone huts in the olive groves, he travelled long distances by night, to organise 150 followers in two main groups divided into sections. He attempted to give his *comitiva* military discipline, calling it "The Company of the Sergeant from Gioia." Looting was forbidden and his men had to attend Mass on Sundays, often in the chapel of the Masseria dei Monaci near Altamura, a service that was known by locals as 'The Brigands' Mass'. Even so, embittered by the Piedmontesi's deliberate murder of his fiancée Lauretta, he never took prisoners.

However, the odds were growing much greater. The new rulers had started to buy the support of Southern landowners, just as they had bought the Borbone officers by guaranteeing their pensions. At first, a fair number of the *galantuomini* (gentlemen) had encouraged the brigands, sheltering them, even providing supplies and ammunition; they disliked being bullied by Piedmontese and had feared that their estates would be confiscated. Now however, the regime guaranteed their property, encouraging them to raise private armies and fight the brigands. They cowed their peasants, who stopped helping the men in the forests and grottoes.

During 1862, "a regular battle was fought near Tàranto, when twenty-six brigands were killed, and eleven shot the next day in the market-place", Janet Ross was told twenty years later. "After that the Tarentine gentlemen could visit their *masserie* without the fear of being held up for ransom, or having to take a body of armed men to protect them." Many brigand leaders were caught between December and the following June. Giuseppe Valente – known as 'Nenna-Nenna', a deserter from Garibaldi's army – was captured near Lecce and swiftly given forced labour for life. 'Il Caparello', operating between Santeramo and Gioia del Colle, was killed in January, and Cosmo Mazzeo, an ex-Borbone soldier from San Marzano di San Giuseppe, was taken prisoner in June, to be shot in November.

On 5 January 1863 Sergeant Romano attacked his home town of Gioia del Colle with 28 men. The National Guard and a troop of Piedmontese cavalry proved too strong; 22 were killed and the rest were captured and shot. Among those who fell in the battle was Romano himself – despite begging for a 'soldier's death' by a bullet like the others, he was bayoneted in cold blood. From a diary found on his body, it is clear he knew that some of his men were no better than "bandits." Even so, they had been "bound to obey all orders given by me to further the cause of our rightful king." Also found was a copy of the oath he made them swear to King Francis and "our column commander." The sergeant is still a hero at Gioia del Colle, where a street was named after him in 2010.

Cosimo Pizzichiccio took over command of Romano's *comitiva*. During a battle with Piedmontese troops – in June 1863 at the Masseria Belmonte, east of the Statte-Crispiano road – he lost thirty-seven men killed, wounded or taken prisoner, although he himself got away with the remainder of the band to the woods in an area bounded by Mottola, Martina Franca and Alberobello. From here he continued to rob *masserie* and take hostages for ransom. His brother was caught in July while what was left of the *comitiva* were ambushed in a wood a few days later, but managed to escape. Like Romano, Pizzichiccio was blamed for fewer murders than most *capobande*. In October, however, he kidnapped a blacksmith, Giuseppe Marzano, who unwisely boasted he would eat his captor's brains 'like a sheep's head'. Pizzichiccio promptly cut him down with a cavalry sabre.

Throughout, the soldiers from Piedmont retaliated with the utmost savagery. Admittedly they were under enormous pressure, constantly ambushed, besides knowing that they would be tortured and murdered if captured. They were also decimated by malaria – at one point, out of each company of a hundred men only thirty-five were fit for service. A former British Foreign Secretary, the Earl of Malmesbury, commented with some exaggeration that "The cruelties of the Piedmontese armies to the Neapolitan royalists were unsurpassed in any civil war."

Undeniably, it was a horrible war, with reports of men being burned alive or crucified by both sides. Hundreds of Apulian non-combattants were killed, many others fleeing to the cities, leaving their farms deserted or their shops boarded up. Most of the towns and the *masserie* were ringed by trenches and stockades. It was impossible to travel anywhere without a heavily armed escort, while Bari was cut off by land. The only reasonably safe people were those landowners who, like the old feudal barons, had recruited private armies.

All over Apulia men were imprisoned without trial simply because some enemy had seized the opportunity of settling an old score, charges of collaboration with brigands being easily fabricated. Landowners whose *masserie* had not been raided fell under suspicion automatically while senior officials were often accused without any justification of supplying rifles and ammunition. Despite having shown slavish loyalty to the new regime, the *sindaco* of Alberobello was charged with taking bribes and with helping a notorious brigand, Giorgio Palmisani, to break out of prison. He was only acquitted after spending months under house arrest.

New brigand leaders were always emerging to fill the places of those who had been killed or captured. Among the most notorious were the psychopath Caruso, Crocco's lieutenant 'Ninco Nanco' Coppa, a former Borbone soldier, and Varanelli, who was rumoured to eat human flesh. Lesser men included 'Brucciapaese', 'Mangiacavallo' and 'Orecchiomozzo', each one with a small band of followers.

Caruso, once a cowherd of the Prince of San Severo, possessed real military talent. By the end of 1862 he was leading the largest surviving *comitiva* in Apulia, 200 mounted men according to the Piedmontese garrison commander at Spinazzola. He never took prisoners, invariably killing enemy wounded. Having demanded bread, sheep and fodder from a peasant named Antonio Picciuti, after receiving them he seized Picciuti's hand, laid it on a table and chopped it off, as a warning that he would need more next time. On another occasion he hacked off the arms and legs of a suspected informer before throwing him into a cauldron of boiling water. During the single month of September 1863 he is said to have personally killed 200 people. By then he had been driven into the Benevento where, after further atrocities, his band was wiped out. In December, accompanied by a sole surviving follower, Caruso was captured in the hovel of his sixteen year old mistress Filomena and immediately shot.

'Ninco-Nanco', a game-keeper formerly in prison for murder,

operated with fifty horsemen in the Murgia between Altamura and Minervino, hiding in the ravines. During the terrible winter of 1863–4 his *comitiva* was hunted down and broken, 'Ninco-Nanco' being apparently killed in the storming of a *masseria* where he had taken refuge. But somehow he got away, escaping to the Papal States, from where he sent a defiant message, "Ninco-Nanco lives!"

Other brigands held out in the Abruzzi and the Piedmontese garrisons dared not relax. This explains Mme Figuier's alarming experience in her *locanda* at Trani during the winter of 1865. She had observed some suspicious looking men muffled in cloaks standing round the stove when a young chamber-maid warned her that she and her husband were in the gravest danger, telling her how to answer questions she was going to ask in front of them.

"'You are Spanish, surely Signora, aren't you?', the little servant girl asked me loudly. 'You have never had a father, a brother or a fiancé who was a soldier, have you? Isn't it true that you trust in the Virgin and that you think brigands are good men who earn a living by taking what the rich can easily spare?'" Realising that her husband had been mistaken for a Piedmontese officer – Piedmontese officers often spoke French among themselves – Mme Figuier hastily agreed. Knowing the brigands' sympathy for the Carlist guerillas in Spain, she added that the bands in the Abruzzi were being joined daily by Spaniards. Smiling, the men doffed their hats, offering to protect the lady and her husband during their stay.

In 1865–7 the Piedmontese officials at Naples made certain of the co-operation of the Southern monied classes by allowing them to buy up the confiscated crown and church lands, producing the wretched social consequences that have been described in earlier chapters. As Francis II's brother-in-law, the Austrian Emperor Franz-Joseph was understandably eager to see him restored, but in 1866 Austria's defeat by Prussia and the new Italian state finally dispelled all hope of a restoration. The kingdom of the Two Sicilies degenerated into *La Questione Meridionale* (The Southern Question) – poverty stricken, despised Southern Italy.

The handful of Apulian brigands who survived in the Abruzzi fled across the Papal frontier. Whether genuine royalists like Sergeant Romano or psychopaths like Caruso, they had been the last defenders of the ancient *Regno*. Now that they were eliminated, the *Risorgimento*'s asset-stripping could be completed without any fear of interference. Nothing remained to deter speculators from investing in the 'Apulian Texas', and a new way of life lay ahead for the labourers on the Tavoliere.

Occasionally those who found conditions in the labour gangs beyond endurance still took to the ravines in the Murge, from where they raided lonely *masserie*, but by 1900, brigands who rode out from caves had been replaced by urban gangsters and were passing into folk-memory.

There is a bitter legacy. As a young man in Turin, Antonio Gramsci, one of the founders of the Italian Communist Party, met Piedmontese veterans of the Brigands' War, and he always remembered the hatred they felt for their 'Southern brothers." Apulia, on the other hand, has neither forgotten nor forgiven its "liberation."

Part XIV

Epilogue

Apulia Today

THERE HAS BEEN A COMPLETE TRANSFORMATION since 1945. For all its beauty, the old Apulia was a harsh, cruel land, most of whose inhabitants lived a wretchedly hard life. In contrast today's Apulians have grown rich. Yet the region remains strikingly different from the rest of Italy, with strong echoes from the past – a dramatic folk-piety and even witchcraft surviving in high-rise flats.

The transformation is partly due to "the coming of the water." Often attributed to the great aqueduct completed by the Duce in 1939, in reality this owes far more to modern wells 200 metres deep; the rainfall in winter has always been high and, as Henry Swinburne observed, it must go somewhere. Not only has the water made life more agreeable for everybody, but it has done wonders for farming. Malaria has been eradicated – before 1945, quinine was part of the staple diet in low-lying areas, but pesticides have wiped out the anopheles mosquito.

The *latifondisti* now farm the land themselves, using the latest machinery instead of work-gangs. (Several of these gentleman-farmers bear some of the oldest names among those of the historic nobility.) Seventy per cent of Italy's fruit and vegetables comes from Apulia, while Apulian oil provides a third of the peninsula's entire output and Apulian wine a sixth. In addition, early vegetables for Northern Europe are grown here on a massive scale. Even so, the old high-wheeled Apulian cart can occasionally be seen, while the short-handled mattock that crippled their fathers is still used by a few peasant smallholders, although these are a fast dwindling breed.

Bari, whose population has risen to 350,000, flourishes so much that Northerners call it the 'Milan of the South'. Besides producing tyres and other rubber goods on a huge scale, it has factories that specialise in electronics and micro-chips, while the port is busier than ever, playing an increasingly vital role in the commercial life of the Adriatic. The university has a particularly fine record of industrial research, although it is probably best known for a faculty of agriculture from which the entire region benefits. It also supplies Italy with countless lawyers, including many judges and a host of distinguished advocates.

The Feast of St Nicholas is celebrated as devoutly as ever. Nowadays Russian pilgrims come too, his crypt chapel in the basilica resounding with Slavonic chant since he has always been one of the great miracle-workers of Holy Russia. These pilgrims also recall how another St Nicholas (canonised in 2000) prayed here in 1892, when he was still the young Tsarevich.

Mercifully, industrialisation affects only one or two other small areas, such as the steel-works at Tàranto or the oil-refinery at Brìndisi. What really does hurt the landscape, however, are the blocks of hideous high-rise flats, tall, grey and forbidding, that are starting to obscure some of the little white cities.

In many places serious social problems have resulted from moving large numbers of people into flats like these, problems compounded by the spread of drugs since the early 1980s. Another worry is the influx of would-be immigrants who enter from Albania, Montenegro or North Africa; troops based at Bari patrol the coast to intercept them. (If caught, these unfortunate people are treated with considerably more humanity than in other Mediterranean countries.) Yet there is plenty of hope for the future, and with their growing wealth the Apulians feel a justifiable optimism.

Judging from all the books published at Bari, the Apulians must be fascinated by their history. Castles and cathedrals are very well maintained, with an admirable programme of restoration. (Sadly, despite the efforts of the World Monuments Fund this does not apply to the grotto churches, where the frescoes continue to fade). Traditional peasant food, not so long ago considered quite unfit for gentry, now appears in the smartest restaurants. *La Cucina Pugliese* (The Pugliese Cuisine), based on fish, pasta and vegetables, has seen a triumphant revival, the difference being that while in former days one of its dishes was an entire meal, often a selection of them are now served as an hors d' oeuvres. Even the Apulian mafia bear a title redolent of history, *La Sacra Corona Unità* (United Sacred Crown), which seems to hint at memories of the old brigands and the war to save the *Mezzogiorno* from Northern invasion – although the brigands never dealt in drugs, Russian prostitutes or illegal immigrants – nor did they blow up school children, as happened recently in Brìndisi.

With its low white cliffs along the Adriatic and its long sandy beaches along the Ionian Sea, and with some really excellent hotels, Apulia's tourist potential is beginning to be exploited. This is scarcely surprising since the region has so many attractive features. It will always be a paradise for everybody interested in classical history or architecture while, if reserved, its charming inhabitants seem to welcome visitors.

Although hardships of the sort described in our book are fortunately a thing of the past, they have bequeathed some very impressive qualities. Amongst them is an awe-inspiring capacity for grinding hard work and a razor-sharp instinct for survival, which will ensure Apulia's success in the difficult new Europe.

Acknowledgements

WE WOULD LIKE TO THANK, in particular: H. E. Dr. Boris Bianchieri, formerly Italian Ambassador in London; Professor Rosangela Barone of the Italian Cultural Institute; Professor Antonio Graniti of Bari University, Don Riccardo Tomacelli-Filomarino (Duca di Torre a Mare) and Donna Irene Tomacelli-Filomarino, and our agent Andrew Lownie.

We are also grateful to Don Gennaro del Balzo, Don Grazio Gianfreda (Parocco of Otranto Cathedral), Don Giuseppe Civerra of the Santuario S. Salvatore, Andria, and Dr. Italo Palasciano, who gave us otherwise unobtainable information.

We owe a lot to the people of Gioia del Colle, above all to the brothers Giuseppe, Giovanni and Lucio Romano.

We would also like to thank Ellie Shillito of Haus Publishing for her patience and unfailing help in preparing the new edition.

Picture credits

The authors and publishers wish to express their thanks to the following sources of illustrative material for permission to reproduce it. They will make the proper acknowledgements in future editions in the event that any omissions have occurred.

London Library: pp. 67, 113, 178, 243, 284, 289. Marcok: p. 83. Susan Mountgarret: pp. 21, 45, 88, 96, 121, 124, 138, 157, 164, 165, 174, 184, 232, 234, 251, 261. Zhebiton: p. 189

Further Reading

THE BOOKS used by eighteenth century travellers were Pietro Giannone's "Istoria Civile del Regno di Napoli", first published in 1723, and the 25 volume "Raccolta di tutti i più rinomati scrittori dell'Istoria Generale del Regno", published between 1769 and 1777, and which includes the early histories of such writers as Pontano and Porzio (see below). For art they consulted Bernado de Dominici's delightfully scandalous "Vite dei Pittori, Scultori ed Architetti Napoletani", which appeared in 1742. Nineteenth century travellers supplemented these with Coletta's "Storia del Reame di Napoli dal 1734–1825", which came out in 1848, and Giustiniani's "Dizionario Geografico", published in ten volumes between 1797 and 1805. The English read Swinburne and Keppel Craven but Berkeley remained unknown until the 1870s.

Accounts by travellers

Berkeley, G.: *The Works of George Berkeley*, Oxford 1871
Bertoldi, G.: *Memoirs of the Secret Societies of the South of Italy*, London 1821
Blewitt, O.: *A Handbook for Travellers in Southern Italy; being a guide to the continental portion of the Two Sicilies*, London 1853
Bourget, P.: *Sensations d'Italie*, Paris 1891
Castellan, A.L.: *Lettres sur l'Italie*, Paris 1819
Church, E.M.: *Sir Richard Church in Italy and Greece*, London 1895
Courier, P.: *Oeuvres complètes*, Brussels 1828
Craven, R. Keppel: *A Tour through the Southern Provinces of the Kingdom of Naples*, London 1821
Diehl, C.: *L'Art Byzantin dans l'Italie Méridionale*, Paris 1894
——*Manuel d'art byzantin*, Paris 1925

Douglas, N.: *Old Calabria*, London 1915

Figuier, C.: *L'Italie d'apres nature*, L'Italie Méridionale, Paris 1868

Gissing, G.: *By the Ionian Sea*, London 1901

Gregorovius, F.: *Wanderjahre in Italien: Apulische Landschaften*, Leipzig 1889

Hare, A.J.C.: *Cities of Southern Italy*, London 1883

Horace, Q.F.: *Satires and Epistles* (trans. N. Rudd), London 1973

——*Odes and Epodes* (trans W.G. Shepherd), London 1983

Hutton, E.: *Naples and Southern Italy,* London 1915

Lear, E.: *Journals of a Landscape Painter in Southern Calabria and the Kingdom of Naples,* London 1852

Lenormant, F.: *A Travers l'Apulie et la Lucanie*, Paris 1883

——*La Grande Grèce, Paris 1881–84*

Macfarlane, C.: *The Lives and Exploits of Banditti and Robbers*, London 1833

——*Popular Customs, Sports and Recollections of the South of Italy,* London 1846

Pacichelli, G.B.: *Il Regno di Napoli in prospettiva*, Napoli 1703

Ramage, C.T.: *The Nooks and By-Ways of Italy*, Liverpool 1868

Richard, J.C. Abbé de Saint-Non: *Voyages pittoresques ou descriptions du Royaume de Naples et de Sicile*, Paris 1781–86

Riedesel, H von,: *Reise durch Sizilien und Gross Griechenland*, Zurich 1771

Ross, J.: *The Land of Manfred*, London 1889

——*The Fourth Generation: Reminiscences*, London 1912

Salis Marschlins, C.U. de: *Reisen in verschiedenen Provinzen des Konigreichs Neapel*, Zurich 1793

Sitwell, Sir O: *Discursions on Travel, Art and Life*, London 1925

Swinburne, H.: *Travels in the Two Sicilies in the Years 1777, 1778, 1779 and 1780*, London 1783

Yriarte, C.: *Les Bords de l'Adriatique et de Montenegro*, Paris 1878

Chronicles and early histories

Benjamin of Tudela, *The Itinary of Benjamin of Tudela*, London 1907

Bernard the Wise: *The Voyage of Bernard the Wise (in Early Travels in Palestine,* ed. T. Wright), London 1848

Caesar, Julius: *The Civil War* (trans. J.F. Gardner), London 1967

Chirulli, I.: *Historia Cronologica della Martina Franca*, Venice 1752

Comnena, A.: *The Alexiad* (trans. E.R.A. Sewter), London 1969

De Dominici, B.: *Vite dei Pittori, Scultori ed Architetti Napoletani*, Naples 1742

Diogenes Laertes, *Lives of the Philosophers*

Doria, P.M.: *Vite civile*, Naples 1710

——*Massime del governo spagnolo a Napoli*, Naples 1973

Frederick II of Hohenstaufen: *The Art of Hunting with Birds* (trans. A.C. Wood and F.M. Fyfe), Boston 1955

Giacomo the Notary: *Cronica di Napoli. Notaro Giacomo* (ed. P. Garzilli), Naples 1845

Giannone, P.: *Istoria Civile del Regno di Napoli*, Naples 1723

Gibbon, E.: *Decline and Fall of the Roman Empire*, London 1963

Giovio, P.: *Historiarum sui temporis* (in *Opere scelte* ed. C. Panigada), Bari 1931

——*Commentatarii delle cose de Turchi...e la vita di Scanderbeg*, Venice 1541

Guicciardini, F.: *Istoria di Italia*, Pisa 1819

Livy: *Rome and the Mediterranean* (trans. H. Bettenson), London 1976

——*The War with Hannibal* (trans. A de Selincourt), London 1965

Matteo di Giovenazzo: *I Diurnali di Matteo Spinelli di Giovinazzo 1247–68* (in *Cronisti e scrittori sincroni napoletani* ed. G.del Re), Naples 1845

Misson, M.: *Voyage d'Italie*, 5th ed. Paris 1722

Nicholas of Jamsilla: *Delle geste di Federico II imperatore e de' suoi figli Corrado e Manfredi, re di Puglia e di Sicilia* (in *Cronisti e scrittori sincroni napoletani* ed. G. del Re), Naples 1845

Nugent, T.: *The Grand Tour*, London 1756

Pliny the Elder: *The Natural History of Pliny* (trans. J. Bostock & H.J. Riley), London 1855–57

Plutarch: *The Age of Alexander* (trans. I. Scott-Kilvert), London 1973

Polybius: *The Rise of the Roman Empire* (trans. I. Scott-Kilvert), London 1979

Porzio, C.: *La Congiura de' Baroni del Regno di Napoli contro il Re Ferdinando Primo*, Rome 1565

——*Relazione del regno di Napoli ... tra il 1577 e 1579* (in *Collezione di opere inedite orare di storia Napoletana* ed. S. Volpicella), Naples 1839

Pratilli, F.M.: *La Via Appia, riconosciuto e descritta da Roma a Brindisi*, Naples 1745

Saewulf: *Early travels in Palestine, comprising the narratives of Arnulf, Willibald ... Saewulf*, London 1848

Sandys, G.: *A relation of a journey begun in An. Dom. 1610*, London 1615

Salimbene: *From St Francis to Dante ... the Chronicle of the Franciscan Salimbene*. Ed. G.C. Coulton, London 1908

Strabo: *The Geography* (trans. A.C. Jones), London 1917–32

Villani, G.: *Croniche fiorentine*, Florence 1823

Virgil: *The Aeniad* (trans. Dryden), London 1906

——*The Georgics* (trans. C. Day Lewis), Oxford 1983

William of Malmesbury: *Gesta Regum Anglorum*

Other works

Absalom, R.: *Italy since 1800*, London 1995

Abulafia D.: *Frederick II. A medieval emperor* London and NY, 1988;

Acton, Sir H.: *The Bourbons of Naples*, London 1956

——*The Last Bourbons of Naples*, London 1961

Belli D'Elia, P. et al.: *La Puglia fra Bisanzio e l'occidente*, Milan 1980

——*La Puglia tra barocco e rococo*, Milan 1983

——*Les Pouilles Romaines*, Paris 1988

Béraut, J.: *La colonisation greque de l'Italie méridionale et de la Sicile dans l'antiquité,* Paris 1957

Bertaux, E.: *L'Art dans l'Italie Méridionale*, Paris 1904

Blunt, A.: *Baroque and Rococo*, London 1978

Blunt, J.J.: *Vestiges of Ancient Manners and Customs Discoverable in Modern Italy and Sicily*, London 1823

Boardman, J.: *The Greeks Overseas*, London 1964

Bologna, F.: *Pittori alla Corte Angioina*, Rome 1969

Brandi, C.: *Martina Franca*, Milan 1968

Briggs, M.: *In the Heel of Italy*, London 1910

Bronzini, G.B.: *Homo Laborans*, Manduria 1985

Calò Mariani, M.S.: *L'Arte del Duecento in Puglia*, Turin 1984

Carano Donvito G.: *Storia di Gioia del Colle dagli origini ai primi del secolo XX*, Putignano 1966

Cassiano, A.: *Il Barocco a Lecce e nel Salento*, Rome 1995

Cazzata, M.: *Guida ai castelli pugliesi: i. La provincia di Lecce,* Galatina 1997

Chalandon, F.: *Histoire de la Domination Normande en Italie et en Sicile,* Paris 1907

Coco, P.: *Francavilla Fontana nella luce della storia,* Taranto 1941

Colletta, P.: *Storia del reame di Napoli del 1734 sino al 1825,* Florence 1848

Cornell, T.J. *The Beginnings of Rome,* London 1995

Croce, B.: *Storia del Regno di Napoli,* Bari 1931

Cucciolla, A. and Morelli, D.: *The Urban Development of Bari,* Berlin 1984

Cutolo, A.: *Gli Angioini,* Florence 1934

De Cesare, R.: *La Fine di un Regno,* Citta di Castello 1909

Dell'Aquila, Franco & Massina, Aldo, *Le Chiese Rupestri di Puglia e Basilicata,* Bari 1998

De Sivo, G.: *Storia delle Due Sicilie del 1847 al 1861,* Trieste 1868

De Vita, R.: *Castelli torri ed opere fortificate di Puglia,* Bari 1974

——*Dizionario Biografico degli Italiani,* Rome 1960

Di Benedetto, D., Greco, A., and Del Vecchio, F., *Guida bibliografica di cripte, ipogei e insidiamenti rupestri dell' Puglia,* Bari 1990

Dunrobin, J.: *The Western Greeks,* Oxford 1948

Fagiolo, M. and Cazzolo, V.: *Lecce,* Bari 1984

Farase-Sperken, C.: *La pittura dell' Ottocento in Puglia: i protagonisti, le spere, i luoghi,* Bari 1996

Flaubert G.: *Voyages,* Paris 1948

Forsyth, J.: *Remarks on Antiquities, Arts, and Letters during an excursion in Italy in the years 1802 and 1803,* London 1816

Frazer, J.G.: *The Golden Bough,* London 1907–13

Fronda Michael P.: *Between Rome and Carthage; Southern Italy during the Second Punic War,* C.U.P 2010

Galanti, G.M.: *Relazione sull'Italia Meridionale,* Milan 1791

Galiano, A.: *Il Guercio delle Puglia,* Mian 1967

Gattini, M.: *I priorati, i baliagi e le commende del Sovrano Militare Ordine di San Giovanni nelle provincie meridionali d'Italia,* Rome 1928

Gay, J.: *L'Italie méridionale et l'Empire byzantin,* Paris 1904

Gelao, Clara & Tragni, Bianca: Il Presepe Pugliese, Bari 2000

Gianfreda, G.: *Basilica Cattedrale di Otranto,* Galatina 1987

——*Il Monachesimo Italo-Greco in Otranto,* Galatina 1977

Ginsborg, P.: *A History of Contemporary Italy*, London 1990

Gorze, H.: *Castel del Monte, geometric manual of the Middle Ages*, Munich 1998

Guillou, A: *Studies in Byzantine Italy*, London 1970

Kantorowicz, E.: Frederick *II 1194–1250*, New York *1957*

Lacaita, C.: *An Italian Englishman: Sir James Lacaita*, London 1933

Leonard, E.G.: *Les Angevins de Naples*, Paris 1954

Levi, C.: *Christ stopped at Eboli*, London 1987

Lucarelli, A.: *Il brigantaggio politico del Mezzogiorno d'Italia doppo la seconda restaurazione borbonica, 1815–1818: Gaetano Vardarelli e Ciro Annichiarico*, Bari 1942

——*Il Brigantaggio politico delle Puglie doppo 1860: Il Sergente Romano*, Bari 1946

Lucarelli, A.: *La Puglia nella rivoluzione napolitana del 1799*, Manduria 1998

——*La Puglia nel Risorgimento*, Bari 1931–53

Lumley, R. and Morris, J., *The New History of the Italian South*, Exeter 1997

Maffei, A.: *Brigand Life in Italy: a history of Bourbonist reaction*, London *1865*

Merlino, F.S.: *L'Italie telle qu'elle est*, Paris 1890

Mola, M. de, and Palasciano, G.: *Le chiese rurali del territorio di Fasano*, Fasano 1987

Mommsen, T., *The History of Rome*, London 1894

Mongiello, L.: *Le masserie di Puglia: organismi, architettonici ed ambiente territoriale*, Bari 1996

Monnier, M.: *Histoire du Brigandage dans l'Italie méridionale*, Paris 1862

Norwich, J.J.: *The Normans in the South*, London 1967

——*The Kingdom in the Sun*, London 1970

Palasciano, I.: *Alberobello nel sette e ottocento*, Fasano 1987

Paone, N.: *La Transumanza*, Isernia 1987

Pasculli Ferrara, M.: *Arte napoletana in Puglia del XVI al XVIII secolo*, Fasano 1983

Patrunio, L.: *Puglia e Basilicata: mura, castelli e dimore*, Milan 1995

Patrunio, L.: *Puglia e Basilicata: l'uomo e le sue tradizioni*, Milan 1997

Penkovsky, V.: *Private Army*, London, 1950

Perkins, C.: *Italian Sculptors*, London 1868

Petrignani, M. and Porsia, F.: *Bari*, Bari 1982

Pizzigallo, M.: *La collegiata di Martina Franca*, Fasano 1976

——*Uomini e vicende di Martina*, Fasano 1986

Potter, T.W.: *Roman Italy*, London 1987

Prandi, A.: *In terra di Tàranto,* Milan 1970

Reumont, A von.: *Die Carafa von Maddaloni*, Berlin 1851

Ripabottoni, A.: *Padre Pio of Pietrelcina*, San Giovanni Rotondo 1987

Ruotolo, G.: *La Quarta mafia: storie di mafia in Puglia*, Naples 1994

Ruppi, C.F.: *Alla scoperta di un angolo di Puglia*, Conversano 1971

Simone, L. De: *Lecce e I suoi monumenti,* Lecce 1964

Smith, Sir W.: *A Dictionary of Greek and Roman Biography*, London 1904

——*A Smaller Classical Dictionary*, London 1910

Snowdon, F.M.: *Violence and Great Estates in Southern Italy: Apulia 1900–1922*, C.U.P. 1986

Tancredi, G.: *Il Gargano nel Risorgimento*, Foggia 1948

Touring Club Italiano: *Puglia*, Milan 1978

Villari, R.: *Il Sud nella storia d'Italia*, Bari 1966

——*La rivolta antispagnola a Napoli,* Rome 1967

Wuillermier, P.: *Tarente des origine a la conquete romaine,* Paris 1939

Short Chronology

	Disfida di Barletta
1528	Apulia invaded by French army under Lautrec
1656	Plague
1714	Austrian rule over Apulia recognised at Peace of Rastadt
1734	Austrians defeated by Spaniards under Charles of Bourbon at Bitonto
1799	Foundation of Parthenopean (Neapolitan) Republic and campaign of Sanfedisti
1801	French garrisons admitted to Apulian ports
1806–15	French occupation
1815	Restoration of Borboni
1860	Garibaldi overthrows Borbone regime, Unification of Italy
1861–5	Brigands' War
1865	Tavoliere opened up to cultivation; new era of *latifondismo*
1906	Work begins on construction of Apulian Aqueduct
1920	Workers rising in Bari
1939	Completion of Aqueduct
1940–5	Second World War
1943	In September King Victor Emanuel III establishes seat of government at Brìndisi

Rulers of Apulia from Norman Times

The Hautevilles

1042–46	William, Count of Apulia
1046–51	Drogo, Count of Apulia
1051–57	Humphrey, Count of Apulia
1057–85	Robert Guiscard, Count and Duke of Apulia
1085–1111	Roger Borsa, Duke of Apulia
1111–27	William, Duke of Apulia
1127–30	Roger, the Great Count of Sicily
1130–54	Roger II, King of Sicily
1154–66	William I – 'The Bad' – King of Sicily
1166–89	William II – 'The Good' – King of Sicily
1189–94	Tancred, King of Sicily
1194	William III

Tancred had been illegitimate and the Emperor Henry VI claimed the throne as husband of the rightful heir Constance, daughter of Roger II, deposing and murdering Tancred's son, the infant William III.

The Hohenstaufen

1194–97	Henry VI, Holy Roman Emperor
1197–1250	Frederick II, Holy Roman Emperor
1250–54	Conrad IV, Holy Roman Emperor
1254–66	Manfred, King of Sicily

The Pope offered the Kingdom of Sicily to Charles of Anjou (brother of Louis IX of France) who defeated and killed Manfred, taking his throne. In 1282 the Sicilians rose against him in the Sicilian Vespers, choosing as their king Pedro III of Aragon who had married Manfred's daughter. There were two kingdoms of Sicily – that on the mainland (including Apulia) ruled from Naples and that on the island ruled from Palermo.

The Angevin Kings

1266–85	Charles I – 'Charles of Anjou'
1285–1309	Charles II – 'The Lame'
1309–43	Robert – 'The Wise'
1343–81	Giovanna
11381–66	Charles III – of Durazzo
1386–1414	Ladislao
1414–35	Giovanna II
1435–42	Réné of Anjou

In 1442 Alfonso King of Aragon and Sicily conquered Naples from Réné of Anjou (father-in-law of Henry VI of England) and styled himself 'King of the Two Sicilies'. He left Naples to his bastard son Ferrante, his descendants ruling it until the Spanish conquest in the sixteenth century.

The Aragonese Kings

1442–58	Alfonso I – 'The Magnaminous'
1458–94	Ferdinand I – 'Ferrante'
1494–95	Alfonso II
1495–96	Ferdinand II – 'Ferrantino'
1496–1501	Federigo

In 1501 Federigo was deposed by his cousin King Ferdinand of Spain and for over 200 years the kingdom was governed by Spanish viceroys.

In 1713 it passed to the Emperor Charles VI, being governed by Austrian viceroys. In 1738 Charles of Bourbon (technically Charles VII but generally called Charles III) drove out the Austrians, re-established the Two Sicilies as an independent monarchy and founded the 'Borbone' dynasty. On becoming King of Spain he abdicated in favour of his third son, Ferdinand IV, who in 1816 become known as Ferdinand I to mark the administrative reunion of the Two Sicilies.

The Borbone Kings

1734–59	Charles III
1759–99	Ferdinand IV
1799	The Parthenopean Republic
1799–1806	Ferdinand IV
1806–8	Joseph Napoleon (Bonaparte)
1808–15	Joachim Napoleon (Murat)
1815–25	Ferdinand IV and I (from 1816)
1825–30	Francis I
1830–59	Ferdinand II – 'Bomba'
1859–60	Francis II – 'Franceschiello'

Since 1860 the kingdom of the Two Sicilies has been part of united Italy (although the Holy See recognised its exiled kings until 1902).

Historical Gazetteer

Alberobello

One of the most visited towns in Apulia, it is unique in that the old centre is comprised entirely of *trulli*. The *trullo* church of Sant'Antonio was built in the twentieth century. **133, 173, 175, 176, 186, 237, 291, 293, 294, 310**

Altamura

In 1999 over 3000 footprints of five types of dinosaur were discovered in the area, the largest collection in Europe. The area was widely inhabited since Neolithic times but the discovery in 1993 of **Altamura Man**, the only complete fossilised skeleton from the Middle Lower Paleolithic era (200,000 BC), suggests its occupation by man started much earlier. (There is a conducted tour to this and the **Pulo di Altamura** – an impressive karst sink-hole north of the city). The city was one of the most important Peucetian settlements from at least the fifth century BC, surrounded by 6 metre high walls which ran for 4 kms. With the advent of the Via Traiana and the decline of the Via Appia it lost its importance. Destroyed by the Saracens who came from Metaponto up the Bradano valley it remained uninhabited until 1230 when Frederick II founded the modern town on the site of the old acropolis. The previous inhabitants had fled to the *gravine* – as they were to do again – and there are several rupestrian churches with traces of frescoes. The **cathedral**, one of the four palatine basilicas of Puglia, was founded by Frederick II in 1232 but considerably altered after the earthquake of 1316; the late fourteenth century portal with its bas relief of the Annunciation is particularly fine, as is the rose window from the thirteeth century. **90, 140, 143, 149–152 , 165, 204, 241, 292, 295**

Andria

Frederick II's most loved city although now, with a population of 100,000, one of the largest in Apulia is still an attractive town and a good base from which to explore the cathedral cities of Trani, Barletta, Giovinazzo and Bisceglie. It is also the nearest town to the unmissable **Castel del Monte.**

The first inhabitants of the area lived in the grottoes but in the Iron Age they built round houses very similar to the *trulli*, many of which have been discovered between Andria and Castel del Monte Apulo from 1000 BC. it became a Peucetian settlement from the seventh century and then the Greek Netium. The inhabitants of Cannae fled here after the battle and destruction of their village in 216 BC. Under the Romans the town became a station on the Via Traiana. In 44 AD, on their way to Rome, St Peter and St Andrew evangelised the city which became a See in about 492. Basilian monks, fleeing from the iconoclast Byzantine emperors, settled in the surrounding grottoes and created their churches – **Santa Croce** still has frescoes. From 1064, under the Normans, the town was walled and fortified. The Emperor Frederick II regarded it as one of his most loyal cities and two of his wives had mausolea, destroyed by Charles of Anjou, in the **cathedral** crypt, the former seventh century Church of San Pietro. The cathedral also contains relics of San Riccardo and a thorn from Christ's crown of thorns. Under the Angevines it became a duchy and was given in fee to Charles II's daughter Beatrice on her marriage to Bertrando Del Balzo. Given to Gonsalvo de Cordoba in 1507 by the Spanish King Ferdinand the Catholic, in 1552 it was sold by his nephew to the Carafa family to whom it belonged until 1806. Fabrizio Carafa built the basilica of **Santa Maria dei Miracoli** just outside the city. Andria was the birthplace of the famous eighteenth century *castrato* Farinelli, but he does not seem to have performed publicly in his native city after he was castrated on the suggestion of his brother and sent to Naples to study singing.

Bari

Bari is now a thriving town and a very interesting place to visit for a couple of days. In the new town the **Petruzzelli Theatre** has been restored and is staging world class operas and nearby Via Sparano and the streets off it are full of internationally renowned shops. But the real reason to go to the city is to visit **Old Bari,** a tangle of very narrow streets opening out into squares containing the wonderful **Romanesque Cathedral of San Sabino,** the **Basilica di San Nicola** and the **castle** built by Fredrick II. 2, 8, 13, 17, 22–4, 51, 60, 63, 67, 73, 81, 82, 97–116, 119, 123, 125–7, 138, 143, 151, 152, 176, 179, 201, 204, 219, 223, 226, 228, 249, 255, 265, 266, 274, 283–5, 289, 292, 294, 299–300, 307, 309–10, 312–13, 322, 333, 335

Barletta

Inhabited from at least the fourth century BC it was the port for Canosa in Roman times. The Lombard invasion in the sixth century AD caused the inhabitants of Canosa to seek refuge in Barletta, as did the Norman Robert Guiscard's sack of Cannae. The Normans built the church of **San Sepolcro** in front of which stands the statue of **Eraclio/Are.** The church has been heavily restored after falling out of use in the nineteenth century. Following the Muslim conquest of the Holy Land, the Archbishop of Nazareth took refuge in Barletta and the diocesan offices moved permanently there in 1327. Under the Anjou dynasty the city enjoyed its most prosperous period; the Romanesque **cathedral** was extended to the east in Gothic style by Pierre d'Angicourt, who also built the cathedral at Lucera and restored the castle at Canosa. But in 1456 an earthquake caused extensive damage. The Aragonese rebuilt the Norman **castle** to withstand Turkish bombardment but it was badly damaged by the Austrians in the First World War; it has been restored and is one of the most impressive in Puglia. From the baroque period very few *palazzi* of note have survived, one of which – the **Palazzo della Marra** – now houses the **Pinecoteca De Nittis.** An interesting modern monument is the **Ossario Commemorativo dei Caduti Slavi** – memorial and ossuary for the Yugoslavian partisans who, wounded in the Balkans during the war and brought across the Adriatic to hospitals in Puglia, died of their wounds. 46, 51, 70–1, 82–90, 92, 178, 182, 213, 230, 233, 243, 313, 337, 339

Bisceglie

Judging by the evidence of numerous **dolmens** in the hinterland of the city, the area was inhabited from early times; but it is first mentioned in 1042 when it fell to the Norman Robert Guiscard who gave it in fee to Pietro, Count of Trani. The latter fortified the town in

1060 and encouraged the inhabitants of the surrounding villages to move to Bisceglie. It was greatly enlarged by Frederick II who built the first **castle,** and became a prosperous city under the Angevines. During the fourteenth and fifteenth centuries it belonged to the Del Balzo but then passed to the Spanish Crown which in 1512 raised the present walls. The Spanish expelled the Jewish community and all heretics from the city – they were allowed to visit it on business for 3 days but staying any longer resulted in forfeiture of goods and corporal punishment. The **Cathedral,** founded by the Normans in 1073, like so many, was considerably altered in the eighteenth century. Bisceglie welcomed the Napoleonic troops but the French were kicked out by a Russian fleet who returned the city to the Bourbons. **46, 85, 317, 325, 337**

Bitonto

An important city in pre-Roman times when it became a Municipium on the Via Traiana. Sacked by the Catapan Zaccaria in 975, from the eleventh century it gradually recovered and its prosperity (derived from the olive oil which the Venetians considered the best in Italy) is shown by the splendid thirteenth century Romanesque **cathedral,** one of the finest in Apulia. From 1507 (amongst several other cities) it was the fief of Gonzalo de Cordoba, The Great Captain. In 1551 the city bought its independence at the cost of 86,000 ducats. **126, 233, 313**

Bovino

Bovino was the Roman Vibinum, an Osco-Samnite city where Hannibal established himself in 217 BC before the battle of Cannae. A fortified centre in the early Middle Ages, it was part of the Duchy of Benevento. The **castle** (in which one can now stay) was built by the Normans, who reorganised the Byzantine **cathedral,** which was then altered again in the fourteenth century. During the Brigand's War Bovino was occupied by Carmine Donatello Crocco. Now, according to a large sign on the road from the valley, it is considered one of the most beautiful cities in Italy. **61, 186, 190, 237–41, 272**

Brìndisi

Settled by the Messapians in the Bronze Age, Brìndisi traded with the Mycenaeans. It became a Greek city, then in 244 BC a Roman colony and naval base, connected with Rome by the Via Appia and the Via Traiana. In the early Middle Ages it belonged to Goths, Byzantines and Lombards, the latter holding it from the seventh to the tenth centuries when it reverted to Byzantine rule. During this period it was destroyed by the Holy Roman Emperor Ludwig II, in 868, and sacked by the Saracens. In 1071 it became part of the Norman Principality of Tàranto and, until the death of Frederick II Hohenstaufen (who built the Swabian castle), was the principle point of departure for crusades and pilgrimages to the Holy Land. In 1456 it was destroyed by an earthquake, but was rebuilt by Ferdinand I. From 1496 -1509 it was ruled by Venice, but was reconquered by Spain and began a long decline. Then it came under Austrian rule and finally to the Bourbons who cleared the harbour and brought new prosperity to the city. The main sites of historical interest in the city are the **Roman column** at the end of the Via Appia, the **mosaic floor in the cathedral** and the **Templar church of San Giovanni al Sepolcro**. Outside the city is one of the few Gothic churches in Apulia, **Santa Maria del Casale**. Built by Phillip of Anjou, it has notable frescoes from the fourteenth century. **5, 23, 101, 115, 142, 147, 179, 191–215, 224, 250, 255, 259, 301, 308, 313, 327**

Canosa di Puglia

One of the oldest uninterruptedly inhabited cities in *Italy*. The site was occupied by the Dauni since 6000 BC and the city itself was founded by Greeks. An ally of Rome at the Battle of Cannae it became first a colony of veterans and subsequently an important municipium on the Via Traiana with temples, baths and an **amphitheatre**. Canosa has suffered extensive damage from earthquakes over the centuries and from bombing during the Second World War but the seventh century crypt of the **Cathedral of San Sabino** which contained the saint and first bishop's remains escaped, as did the **mausoleum of Bohemond** and the **pulpit** built by Acceptus. Other important sites include the **Roman/Medieval bridge** over which ran the Via Triaina, the Daunian **Hypogeum of Lagrasta** and the **Basilica of San Leucio** – a pagan temple dedicated to Minerva, transformed into a Christian church. **39, 123–5, 132, 147, 318, 339**

Casarano

A hamlet founded in Roman times. Ninth century incursions by the Saracens forced the inhabitants to flee to a low hill to the north. This new settlement became the town of Casarano and in the thirteenth century, after the defeat of Manfred, was given to the Tomacelli and the Filomarino families, supporters of the Angevines. In the original settlement **Santa Maria della Croce** (or Casaranello) is one of the most beautiful early churches in Apulia with **mosaics** dating from the fifth century and frescoes from the eleventh. 250

Cerignola

The area around present day Cerignola was inhabited since at least the Bronze Age and reached the height of its prosperity in the fourth century BC. It was destroyed by Alexander I of Epirus during the Greco-Roman War but recovered, and in Roman Imperial times, being on the Via Traiana and the centre of the wheat growing Tavoliere, it thrived; the **Piano delle Fosse** on the edge of the town has the only remaining ancient pits for grain storage in Apulia. After the usual incursions of Goths, Lombards and Saracens it slowly regained its prosperity, although described in the thirteenth century as "a walled city with a moated fortress and few inhabitants". In the following century it was destroyed in the war between Giovanna I and Louis I of Hungary. Under the Aragonese it prospered but went through a bad period with the Spanish and continued to do so until the devastating earthquake of 1731 which destroyed most of the city. The thirteenth century **Chiesa Matrice** and former cathedral survived and has an interesting roof with six hexagonal cupulas. The town was rebuilt at the end of the eighteenth century and increased in size enormously during the nineteenth. The Teatro Mercadante dates from this period, as does the new cathedral – the home for half the year of the Byzantine icon of the Madonna di Ripalta (the other six months being spent at the **Santuario della Madonna di Ripalta** to the south of the city near the River Òfanto. This was built on the site of a temple dedicated to the Roman goddess Bona Dea). Cerignola is one of the few Apulian cities to be built on the exact site of the Roman municipium and it is sad that very little remains of the old city, but it is now one of the main agricultural centres in Apulia, famous for its olives. 65–9, 76–8, 115, 239–40, 312

Conversano

Founded by the Iapigi in the eighth century BC and surrounded by **walls**, Norba had a large sixth century necropolis in which many tombs have been found with Greek vases. In 268 BC it came under Rome and was an important city on the junction of the Via Appia and the Via Minucia Traiana, trading with the indigenous population of the interior and the Greeks on the coast. It was destroyed by the Visigoth Alaric in 411 AD but was quickly re-populated during the Byzantine and Lombard eras but with a new name – Casale Cupersanem. Geoffrey of Hauteville created the county of Cupersani which stretched from Bari to Lecce and in 1054 built the **Norman Castle** which has undergone considerable modification, particularly in the fifteenth and seventeenth centuries (It now contains the 10 **paintings by Finoglio of Tasso's** *Gerusalemme Liberata*). Robert Curthose, son of William the Conqueror, stayed here on his way back from the First Crusade and married Sibilla of Conversano. The Romanesque **Cathedral** suffered greatly from a fire in 1911 but the thirteenth century façade is still beautiful. Outside the town are the early thirteenth century church of **Santa Caterina** and the church of **Santi Cosma and Damiano**. 111, 133, 138, 174, 176, 182–3, 185, 187, 189, 234, 265–71, 272, 276, 311, 334

Copertino

A paleochristian crypt under the **castle chapel** is the earliest evidence of a settlement. Copertino was a hamlet when the inhabitants of neighbouring villages destroyed by the Saracens in the ninth century fled to the area. Under the Byzantines it increased in size but was not walled until after the death of Frederick II who had built a fortified tower here. This was incorporated into the Angevin castle which in turn was rebuilt in 1540 to form what is now one of the largest in Apulia. A county under the Enghiens, in the fourteenth century it was given to Caterina, daughter of Mary of Enghien, Countess of Lecce and Copertino, on her marriage to Tristan Chiaromonte. Tristan's daughter Isabella, heiress to the Brienne claim to the Kingdom of Jerusalem, who was born in the **castle**, married the Aragonese King Ferdinand I of Naples. It was given in fee to the Castriota Granai but after the disappearence of the last male Castriota, Antonio, it passed to the Viceregent of Spain. At the end of the sixteenth century the city flourished and many palaces were built, for the first time outside the walls. On the edge of the town is the **Santuario della Grotella**, built in 1577 over a rupestrian church, where San Giuseppe da Copertino flew on numerous occasions. The fresco of the Madonna over the main altar was cut from the Byzantine church. Another rupestrian church is the **Cripta di S.Michele Arcangelo** which lies outside the town. **234-5**

Fasano

When the ruins of **Egnathia** – Horace's last stop on the Via Appia – were abandoned after the fall of the Roman Empire of the West the inhabitants sought refuge in the grottoes inland from the coast, forming rupestrian villages with churches such as **Cripta di San Lorenzo** and **Cripta di San Procopio**. After the country was no longer harassed by Saracen raids the inhabitants built the town of Fasano which, from the fourteenth century, belonged to the Knights of Malta whose crest is on several buildings including what is now the **Palazzo Communale**. An interesting church outside the town is the ninth century **Tempio Seppannibale,** a small church with a dome whose design is thought to have been influenced by Saracen architecture. **179-81, 310-11**

Foggia

Owing to the fertility of the soil of the Tavoliere, from 6000 BC the area round Foggia was the largest neolithic village in Europe, the centre of primitive western agriculture. By 2000 BC the site had become the one of the largest and most prosperous Iapigian cities – Arpi, 8 km from modern Foggia. Under Roman rule and because of its distance from both the Via Appia and later the Via Traiana it became a backwater and the land uncultivated, swampy and malarial. It was not until the arrival of Robert Guiscard that the building, in a very limited way, of the present city of Foggia was begun. William the Good began to restore the land and to accelerate the building of Foggia, including the **cathedral** which houses the **Byzantine Icona Vetere**. The cathedral was altered in the baroque period and again after the earthquake of 1731. Frederick II loved Foggia and in 1223 built a large palace in what is now the Via Arpi. This was almost completely demolished by Papal troops after his death in 1250 but a small portion of it now houses the **Museo Civico** and there are several interesting *palazzi* on the site such as the sixteenth century **Palazzo de Vita de Luca**, which survived the devastating earthquake of 1731, and the eighteenth century **Palazzo Del Vento.** Frederick also built another palace outside the city, the Palacium dell' Incoronata, near the modern **Santuario della Madonna dell' Incoronata**.

Other survivors of the earthquake are the fifteenth century **Palazzo della Dogana,** the customs' house for the sheep arriving from the Abruzzi, and the baroque **Chiesa delle Croci** (aka the Calvario) built on the spot where the *tratturi* from Aquila and Celano met at Foggia. 6, 8, 31, 39, 40, 59–64, 68–75, 77, 78, 94, 111, 116, 188, 190, 237, 240, 267, 285, 288, 311, 339

Francavilla Fontana

The area has been inhabited since the Middle Neolithic era and expanded in the Messapic period although it was only a group of farms around Oria until Philip of Anjou founded it round the site of the fountain. Philip gave it in fee to the Antoglietta who built the walls. Subsequent feudatories were Giovanni Antonio Orsini Del Balzo who strengthened the walls and built the castle as a barracks and the Imperiali who built the **Palazzo Imperiali**. The Parish church (**Chiesa Matrice**) was built on the site of an Angevine predecessor after the earthquake of 1743. Amongst the finest palaces is the early eighteenth century **Palazzo Giannuzzi Carissimo**. 182–3, 231, 272–3, 276–9, 309

Galatina

The origins of Galatina are rather vague but it was probably a Messapian and then a Greek city. It is certain that in 1178 it was known as San Pietro in Galatina (the name it retained until 1861) because St Peter was supposed to have visited it on his way from Antioch to Rome. Outside the town are several basilian crypts of which **Santa Maria della Grotta** has the most interesting frescoes. Raimondello Orsini del Balzo began the construction of the **Basilica di Santa Caterina d'Alessandria** in 1369 as a votive offering for his safe return with a relic of St Catherine from a pilgrimage to Mount Sinai. His family lost Galatina to Giovanni Castriota Skanderbeg for services rendered to the Aragonese King of Naples, Ferrante. The Castriota built the walls with five gates (three of which still remain – **Porta**

Nuova, **Porta Luce** and **Porta Cappuccini**) and a castle, which no longer exists. From the Castriota the city passed by marriage to the Sanseverino and then in 1615, in payment of a debt, to the Genoese bankers Spinola. From this period the city expanded considerably with many fine palaces and churches, among them the Baroque church of **Santi Pietro e Paolo**, rebuilt from 1633 on a previous Greek-rite edifice, the octagonal **Chiesa delle Anime Sante del Purgatorio** with an unusually plain exterior but a very exuberant interior and **Chiesa di Santa Maria della Grazia**, the last resting place of Maria Castriota, her sister-in-law Adriana Acquaviva and Nicolò Berardino Sanseverino. Galatina's calm and prosperous existence was shattered in April 1903 when, during a peasants' revolt against the *latifondisti*, the police were called to quell the disturbance leaving two dead and thirty wounded. **205, 235, 236, 242, 244, 251, 266, 309**

Gallipoli

The site of Gallipoli was probably the port for the Messapian Alezio. When Alezio was destroyed Gallipoli was enlarged and became a city with an easily defended site and, as in other ports such as Bisceglie, very narrow streets which did not allow an invader room to fight. It became part of Magna Graecia with territory stretching as far as Porto Cesareo. Gallipoli fought with Tàranto and Pyrrhus against Rome but was defeated and became a Roman colony and municipium. Sacked by the Vandals and the Goths it was rebuilt by the Byzantines and enjoyed a period of prosperity. Then came the Normans and later the Angevines, against whom the citizens revolted. When Charles of Anjou besieged the city the inhabitants fled to Alezio, returning only in 1300 when the city was walled. The Spanish rebuilt the **walls** and the **castle** and founded the Baroque **cathedral** on the site of a Byzantine church. Gallipoli flourished under the Borbone and became the most important port trading in lamp oil in the Mediterranean. **90, 219, 251–3, 258, 268**

Gioia del Colle

The actual site of Gioia del Colle grew up round a Byzantine castle and was enlarged by the Normans, only to be destroyed by William the Bad. On his return from the Crusades in 1230 Frederick II rebuilt the city and the **castle**, part of which he used as a hunting lodge, the greater part being used as a barracks for the soldiers guarding the fertile countryside. Bianca Lancia, Frederick's mistress by whom he had three children, was incarcerated here on suspicion of treason. The Angevines completed the castle which under the ownership of the Aquaviva d'Aragona lost its fortifications. In the twentieth century it became the property of the Marchese di Noci who organised its restoration and gave it to the Town Council. It now houses the Archeological museum and is used for exhibitions. About 5 km from the town lies the most important of all the Peucetian settlements – **Monte Sanacce.** Inhabited from prehistoric times it flourished from the sixth till the fourth centuries BC . It was surrounded by five rows of walls and in the fifth century the streets were built on a Greek plan. Corinthian and Attic vases of the seventh and sixth century have been found in the tombs, as well as local wares. When the Romans conquered Apulia Monte Sanacce was abandoned. **119, 126–8, 140, 150, 165, 187, 262, 265, 292–3, 303, 308**

Giovinazzo

The Roman Natolium was built on the ruins of the Peucetian Netium destroyed during the Punic Wars. Until the arrival of the Normans it was no more than a small fishing port but later became a commercial centre trading with the Venetian ports of Dalmatia. The **cathedral**, dedicated to **Santa Maria Assunta** (twelfth to thirteenth century), has a baroque interior over the original crypt. The port is one of the prettiest in Puglia and is a popular background for wedding photographs. **85–6, 88, 204, 307, 317**

Giurdignano

The human presence in the area of Giurdignano dates to as early as the Bronze Age, as testified by the presence of twenty-five menhirs and dolmens. Later it was conquered by the Romans (archaeological findings include a second to third century AD necropolis). In the ninth century Basilian monks built the rupestrian **Cripta di S.Salvatore** which has frescoes dating from the twelfth century. **251**

Gravina in Puglia

Thanks to its stragegic position the story of Gravina has an extremely ancient history; the territory was inhabited continuously from at least the seventh century BC, as is seen in the settlement of **Botromagno**, and, in the Dark Ages, the paleochristian churches of San Paolo and Santo Stefano e Santo Staso. It came under the influence of Tàranto and was then occupied by Rome and became a staging post on the Via Appia but was destroyed by the Vandal Genseric. The citizens took refuge in the *gravina* and later built their city on the opposite side of the ravine. The **cathedral** was begun in 1092 by the Normans but destroyed by fires and earthquakes in the mid-fifteenth century. (Fortunately the most precious relic, an arm of St Thomas à Becket obtained by Bishop Roberto in 1179, has survived). Rebuilt later in the century, it is now closed for restoration. Outside the town is the ruin of **Frederick II's castle**, a hunting box used for falconery. The most unusual church is the early seventeenth century **Madonna delle Grazie** whose façade is almost covered by an enormous carved eagle, the crest of the founder Monsignor Giustiniani, in whose memory the eagle was added in 1704.

Grottaglie

A city on the edge of the Murge, Grottaglie grew up round a rupestrian settlement – the Lama Fullonese – inhabited by local peasants and fugitives from Gothic raids who, in the seventh century had built the church of Saints Peter and Paul (later called St Peter of the Jews). These were joined by a group of Jews fleeing from the Saracen sack of Oria. In the fifteenth century Grottaglie was fortified and given the **castle** and **Parish Church**. The most important sights in the city are the monastery of **San Francesco di Paola** and the **Chiesa del Carmine** with a wonderful **Nativity** by **Stefano di Putignano**. In the seventeenth century it suffered under the Spanish but the ceramics industry, which is now famous, was started under their rule. **155, 228, 231–2**

Lecce

Undoubtedly the most beautiful city in Apulia, which saw its architectural zenith in the seventeenth century when many of the monasteries, churches and palaces were built. Founded by Messapians who successfully repelled all advances from Tàranto it became the Roman Lupiae. During the reign of Hadrian the centre was moved three kilometres to the northeast and took the name Litium. The Via Traiana was extended to Lecce and its port at present day San Cataldo became the busiest in the Salento after Brìndisi while Lecce itself, by now with a theatre and amphitheatre, became the most important town. During the Dark Ages it was sacked by Totila but recovered for the Byzantines in 549 but did not flourish until the Norman Conquest in the eleventh century. The Normans built the **Chiesa dei Santi Niccolò e Cataldo** which, although considerably altered in the Baroque period, still retains its original portal. From the end of the fifteenth century during the reign of Ferrante d'Aragona it had commercial dealings with Florence, Venice, Genoa, Greece and Albania becoming one of the richest and most cultured cities of the Italian peninsula. Owing to Turkish incursions new walls and a **castle** were built under Charles V. From 1630 under Spanish rule a building frenzy created numerous religious institutions and palaces. However in 1656 the plague killed thousands of the inhabitants, only being brought to a halt by the intercession of Sant' Oronzo who, from this time, became the city's patron saint. The most outstanding ecclesiastical buildings are **Santa Croce** and the adjacent **Palazzo dei Celestini**, the **Cathedral, Sant'Irene dei Teatini, Basilica di San Giovanni Battista al Rosario, Chiesa del Carmine, Chiesa di San Matteo** and the **Cloister of the Dominicans.** Other interesting edifices are the gates of the city – **Porta Napoli**, **Porta Rudiae** and **Porta San Biagio** and the towers – the moated **Belloluogo Tower** where Maria d'Enghien spent the last years of her life and in which is a tiny chapel with frescoes of the life of Mary Magdalene, and the *Torre del Parco* where Maria D'Enghien's son, Giovanni Antonio Orsini del Balzo, kept his bears. The latter is now an hotel. 3, 6, 9, 133, 178, 188, 202, 212, 217–245, 252, 258, 267, 292, 308–11, 322

Lucera

According to Strabo Lucera was founded by Diomede King of Etolia who after the fall of Troy fled to Apulia and established himself and his followers nearby. In 314 BC it became an autonomous Roman colony. The **amphitheatre** was built in honour of Octavian who visited it on several occasions to watch fights between gladiators and wild beasts. During the first century AD one of the first Christian communities in Europe was founded, with St Peter, on his way to Rome, baptising them in the River Vulgano. The first bishop, Basso, was martyred under Trajan in 118. The Byzantine emperor Constans II sacked the Lombard city in 663 but in 743 the Lombards returned and rebuilt the cathedral. The Emperor Frederick II built the **castle** which was much enlarged by Charles I of Anjou. After the destruction of the city by Charles II of Anjou in 1300 he rebuilt it and renamed it "Civita Sancte Marie". The demolished mosque became the **Cathedral** of the Assumption. Robert of Anjou re-populated it with colonists from Provence and the Pope sent the Croatian bishop Agostino Kazotic to convert the area. In 1323 the bishop was mortally wounded by a Muslim. **54, 60, 65–9, 130, 132, 187, 239, 244, 267, 283, 318**

Manduria

An important Messapian city which fended off various attacks from Tàranto thanks to the three defensive walls encircling the city. The Spartan king Archidamus III lost his life beneath these walls in 338 BC. Manduria sided with Hannibal and for this thousands of its citizens were sold into slavery when the Romans took the city. After its destruction by the Saracens it remained uninhabited until it was re-founded in the thirteenth century but occupied only a small portion of the Messapian site. During the Middle Ages Manduria had an important Jewish community living in the **Ghetto**. Having been owned by various families it ended up in 1719 in the possession of the Imperiali di Francavilla, who held it until 1799, and built the fine **Palazzo Imperiali**. In the northeast of the city lies the **Archeological Park of the Messapian Walls** where the largest Messapian necropolis ever found has been excavated amounting to about 2500 tombs, as well as segments of the **three defensive walls** surrounding the ancient city. In the same area are **Pliny's Fountain** and the church of **San Pietro Mandurino** – the latter founded in the eighth century by adapting a Messapian chamber tomb. **230, 258–62, 278–9, 308, 310**

Manfredonia

Siponto was a Daunian settlement then a flourishing Greek port which, having been defeated by first the Samnites and then in 335 BC by Alexander I, King of Epirus, became in 189 BC a Roman colony. It was a bishop's See as early as 465 and probably had been converted to Christianity following St Peter's sojourn in Apulia on his way to Rome. The Byzantine Emperor Constans destroyed it in the process of returning the region to the Empire. It was occupied by the Saracens for several years in the ninth century. An earthquake and possibly a tsunami destroyed it in 1255 and Manfred established his new city of Manfredonia two kilometres away from the malarial swamps which had formed round the old site. Siponto is now a holiday resort but the Romanesque churches of **Santa Maria Maggiore**, whose Byzantine icon of the Virgin is now in the cathedral of Manfredonia, and **San Leonardo** are well worth visiting. In Manfredonia itself the Angevins rebuilt the **castle** and built the **cathedral.** During the fourteenth century the port became the most important in the Capitanata but by the fifteenth century the fortifications had to be strengthened owing to the Turkish threat. These were of no avail as in 1620 the Ottoman Ali Pasha with fifty-six galleys attacked Manfredonia and destroyed the medieval city. The only buildings that remained were the church of St Mark, the castle and the walls. The cathedral was rebuilt from 1624. **8, 18, 20, 29–33, 83, 151, 240, 267**

Martina Franca

Founded by fugitives from Tàranto escaping the Saracens it was recognised as a city in the fourteenth century. Martina Franca has a very attractive old part filled with baroque palaces and churches; the **town hall** with murals by Carella (at the moment being restored) is well worth seeing, as is the **Church of San Martino** with its simple Nativity by **Stefano di Putignano**. **140, 173–5, 180, 182–3, 186, 188, 230–1, 265, 271–5, 293, 306, 311, 334**

Massafra

The most northern of Messapian centres, it came under Greece and then it is thought was given to North African fugitives fleeing from the Vandals. They sought help from the archbishop of Tàranto, who gave them land between the two ravines where they lived in the grottoes. The first documentary evidence is from the tenth century when the Lombards appointed a local administrator.

Under the Normans it was given to Robert Guiscard's nephew Richard the Seneshal, who restored the castle. The Angevins took back Massafra from Oddone di Soliac in 1296 and joined it with the Principality of Tàranto. In the fifteenth century it became a free city and a centre for horse breeding. Later it again became a fief and was given to the Pappacoda family from Naples then to the Imperiali who owned it from 1661 until 1778 and planted olives, vines and fruit trees on their land, modernised the castle and built the clock tower. Apart from the **castle** and the **Convento di San Benedetto** there is little of note in the upper town – the ravines are the reason to visit Massafra. The churches which still have frescoes are **Chiesa di Santa Lucia**; **Chiesa della Candelora**; **Chiesa della Madonna della Buona Nuova** (part of the Chiesa della Santa Maria della Scala); **Chiesa di Sant' Antonio Abate**; **Chiesa di San Simine in Pantaleo**; **Chiesa di San Simeone a Famosa** and **Chiesa della Santa Marina**. **128, 140–1, 155, 158–9, 260, 277–9**

Matera (now in Basilicata)

Like all the cities which grew up round ravines Matera was inhabited in the Neolithic era. The city itself probably has Greek origins, settled by the inhabitants of Metaponto fleeing from Hannibal. It suffered the usual depredations from Goths, Lombards and Saracens and was sacked by the troops of Emperor Louis II while they were trying to exterminate the latter. At the beginning of the eighth century it saw the emigration of basilian monks from the Eastern Empire who established themselves in the caves of the ravines and carved out churches in the *Sassi*. From 1043, with the arrival of the Normans, the city enjoyed a long period of stability during which Frederick II founded the cathedral which was completed in 1270. As well as the rupestrian churches, two others are worthy of note – the **Chiesa del Purgatorio and the Convento di Sant'Agostino**. The most important churches of the *Sassi* are **Santa Lucia alle Malve, Convicinio di Sant' Antonio, Santa Maria di Idris, Madonna delle Virtù, San Pietro Barisano** and **Santa Maria della Valle**. Further afield the **Cripta del Peccato Originale** has Lombard frescoes. **100, 150, 155–6, 163, 167–70**

Melfi (now in Basilicata)

The first record of Melfi comes in the eleventh century when Basil Boiannes was *catapan* but the site was occupied in at least the Bronze Age. With the Roman conquest of the area it seems the inhabitants were sent to the new colony of Venusia. Its period of greatness came with the Normans who made it their headquarters in the conquest of Puglia. Robert Guiscard married Sichelgaita of Salerno in Melfi. In 1059 Pope Nicholas II at the First Council of Melfi made Robert Duke of Puglia and Calabria and a vassal of the Holy See. Frederick II spent a great deal of time in Melfi owing to the good hunting in the area. His Constitutions were set out here and in 1241 he imprisoned two cardinals and numerous French and German bishops who had attended a Council called by the Pope with the object of deposing him. The Angevines greatly enlarged the castle to control the surrounding population who were supporters of the Hohenstaufen and loathed the French.

In 1531 the Aragonese King Carlos V who was short of money after the Thirty Years' War removed the Caracciolo family from the Principality of Melfi and sold Melfi to the Genoese Andria Doria for 25,000 ducats. It then went into steady decline, not helped by earthquakes – the last in 1930 destroying much of the city – and, after the Unification of Italy, the presence of brigands including the notorious Carmine Donatello Crocco. The **castle** now houses the archeological museum, and the **Cathedral** and the eighteenth century **Bishop's Palace** have been restored. The walls which in Norman times were four kilometres in circumference have mostly been destroyed by earthquakes but small stretches remain as well as the **Venosa Gate**. Outside the city are two rupestrian churches with frescoes – **Santa Margherita** and **Santa Lucia**; the former is particularly interesting as one of the frescoes shows Frederick II holding a hawk with his wife, Isabella of England, and his son Corrado on his right, and on his left three skeletons. An interesting church historically is the **Chiesa di Santa Maria ad Nives** which was built in 1570 by the Albanian Giorgino Lapazzaia. It still retains the arbëreshë rite which is basically Greek Orthodox and serves a community who speak a dialect of Albanian going back to the sixteenth century. Melfi is a pleasant place with lovely views of Monte Vulture. **23, 40, 83, 102, 139, 143–4, 288, 312**

Monopoli

The area immediately around has been inhabited for the last 80,000 years but the city itself was founded by the Messapians in about 500 BC. They walled the city and built a fortress. In the Roman era the port was used primarily for military purposes. After Gothic and Saracen raids the people of Egnathia fled to Monopoli which was then taken by the Byzantines. In 1041 the inhabitants called in the Normans and resisted all efforts by the Byzantine general George Maniaces to retake it; in retribution he laid waste to all the surrounding territory. The medieval city was laid out by the Normans on the peninsula between the two natural harbours. It was during their rule that the famous icon of the **Madonna della Madia** (now in the **cathedral**) is alleged to have arrived on a raft with a consignment of wooden beams required for the roof of the new church. This church had been superimposed on an earlier one, which in its turn had been erected on the site of a pagan temple. In 1742 it was decided to enlarge the building, which had been already altered in the sixteenth century, and the present cathedral was built – a fine example of late eighteenth century Baroque. In a room up a flight of stairs from the vestry is a fascinating collection of ex-voto paintings. There are several rupestrian churches in and around the city including the crypt of **Chiesa di Santa Maria Amalfitana**, Madonna del Soccorso and **San Leonardo.** During the long minority of Frederick II the barons in Puglia rebelled but Monopoli remained loyal to the emperor. The walls were damaged but restored and strengthened by Frederick when he was older, thanks to which the city was never attacked by the Turks. They also withstood a three month siege by the Spaniard Alfonso d'Avalos during the struggle for Puglia between the Venetians and the Spanish in 1529. After the armistice Monopoli belonged to Charles V. The castle, superimposed on the Messapian walls and the Roman gate to the port, was built in the sixteenth century under the hated Spanish rule. The city went into a decline from this period and in July 1647 during a popular rising the governor was lynched, followed by reprisals by troops stationed at Bari. **24, 46, 138, 179, 188, 233, 336**

Monte Sant' Angelo

Under the Lombards the city grew up around the **Sanctuary of St Michael** (still a place of pilgrimage), and was enlarged by the Normans who founded the **Chiesa di Santa Maria Maggiore**, and the **Tomba di Rotari** – in reality a baptistery. Charles of Anjou erected the building now housing the sanctuary and the elegant *campanile* over the grotto. The **castle** was built by Orso, bishop of Benevento in the ninth century but he could not prevent the sack of the city by the Saracens in 871. Normans, Hohenstaufen, Angevins and the Aragonese enlarged and strengthened it to withstand contemporary warfare. 16–21, 25–6, 29, 53, 63, 87, 261, 312

Mottola

Although it was inhabited in the Bronze Age and remains of Greek walls have been discovered round the centre there is no documentary evidence for its existence until the beginning of the eleventh century when the *catapan* Basil Boioannes founded a castle here against the incursions of the Saracens. Under the Normans who attempted to stamp out the Greek rite, rupestrian churches were made in the ravines of Petruscio and Casalrotto by followers of the rite. These include **San Nicola**, **Sant'Angelo**, **San Gregorio** and **Santa Margherita**, all with frescoes – those of San Nicola some of the best in Apulia. During the Second World War Polish soldiers hid from the Germans in the **Villagio ipogeo di Petruscio**, an amazing settlement of underground dwellings and churches dating from early times. In 1653 the fee of Mottola was sold to Francesco Caracciolo VII, Duke of Martina Franca, who retained it until the end of feudalism in 1806. 157–8, 195, 272, 293

Nardò

One of the most attractive and largest cities in the Salento, it is near the Ionian coast with the interesting series of watchtowers (six of which are in the parish) built by Charles V to defend Puglia from the Muslim pirates of North Africa and the Balkans. A Messapian settlement from the tenth century, it was frequently at war with Tàranto but joined them in the fight with Pyrrhus against Rome and was severely punished by the victorious Romans after the Social Wars. Under Augustus, the city, which had been abandoned for decades, was reinstated as Neritum; new roads were built to link it with the Via Appia and it flourished until the arrival of the Goths. Taken by the Byzantines and Lombards it became a haven in the ninth century for basilian monks who built the Abbazia di Santa Maria di Nerito, now the very much altered **cathedral of Santa Maria Assunta.** After the city was conquered by the Normans in 1058 the abbey was handed to the Benedictines. Nardò was loyal to Frederick II in his battle with the Papacy, and to Manfred after his father's death. The papal troops took the city but Manfred recaptured it with a force of Saracen mercenaries and returned it to his loyal vassal, Tommaso Gentile. It was then attacked by cities loyal to the Pope – Brìndisi, Mesagne and Òtranto – whereupon Manfred besieged and destroyed Brìndisi. Nardò was once again given back to Tommaso Gentile in 1255 but he died the following year, to be succeeded by his son. The next feudatory was Luigi Sanseverino, Prince of Salerno, who governed well and created a renowned School of Studies, but he rebelled against Giovanna II and was deposed in favour of the Del Balzo Orsini. On the death of Giovanni Antonio in 1463 Nardò returned to the Crown but, after the Ottoman attacks in 1480 at Tàranto, Òtranto and Nardò, in 1497 the Aragonese King Federico I sold the city to the Acquaviva Counts of Conversano for 11,000 ducats. The new owners built the fine Baroque palaces, including the beautiful **Palazzo del Tribunale**, and the **Guglia** in the **Piazza Salandra** – and it remained in the family until the end of feudalism in 1806. **233-4, 266-8**

Ostuni

The site was inhabited since the Stone Age, became a town under the Messapians and was destroyed by Hannibal. Re-built by the Greeks it suffered the usual depredations of Goths and Saracens before being once more rebuilt under the Byzantines who made it a diocese. From 1294 to 1463 it was part of the Principality of Tàranto and from 1507 passed first to Isabella Sforza, Duchess of Bari and then to her daughter Bona. In 1639 it was sold by the Spanish King Phillip IV to the merchant family of Zevallos who taxed the inhabitants harshly and caused a decline in the population. Known as the White City on account of its whitewashed houses (to which it owed its immunity from the plagues of the seventeenth century) it revived under the Bourbons and expanded onto the neighbouring hills. The main sights of the old town are the fifteenth century **Cathedral**, the **Bishop's palace**, the **Guglia di Sant'Oronzo, Chiesa di San Vito Martire,** and in the newer town the **Chiesa dell'Annunziata**, but there are also numerous palazzi in the old town making it one of the most attractive in Apulia. Outside the town is the church of **Santa Maria la Nova**, built in 1561 above a rupestrian church with traces of frescoes. **107, 179, 180, 182-5, 188, 233, 249, 269**

Òtranto

Òtranto was a town of Tarentine Greek origin which became a Roman municipium and an important port of embarkation for the east. The Via Traiana was extended to the city after the temprorary demise of Brìndisi. It remained part of the Byzantine empire – during which the **Church of San Pietro** was built – until it was among the last cities of Apulia to surrender to Robert Guiscard at the end of 1070. The **cathedral** was founded in 1080 and finished in the twelfth century, when the marvellous **mosaic floor** was laid. In the Middle Ages there was a large population of Jews who had a school there but these were expelled by the Aragonese. Òtranto was occupied from 12th August 1480 until 18th September 1481 by the Turks. After it was recovered by Alfonso, Duke of Calabria, the walls were strengthened and the **castle** rebuilt but it still suffered from attacks by Venetians and Turks, including being briefly taken by the notorious corsair Barbarossa. Today Òtranto is a popular place for day trippers but in the evening or early morning it is one of the most fascinating and attractive cities in the Salento. **13, 24, 73, 89, 99, 100, 160, 168, 178, 188–9, 194, 213, 219, 220, 227, 229–30, 240, 249, 251–9, 266, 303, 309, 312–3, 336**

Poggiardo/Vaste

The history of Poggiardo is that of most of the Salento south of Òtranto. Vaste was an important Messapian settlement from the seventh century BC, subsequently destroyed by Goths and Saracens, and finally by William the Bad who in 1147 razed it to the ground. The inhabitants moved to neighbouring Poggiardo which, from a small village, began to expand at the end of the fourteenth century after it had sided with Charles of Anjou against Manfred. A century later it became part of the Principality of Tàranto and was defended with walls and a castle. After the destruction of nearby Castro by the Turks it became the seat of the bishop. The fifteenth **bishop's palace** was sold to the Guarini after a rising against the bishop in 1756 and was subsequently a prison and a tobacco factory. In the Piazza Episcopo is the **museum of frescoes** from the rupestrian church of **Santa Maria degli Angeli.** Between Poggiardo and modern Vaste lies the **Parco dei Guerrieri di Vaste**, an archeological area which includes the Messapian remains of Vaste and the **Cripta di Santi Stefani** whose frescoes are in a bad state of repair, the church having been used as a tobacco drying barn within living memory. **250–1**

Putignano

An ancient Peucetian settlement it became a Roman municipium. In the early eleventh century the land belonged to the Benedictine monks of Monopoli and their labourers gathered to form a village on the old site. In the thirteenth century Frederick II built a fortified hunting lodge just outside the walls but because he had been excommunicated by the Pope on the advice of the monks, Putignano denied him access. In a rage he demolished the castle and partially destroyed the town walls. In 1317 the Pope gave Putignano to the Knights of Malta. Because of the increasing danger of Turkish raids the Byzantine icon and relics of St Stephen were brought from Monopoli and housed in a new church. The Putignano Carnival which is still held every year dates from the arrival of the icon. The walls were rebuilt in the fifteenth century by the *Balì* Carafa who also greatly enlarged the original church of **San Pietro**. Napoleon's troops removed most of the church bells in Putignano and stole many church treasures. 138, 174, 180–1, 189, 270, 308, 327, 330

Ruvo di Puglia

A flourishing Peucetian centre from the ninth century BC trading with Greece in ceramics, wine and oil, between the fifth and third centuries BC it was colonised by Greeks from Arcadia. By the fourth century BC its territory included modern Molfetta, Corato, Trani, Terlizzi and Bisceglie. A large collection of Apulian and Attic pottery from the extensive necropolis is in the **Museo Jatta.** A Roman municipium on the Via Traiana, with the rise of Molfetta, Trani and Bisceglie, it had lost a lot of its territory by the fifth century when it was sacked by the Goths and totally destroyed. The new city was surrounded by high walls with four gates and in the centre a tall tower, now the *campanile* of the wonderful **Romanesque cathedra**l. During the reign of Roger II of Sicily the city rebelled and, having withstood a lengthy siege, was betrayed by one of the citizens and partially destroyed. It bounced back in the twelfth century, when the cathedral was founded, and flourished again. The walls were strengthened under the Angevins who built the castle on the site of Frederick II's fortress but were destroyed once more in 1350, this time by Ruggiero Sanseverino. In 1503 the Duc de Namours billeted his men in Ruvo and sent out the thirteen Frenchmen who took part in the Disfida di Barletta. From 1510 Ruvo belonged to the Carafa family and during their rule and the arrival of the Dominican monks the city became enriched with churches, palaces and monasteries. When Napoleon's troops arrived in 1799 the people of Ruvo flew the tricolore from the clock tower and planted a Tree of Liberty which was swiftly cut down when a rumour that the British Navy was about to bombard any city which had planted the tree – they seem to have had a strange idea of the fire power of the navy at the time, Ruvo being about twelve kilometres from the the coast. Ettore Carafa and Giovanni Jatta, although on opposing sides, managed to make Ruvo avoid the worst excesses of this violent period and after the Unification of Italy Ruvo once again flourished as a centre for olive oil and wine. **46, 125, 133**

San Giovanni Rotondo

Most people who come to this town do so to visit the tomb of Padre Pio but it is worthwhile wandering round the old part with its gateways, churches and sixteenth and seventeenth century palaces. Such is the fervour of devotion to Padre Pio that another new church had to be built to accommodate the thousands of pilgrims who visit the city. This is next to the one over his tomb, was consecrated in 2004 and is capable of holding more than 7000 people; it is one of the largest and most modern in Italy and was founded almost entirely by contributions from the pilgrims. **15, 26–8, 311**

San Vito dei Normanni

The area was inhabited since at least the Bronze Age but the modern settlement dates from the tenth century AD when it was founded by a colony of Slavs from Croatia. Bohemond d'Hauteville built the fortress as a hunting lodge; it is now the *Comune* where one can obtain the key to the rupestrian **Church of San Biagio** with its wonderful Byzantine frescoes. The town passed from the Hautevilles to the Sambiase then to Raimondo del Balzo Orsini. The church of the **Madonna della Vittoria** was built to commemorate the participation of many of the inhabitants at the Battle of Lepanto. Like many Apulian cities it was greatly increased in size under Mussolini and again in the late twentieth century making it difficult to reach the old part – and making parking a nightmare. **164–5, 250**

Tàranto

One of the most important centres in Magna Graecia, traditionally founded in 706 BC. The **archeological museum** has amongst other things stunning gold jewellery found in tombs in the surrounding area. Also of note are the **Cathedral** and the **Old Town**, the **Fortezza di Laclos** and the **Castello Aragonese** built originally by the Byzantines for protection against the Saracens and Venetians and greatly altered by Ferdinando II d'Aragona in 1486. It is one of the most polluted cities in Puglia, however, and not a place to linger, nor is there much to see in the way of Greek remains – a couple of columns from a temple here, a grave there – and the rupestrian **Cripta del Redentore** with good frescoes dating from the twelfth century is now closed for restoration. 2, 6, 8–9, 21–3, 53, 85, 89, 102, 105, 119–212, 214, 228, 230, 244–5, 249, 251–2, 255, 259–60, 274, 292, 300, 309, 311–12, 320, 325, 327, 329–30, 335–6

Trani

Of all the coastal cities in the Terra di Bari Trani is probably the most attractive place to stay; the old part is less shabby than that of Bisceglie or Molfetta, the port beautiful and there is more to see than at Barletta. The origins of Trani really only date from the the ninth century AD when the seat of the episcopal See was transfered from Canosa to Trani after Canosa was sacked by the Saracens in 813. The fishing port expanded and became important during the Crusades and the **cathedral** dedicated to St Nicolas the Pilgrim was founded in 1097. The bronze doors made by Barisanus of Trani in 1175 are outstanding. From the same period dates the Templars' **Chiesa di Ognissanti.** Frederick II had the greatest influence on Trani's prosperity, building the walls and **castle** and granting privileges to Jews and Florentines who traded with the East. There are still two synagogues – the **Scolanova** restored to the Jewish rite and that which became the **Church of St Anna** but is now a museum. The city declined during the Aragonese period with the expulsion of the Jews but recovered under the Bourbons and now the Jews have returned and form one of the largest communities in Italy. 8, 23, 46–7, 54, 81, 84–5, 88, 91–6, 106, 177–8, 204, 283, 295, 317, 318, 337

Troia

An attractive city on the top of a hill in the predominately agricultural area south west of Foggia. According to legend founded by Diomede in the twelfth century BC. The earliest archeological evidence points to a much later date but it was a Daunian centre and taken by Hannibal after the battle of Cannae. The present city began to be built round a fortress, after the town had been besieged and sacked by the Saracens, in 1019. The **Romanesque cathedral** with two rose-windows and outstanding bronze doors by Odisirio da Benevento was built by the Normans in the twelfth century using material from the Byzantine church and the Roman city. Pope Urban II held the first Council of Troia in 1093 followed by three more – the last in 1127. Owing to its allegiance to the papacy, it was besieged by the Hohenstaufen emperors Henry II and Frederick II. The city sided with the Angevines, the Aragons and then the Bourbons. **65–9, 89, 188, 204, 213, 240**

Vieste

Vieste was inhabited from paleolithic times later becoming a Greek colony and a Roman municipality. During the Middle Ages, because of its strategic position on the tip of the Gargano, it was fought over by the Byzantines, Normans, Lombards, Venetians and Arabs. The **castle** was built by Frederick II in 1240 and later strengthened with bastions and ramparts but was seriously damaged in 1648 by an earthquake. It was attacked by the Turks in 1480, 1554, 1674 and 1678. During the *Risorgimento* many died in violent clashes between supporters of the Bourbons and supporters of the Unification. Now it is a popular sea-side resort with a lovely beach. **31–2, 88**

Venosa (now in Basilicata)

A Roman colony and birthplace of Horace it has evidence of its origins in the stones used to build the **Church of the Santissima Trinità,** many of which come from the Roman city around it. This church built by the Normans and consecrated in 1059 was later given to the Benedictines who began to enlarge it on a vast scale, but had only reached the arches, when they were banished by Pope Boniface VIII in 1297. The Order of Malta to whom it was given established themselves in the city and the building was never finished – hence its modern name of *La Chiesa Incompiuta* (The unfinished church). Next to the church is the **Archeological Park** with remains of the second century AD Roman amphitheatre, a fine mosaic pavement and Roman and medieval buildings. There are two medieval fountains from the Middle Ages – The **Fontana Angioina** erected by Charles of Anjou in 1298 and the **Fontana di Messer Oto** erected in honour of Roger of Anjou. Pirro del Balzo's **castle** in the centre of Venosa was converted from a fortress into an elegant residence by the composer Gesualdo and is now the Archeological Museum. Below the city the **Jewish and Christian catacombs** lie side by side and date from the fourth to sixth centuries. 7, 23, 50, 53, 62, 119, 142–3, 146–8, 178, 288, 312, 332

Index

U

Ugento 188, 194, 250
Ulloa, P Carla 289, 291
Ururi 239
Uthman 201

V

Val de Bovino 61, 190, 238, 239
Val d'Itria 107, 173, 176, 271
Valente, Guiseppe 292
Valentinian 83
Vardarelli Brothers 190, 230,
    237–241, 320
Vaste 251, **336**
Vatican, the 27, 28, 162
Venosa 7, 23, 50, 53, 62, 119,
    142–3, 146–8, 178, 288, 312,
    332, **340**
Vico del Gargano 288
Victor Emmanuel III, King 112,
    152, 214
Vieste 31, 288, **339–40**
Villagio ipogeo di Petruscio
    333
Villani, Giovanni 40, 55, 308
Villari, Rosario 111, 187–8, 265,
    267, 311

W

Virgil 147, 148, 197, 211, 212,
    249, 257, 308
Vlattus of Òtranto,
    Archbishop 249
von Moltke, Field-Marshal 132

W

Walpole, Horace 254
William, Count of Apulia 313
William, Duke of Apulia 313
William I, King of Sicily 102
William II, King of Sicily 313
William III 313
Wojtyla, Carol, Archbishop of
    Cracow 27

Y

Yolande of Jerusalem 48, 211,
    213, 255
Yriarte, Charles **7,** 75, 224, 306

Z

Zacharias, Catapan 126
Zimbalo, Giuseppe 221, 236